MW00576788

Coal Region Hoodoo

Paranormal Tales from Inside the Pit

Maxim W. Furek

BEYOND THE FRAY
Publishing

Copyright © 2023 by Maxim W. Furek

Published by Beyond The Fray Publishing

This book or any portion thereof may not be reproduced or used in any manner whatsoever without the express written permission of the publisher except for the use of brief quotations in a book review. All rights reserved.

ISBN 13: 978-1-954528-65-9

Cover design: Dauntless Cover Design

Beyond The Fray Publishing, a division of Beyond The Fray, LLC, San Diego, CA

www.beyondthefraypublishing.com

Contents

On being entombed in the pit ...

"The blackness of darkness which envelops the victim, the terrific oppression of lungs, the stifling fumes from the damp earth, unite with the ghastly considerations that we are beyond the remotest confines of hope, and that such is the allotted portion of the dead, to carry into the human heart a degree of appalling awe and horror not to be tolerated – never to be conceived."

Narrative of A. Gordon Pym of Nantucket

By Edgar Allan Poe

To my brother, John L. Furek, for introducing me to H. P. Lovecraft, James Herbert, and Messrs. Latimore, Charing, and Grant.

Introduction

As an introduction, please consider that I've been preparing to write this book for most of my life. As a member of the idealistic Baby Boomer generation, I have received the equivalent of a doctorate of education degree in the paranormal sciences.

My coursework consisted of some of the best television ever created—*The Twilight Zone, The Outer Limits,* and *Thriller,* supplemented with a heavy dose of sci-fiction and horror that included the classic masterpieces *The Thing From Another World* (1951), *The Day the Earth Stood Still* (1951), *War of the Worlds* (1953), *Them* (1954), *Earth Vs. the Flying Saucers* (1956), *Invasion of the Body Snatchers* (1956), *The Abominable Snowman* (1957), *The Blob* (1958), and *The Time Machine* (1960).

Collectively, these journeys into the unknown exposed me to themes of evil and benevolent aliens, forbidden planets, radioactive monsters, interdimensional travel, lycanthropy, zombies, resurrection, and everything in between. Like it or not, the paranormal stalked me like a hellhound on the moors.

Richard Sharpe Shaver was born in my hometown of Berwick, Pennsylvania, and Nick Adams, the Rebel, was buried there. Dr. Frederick L. Santee, the white witch, called "the foremost abstract thinker of the twentieth century," practiced his magick five miles from my home. I resided within a thirty-mile drive of Centralia, Sheppton, the Smurl haunting site, and the gritty parameters of the Pennsylvania Coal Region.

The Coal Region, roughly one hundred miles long by thirty miles wide, sprawls snakelike from Scranton to Harrisburg. It boasted anthracite's richest mother lode, the black gold that fueled the engines of the Industrial Revolution, seducing thousands of European immigrants to crawl down into foreboding black pits. Initially, this book was to be about that area, but, as frequently happens with the paranormal, that scheme changed rapidly ... and dramatically, expanding beyond those confines.

Hoodoo is a body of practices of sympathetic magic associated with something that can cast a spell on someone and bring bad luck. It is not unique to any geographical area and can be found in all religions by various names. Coal Region Hoodoo reflects the region's strange brand of Eastern European and Pennsylvania Dutch curses, spells, and Christian witchery. Our secrets and superstitions have been well-kept within this area of abandoned coal mines, desolation, and high strangeness.

Much of this narrative is personal. I was personally acquainted with Dr. Frederick Santee, interviewed demonologists Ed and Lorraine Warren, and Catherine Adamshock, Nick Adams's mother, was my neighbor. My introduction to the Philadelphia Experiment came after a conversation with my first cousin, James Furek. Jim was a Vietnam vet, a medic, who, while living in New Hampshire, befriended Fred Tracey. Jim told me about Fred's service aboard the USS *Antietam*. I interviewed Tracy at his home in Derry, New Hampshire. This was before I read *The Philadelphia Experiment*. I corresponded with William L. Moore, Stanton Friedman, and Richard A. von Doenhoff of the National Archives, Military Reference Branch, during my research.

Coal Region Hoodoo is the result of my previous book, Sheppton: The Myth, Miracle and Music. After publication, it became apparent that the Sheppton mythology was incomplete. It begged for additional research and confirmation. The third man factor, as an example, perfectly complemented and expanded upon Pope John XXIII's miracle, as did other slivers of esoteric data including material about St. Teresa of Avila. Additionally, the Sheppton mythology was strongly embraced by the paranormal community, encouraging me to continue my journey and investigate these topics further. I am grateful for their inspiration and support.

Demonologists Ed and Lorraine Warren pioneered the field of paranormal investigation and were involved in the infamous West Pittston Smurl haunting. The Roman Catholic couple were the inspiration behind the Conjuring franchise, the second-highest-grossing horror franchise of all time, behind only Godzilla. (Maxim W. Furek photograph.)

Chapter 1
Night of the Living Dead

Shot in rural Evans City, Pennsylvania, Night of the Living Dead fleshed out its reputation as birthmother to the zombie film, pushing the boundaries of the horror genre from psychological suspense to buckets full of blood and gore. The beginning is one of cinema's classic opening scenes, with suspense building in every vintage frame. A car (a 1967 Pontiac LeMans) slowly moves up and down steep winding hills, atmospheric music in the background. It finally arrives at a cemetery in rural Evans City.

Evans City

Night of the Living Dead was filmed around the quaint town of Evans City, nestled in a valley surrounded by large hills and a beautiful landscape. It is located just north of Pittsburgh in Butler County. Evans City has approximately 1,800 residents, many sharing the same German heritage as the early settlers. The Evans City Cemetery and nearby community basked in notoriety after *Night of the Living Dead* was released. According to Mayor Dean Zinkhann, his city became a magnet that attracted numerous fans, including couples who renewed their wedding vows at the cemetery chapel. They came from all over the world, including Australia. Nevertheless, this film represents more than just an opportunity for a road trip and a wedding destination.

The Evans City Cemetery, just north of Pittsburgh in Butler County, was the rural location where *Night of the Living Dead* was filmed. In 1999, the film was deemed "culturally, historically, or aesthetically significant" by the Library of Congress and selected for preservation in the National Film Registry. (Photograph by Patricia A. Furek.)

The 1968 American horror film, produced one year before Woodstock's peace and love, was written, directed, and photographed by George A. Romero (1940–2017). In a 2010 interview with film critic Peter Keough, Romero described his zombie films as "snapshots of the time they were made" and influenced by the era's political climate. Moreover, Romero's independent film was cobbled from drips and drabs of other similar themes, hidden gems he successfully mined. For example, Romero and co-writer John Russo found inspiration in Richard Matheson's classic 1954 vampire novelette *I Am Legend*. Matheson's plot is about a virus created to battle cancer, which mutates into a plague turning people into carnivorous vampire-like creatures. Matheson's theme has been imitated in a host of other post-apocalyptic films, such as Vincent Price's *The Last Man on Earth* (1964) and Cormac McCarthy's *The Road* (2006).

House of Usher

If George Romero had a financial incentive in mind, he most likely was influenced by *House of Usher,* famous about a decade earlier. During the early 1960s, America was inundated by eight Poe-derived film adaptations from director Roger Corman. Known as the "Poe Cycle," these films included *House of Usher* (1960), *The Pit and The Pendulum* (1961), *Premature Burial* (1961), *Tales of Terror* (1962), and his 1964 masterpiece, *The Mask of the Red Death.* Corman's final installment in his homage to Poe was *The Tomb of Ligeia* (1964).

These CinemaScope thrillers were highly successful, and, as an example, *House of Usher* became one of the 1960s top five box office hits. Budgeted for only two hundred seventy thousand dollars, it was the most money American International Pictures had ever spent for a film. Although most horror films play to a limited teen audience, *House of Usher* appealed to the masses. Corman had tapped into the American psyche with a macabre mix of brilliant, stylized color sets and suspense, and individuals like George Romero were paying attention.

"Godfather of Gore"

Romero also drew inspiration from Pittsburgh filmmaker Herschell Gordon Lewis (1926–2016), often called the "Godfather of Gore." Lewis is recognized for creating the "splatter" subgenre of horror films. Fred Beldin, writing for *AllMovie,* observed:

> Herschell Gordon Lewis was a pioneer with his better-known gore films, going further than anyone else dared, probing the depths of disgust and discomfort onscreen with more bad taste and imagination than anyone of his era.

Undead Ghouls

Night of the Living Dead's plotline follows seven people trapped in a rural farmhouse in western Pennsylvania, under assault by an enlarging group of cannibalistic, undead ghouls, who have returned to life after an exploded Venus probe exposes them to an unknown form of radiation. The film starred Duane Jones and included friends and relatives, local stage and amateur actors, and residents from the area, providing an opportunity for everyone to be a movie star.

Romero completed the film on a budget of approximately hundred thousand dollars but was quick to see a return on his investment. Just how successful was Romero's film? *Night of the Living Dead* had its theatrical premiere in Pittsburgh on October 1, 1968. The film eventually grossed twelve million dollars domestically and eighteen million dollars internationally, earning more than 250 times its budget and making it one of the most profitable film productions ever made at the time, even though the project was shot on a shoestring budget. That technique was scrutinized by film reviewer Matt Brunson, writing in *Film Frenzy:*

> Here's one of those happy examples when limited resources actually enhance the final product, as the ultra-low-budget—evidenced by natural settings, black-and-white film stock, and a shooting style that frequently borrows from the documentary playbook—is largely responsible for turning this into one of the classic horror films of all time.

The low-budget *Night of the Living Dead*, actualized by special effects guru Tom Savini, was significant for its unforgiving snippets of zombies munching on human flesh but can also be viewed as a metaphor for the Covid-19 pandemic and the post-apocalyptic narrative, "Can we survive?"

Library of Congress

Night of the Living Dead's explicit violence and gore circumvented the Motion Picture Association of America rating system, according to film critic Roger Ebert:

> The new Code of Self-Regulation, recently adopted by the Motion Picture Association of America, would presumably restrict a film like this one to mature audiences. But *Night of the Living Dead*

was produced before the MPAA code went into effect, so exhibitors technically weren't required to keep the kids out.

Still, the film represented more than a mere bloody gorefest. In 1999, the film was deemed "culturally, historically, or aesthetically significant" by the Library of Congress and selected for preservation in the National Film Registry. Of cultural significance was casting Duane Jones, an African-American, in the leading role as a chief zombie killer.

Romero later produced *There's Always Vanilla* (1971) and *Jack's Wife/Season of the Witch* (1972). *The Crazies* (1973) dealt with a bio-spill that induced an epidemic of homicidal madness, while *Martin* (1978) was a critically acclaimed arthouse success dealing with the vampire myth.

Crowned "the Godfather of Zombies," Romero made five more *Dead* movies, including *Dawn of the Dead* (1978) and *Day of the Dead*.

Romero's groundbreaking films were all similarly draped in controversy and negative reviews. Still, the bad publicity attracted a cult following, celebrating the outrage. While *Night of the Living Dead* mimicked the documentary style of *Invasion of the Body Snatchers* (1956), its visual horror and suspense were later visited in films such as Tobe Hooper's *The Texas Chainsaw Massacre* (1974) and the cinema verite–like *The Blair Witch Project* (1999).

The Walking Dead

Romero's nightmare was resurrected forty-two years later when *The Walking Dead*, a post-apocalyptic horror television series based on Robert Kirkman's comic book series, appeared. The AMC series mimicked *Night of the Living Dead* as survivors of a zombie apocalypse try to stay alive under near-constant threat of attacks from zombies known as "walkers."

In 2016 and 2019, *The Walking Dead* TV series, based on *Night of the Living Dead*, was filmed near the southern end of Driftwood Beach on Georgia's Jekyll Island. (Patricia A. Furek photograph.)

The series premiered on October 31, 2010, with most filming taking place at Riverwood Studios near Senoia, Georgia. Driftwood Beach on Jekyll Island was used as the surreal location for one of the filming sites.

AMC later developed the series into spinoffs, *Fear the Walking Dead* (2015) and *The Walking Dead: World Beyond* (2020).

While the series has been nominated for several awards, including the Golden Globe Award for Best Television Series – Drama and the Writers Guild of America Award for New Series, *Night of the Living Dead* continues to receive high praise. *Rotten Tomatoes'* "30 Essential Zombie Movies" listed *Night of the Living Dead* at the number 1 spot, observing:

> It's commonly accepted the subgenre as we know it today didn't rise until 1968, when George A. Romero unleashed *Night of the Living Dead*, an independent film with a budget barely above six figures. *Night* enthralled audiences with its mysterious plot, shocking gore, progressive casting and social commentary, and natch, the unforgettable hordes of the gaunt, hungry undead.

George Romero and Herschell Gordon Lewis are representative of the contributions keystone filmmakers have made, especially in the arena of gore. Romero returned to the scene of the crime in 1973, shooting *The Crazies* near the same Butler County location. *Night of the Living Dead* spawned a franchise that included five official sequels, released between 1978 and 2009, all directed by the ever-prolific Romero.

Cole Paquet, writing for the *Concordian*, noted that the script was developed by Romero and collaborator John

Russo in only three days, but during one of America's most perilous times:

> That same year, a series of 159 race riots exploded across the United States in what became known as the "Long, hot summer of 1967." Concurrently, the Vietnam War continued to rage on, being regularly broadcast to homes across America in vivid, graphic detail. As author Geoff King details in his book *New Hollywood Cinema: An Introduction*, the image of America as a place of freedom and democracy had been irreparably damaged, and led to widespread anti-authoritarian and countercultural sentiments across the western world.

Those anti-government sentiments can still be heard today, a troubling homage to Romero's futuristic vision of violence and anarchy. His zombie opus, influenced by a tumultuous era and a society at war with itself, remains as relevant as ever. And that should make all of us afraid of the horror and uncertainty that lies ahead.

Chapter 2

The Howard Beale Effect

Death is random. It has no timetable. It respects no boundaries. Two years earlier, before Night of the Living Dead assaulted our senses, Charles Whitman and Richard Speck shocked the world in an orgy of carnage. Their killings planted the seed that danger lurked even in the sanctuary of our homes. The concept of "Home Sweet Home" was now in question.

And as art imitated life, Hollywood responded with ideas, scripts, and sets from the former amateurish sci-fi constructs to films steeped in realism. Cinematic themes of murder and retribution became the norm. A pronounced change became apparent as the pendulum swung from conservative '50s repression to the revolutionary '60s.

The next decade oozed with a variation of Romero's theme, marketing entertainment starring sociopaths as leading men. These films drew back the curtain, revealing the bleak realism of Bob Clark's Black Christmas (1974),

John Carpenter's *Halloween* (1978*)*, Wes Craven's *The Hills Have Eyes* (1977), and Tobe Hooper's *The Texas Chainsaw Massacre* (1974), all espousing a hallucination of suburban fear, paranoia, and gore.

But it was *Black Christmas*, recognized as the first in the "slasher film" genre, that spawned the highly successful Halloween franchise.

Halloween: The Night He Came Home is the bloody story of Michael Audrey Myers. After escaping from the Smith's Grove-Warren County Sanitarium, Michael returns to Haddonfield, Illinois, to kill his family. Haddonfield is every idyllic town in America's heartland, with picket fences, tree-lined streets, and children filled with joy and wonder. Michael Myers challenged our innocence and complacency with every bloody slash in a cinematic rendering of Richard Speck's slaughter.

Another example was depicted through the revenge films *I Spit on Your Grave: Day of the Woman* (1978) and *Last House on the Left*. The graphically violent *I Spit on Your Grave*, considered "one of the worst films ever made," portrays the story of an aspiring writer who, after being brutally gang-raped and left for dead, seeks revenge. Similarly, Wes Craven's *Last House on the Left* (1972) explored how far families would go when pushed too far. Both films addressed society's diminished tolerance to accepting the perceived norm of violence and perversion.

At times, a single voice can represent society's zeitgeist, its collective unconscious. People identified with Howard Beale, a fictional character in Sidney Lumet's *Network*

(1976), and Charles Bronson's architect Paul Kersey, portrayed in *Death Wish* (1974). Beale's corporate oppression and resulting emotional outburst, "I'm as mad as hell, and I'm not going to take this anymore," struck a note.

Society can only take so much. *Death Wish*'s vigilante porn and Howard Beale's rant resonated with many. The storyline has Beale, a primary news reporter for UBS TV, fired for low ratings. An angry Beale announces on-air that, in retaliation, he would commit suicide during his nightly national newscast. Beale's threat proved prophetic after Pennsylvania State Treasurer Budd Dwyer, forty-seven, shot himself a decade later. Convicted of bribery and sentenced to fifty-five years in prison, Dwyer held a press conference on January 22, 1987, maintaining his innocence. He then killed himself with a .357 revolver in front of the cameras.

There is a juncture where fear is stuffed into some psychic lockbox and replaced by an instinctive need to survive. We secure handgun permits, arm ourselves, take self-defense courses, and assume control of our personal space. We take back our streets, our home, and ensure our very existence as we scream, "I'm not going to take this anymore."

The Howard Beale effect has always been here, only labeled as something else and never attaining a cultish cinematic connection. The effect was actualized before and after the film *Network*. Events represented by the Beale effect include the Birmingham, Alabama, lunch counter sit-ins (1963); the violent Stonewall riots by members of the Greenwich Village LGBT community (1969); the six-day riots following the assassination of Martin Luther King Jr., affecting over one hundred US cities (1968); the Vietnam War Out Now rally drawing two hundred thousand to Washington, DC, (1971); the Rodney King–triggered Los Angeles Riot (1999); and the Occupy Wall Street protest in Zuccotti Park and the Wall Street financial district (2011). In 2016, the Democratic House of Representatives conducted a sit-in protest over gun control legislation. That same year writer John Horvat penned an article, "What is the Cause of Our Angry Politics," for *Intellectual Takeout:*

> Digging a bit deeper, one finds that, more often than not, people are venting their rage not at any particular individual but rather a class, institution, or grouping of people. Targets include incumbents, corrupt politicians, bureaucrats, lobbyists, politically correct academics, clergy, or just the plain "establishment"—whatever that might mean. This unfocused shotgun approach holds that we must throw the whole lot out and start over again to effect real change.

Frustrations leading to Horvat's "shotgun approach" have been simmering for a long time, impacting every demographic group. Together, the fictional characters in *Network* and *Death Wish* symbolized our refusal to take it anymore.

It was inevitable that art would be deviously imitated. In December 1984, real-life vigilante Bernard Goetz, a thirty-nine-year-old electronics specialist, shot four black men in a Manhattan subway car. Goetz, who had been mugged twice before, said he started firing because he thought the four men were about to rob him. The tabloids labeled Goetz the "subway vigilante." Many subway riders, concerned about subway muggings, applauded his actions and defended him as an "avenging angel," perhaps like Bronson's *Death Wish* character.

An intense debate raged. Some called Goetz a racist because the four men were black. The youths argued that they were not trying to rob him but were only panhandling money, asking for five dollars to play video games.

After one of the four men, Darrell Cabey, was paralyzed in the shooting, his family filed a fifty million dollars lawsuit. The jury found that Goetz had acted recklessly and had deliberately inflicted emotional distress on Cabey. The jury stated that shooting Cabey twice was a critical factor in their decision. Cabey was awarded forty three million dollars—eighteen million dollarsvfor pain and suffering and twenty five million dollars in punitive damages.

Goetz paid the price for his vigilantism. Three years after the shooting, he was convicted of criminal possession of an unlicensed weapon. He spent 250 days in jail. He was, however, acquitted of attempted murder and assault. After the verdict, Goetz's lawyer, Barry Slotnick, said, "I think the true message is that people have a right to protect and defend themselves under justifiable situations."

There is nothing new under the sun. Humankind continues to display an emotional palette of anger, frustration, and intolerance. George Romero's film, although described as prophetic, merely reflected earlier admonitions proposed by writers such as Anthony Burgess, George Orwell, and Aldous Huxley. Even as this book is being prepared for publication (in 2023), our society remains locked in a cold divide, separated by extreme ideologies and zombie-like citizens, all screaming "I'm as mad as hell, and I'm not going to take this anymore."

Chapter 3
Ripperology

 Why are we so intrigued with films like *Night of the Living Dead, Halloween*, and the never-ending carnage from the gruesome *Saw* franchise? Are we all suffering from some strange psychological madness that forces us to take a midnight stroll into horror?

Humans are fascinated by the dark side. And like the moth seduced by the flame, we harbor a curiosity for shadows and ill-defined shapes, what Emily Dickinson called the "cellars of the mind."

Robert Lewis Stevenson walked down into those cellars in his 1886 novel, *The Strange Case of Dr. Jekyll and Mr. Hyde*. His story has gripped us for decades, revealing man's good and evil personas. However, most readers don't realize that Stevenson's horror classic had an unsettling connection to reality. Stevenson found inspiration in the real-life story of Deacon Brodie, a respectable Scottish citizen by day and a thief by night. Another was French teacher Eugene Chantrelle, a killer who poisoned his wife with opium. Stevenson also mined inspiration from earlier literature that had similar themes.

Stevenson's horror classic leaned heavily on the concept of the "double." Gry Faurholt of Denmark's Aarhus University explains that there are two distinct types of the doppelgänger:

> (1) The alter ego or identical double of a protagonist who seems to be either a victim of an identity theft perpetrated by a mimicking supernatural presence or subject to a paranoid hallucination; (2) the split personality or dark half of the protagonist, an unleashed monster that acts as a physical manifestation of a dissociated part of the self.

Like the vampire, the doppelgänger was a product of an early nineteenth-century fascination with superstitious belief. Its roots are in the German Schauerroman and the British Gothic novel. Vicky Lebeau, writing for *Britannica*, stated that the notion of the "double" was widely popular in the nineteenth century, especially in German literary discussions of the doppelgänger:

> Fyodor Dostoyevsky's *The Double* (1846) dealt with this subject, and Mary Wollstonecraft Shelley's

classic *Frankenstein* tale (1818) can be read in this light. The theme was explored explicitly by Oscar Wilde in *The Picture of Dorian Gray* (1891) and by H. G. Wells in both *The Island of Doctor Moreau (1896)* and *The Invisible Man* (1897).

But it was Stevenson's *The Strange Case of Dr. Jekyll and Mr. Hyde* that held readers in a stranglehold of terror as they read his vivid descriptions:

> He put the glass to his lips and drank at one gulp. A cry followed; he reeled, staggered, clutched at the table, and held on, staring with injected eyes, gasping with open mouth; and as I looked, there came, I thought, a change—he seemed to swell— his face became suddenly black, and the features seemed to melt and alter—and the next moment, I had sprung my feet and leaped back against the wall, my arms raised to shield me from that prodigy, my mind submerged in terror.

An untamed beast raged beneath Jekyll's tranquil surface, and Stevenson's portrayal of this psychological aberration connected the thread between Dr. Jekyll's gentility and Hyde's violence. Many psychologists believe that seemingly average individuals also harbor a dark side—a sinister personality trait that psychotherapist Carl Jung aptly named "the Shadow."

Maxim W. Furek

The Shadow

> "Until you make the Unconscious Conscious, it will direct your life, and you will call it fate." Carl Jung

Psychoanalysts Carl Jung and Sigmund Freud helped us understand why millions of individuals enjoy horror movies like *Night of the Living Dead* and *The Exorcist* even though they induce feelings of shock and disgust.

Then, too, novels written by fright masters James Herbert, Clive Barker, and Stephen King are filled with violence, bloodletting, and grotesque monsters—repulsive themes that most tend to avoid. Nevertheless, our fascination with horror remains a paradoxical mystery because people generally seek pleasure and avoid pain. Why, then, are we so strangely drawn to these topics?

Jung's concept of the "archetype" proposed that universal and cross-cultural themes form our personality and behavior patterns. A specific archetype he called the Shadow can help explain our attraction to repulsive themes.

According to Jung, the Shadow represents repressed ideas, shortcomings, weaknesses, chaos, and the unknown. The Shadow comprises hidden aspects of an individual's personality deemed "unacceptable" to society and offensive to our morals and values. These "unacceptable" characteristics include sexual desires, cravings, and urges.

Shadow characteristics are formed mainly by shame and often contain elements of envy, hate, and aggression. When repressed in the hidden parts of the mind, the urges are cast into the shadow—only to show themselves when the environment is safe from judgment. They may be repressed or projected onto others.

Jung represented the Shadow as a picture of Godzilla in his book *Man and His Symbols* (1964, Aldus Books), believing that we expressed the Shadow in dreams or visions with dark images of dragons, snakes, and other exotic figures.

Jung believed that the Shadow was a living creature that could not be repressed out of existence. That would cause internal stress and relationship problems. He wrote:

> If we understand anything of the unconscious, we know that it cannot be swallowed. We also know it is dangerous to suppress it because the unconscious is life, and this life turns against us if buried, as happens in neurosis.

The shadow is a living part of the personality, and therefore wants to live with it in some form. It cannot be argued out of existence or rationalized into harmlessness.

Jung alleged that we needed to confront the Shadow to attain mental balance. That process required an individual to acknowledge every aspect of their Shadow, no matter how grotesque, and then integrate the Shadow into their psyche.

Morbid Fascination

Murderers and psychopaths walk our streets. We are mesmerized by their cruel souls and evil deeds. That morbid fascination has spilled over to popular culture and now provides prime-time entertainment. Note the popularity of programs such as *Fringe, Criminal Minds, Manhunter, Clarice, Hannibal,* and *Dexter*—angry and wounded psychopaths intent on horrible savagery. We watch, transfixed, trying to understand what has damaged their humanity as we look into their tortured inner chamber. These Hollywood images act as our safety valves, allowing us to experience horror in a safe and controlled manner.

"Saucy Jack"

For over a hundred years, Jack the Ripper has gripped us with stories of wanton bloodletting. "Saucy Jack" was a sadistic executioner, and although he didn't wear goat horns or satanic amulets, his pores oozed the hatred of a feral animal. The Ripper murders focused renewed attention on Stevenson's novella published two years earlier.

"Saucy Jack" was a vicious overlord acting out a Victorian horror show. His deviant mind focused only on the next kill as he wantonly slashed throats and mutilated the genitals of Whitechapel prostitutes.

A voracious "Saucy Jack" cult begged for every scrap of information detailing his carnage. Their hunger was fueled by publications such as *Famous Crimes – Past and Present* and the British death inquests routinely published for citizens eager to read the gory details of the murders.

A unique body of work, coined "Ripperology," focused on the Ripper's brutal slayings. Over one hundred nonfiction works deal exclusively with the murders, making it one of the most written about true-crime subjects. The Ripper helped create much of the hysteria. He wrote taunting letters to the newspapers and the Great Scotland Yard, challenging them to "Catch me if you can." In an eighty-nine-line poem, dated November 8, 1887, the Ripper threatened to "destroy the filthy, hideous, whores of the night; dejected, lost, cast down, ragged, and thin."

Walter Sickert

Although the case has never been solved, Patricia Cornwell claims that Walter Sickert, the eccentric world-famous artist, was the Ripper. Sickert's paintings embraced Jung's Shadow Self and were usually macabre and shadowy. He often portrayed London's unglamorous underbelly, including nudes and working-class street scenes. After staying in the Ripper's suspected lodging, he became fascinated with the murders and painted *Jack the Ripper's Bedroom*.

Decades later, Sickert was accused of being the actual Jack the Ripper, as claimed in Jean Overton Fuller's book *Sickert and the Ripper Crimes*. In contrast, Stephen Knight's book *Jack the Ripper: The Final Solution,* asserted that Sickert was only an accessory to the murders, coerced by members of the royal family.

The Sickert-Ripper connection reached a kind of critical mass after crime author Patricia Cornwell published *Portrait of a Killer* in 2002, and according to *All That's Interesting:*

> Adding to the spotted "clues" in his paintings, Cornwell used additional evidence to show that Sickert had the personality and psychology of a serial killer. She even called on a team of forensic experts to analyze the Ripper letters for DNA matches and claimed to find mitochondria DNA that linked at least one Ripper letter to Sickert.

Cornwell believed Sickert had murdered as many as forty victims, something disputed by many historians, including *Artnet,* concluding: "These claims have never been substantiated, and most historians believe them to be without merit."

Gary Heidnik

Dubbed the "House of Horrors" killer, Gary Heidnik's notoriety did not equal that of Jack the Ripper's. Still, he was a sick and twisted psychopath and almost as twisted as the infamous movie character he inspired—Jame "Buffalo Bill" Gumb—from Thomas Harris's 1988 psychological horror classic, *The Silence of the Lambs*.

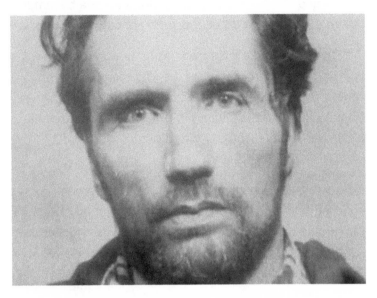

"House of Horrors" serial killer Gary Heidnik was the inspiration behind the *Silence of the Lambs* psychopath, Buffalo Bill. Heidnik was the last person to be executed in the Commonwealth of Pennsylvania. Photo: Philadelphia Police Department via America's Most Haunted. Public domain.

A&E True Crime provided this graphic description—with the *Warning: The following contains disturbing descriptions of violence, including sexual violence. Reader discretion is advised.*

He dismembered his victims and stored their limbs in containers labeled "dog food," allegedly feeding their ground-up remains to those he hadn't yet killed. When Philadelphia police arrested Gary Heidnik in 1987, they found a dismembered head in a stockpot of water on his stove—and three more women chained up in a basement prison pit, where he'd been torturing and raping them.

Bishop Heidnik was a contradiction. He was the self-appointed spiritual leader for the fifty members of his United Church of the Ministers of God. Defense attorney Charles Peruto Jr. explained to A&E True Crime that his client was an intellectually gifted genius with an IQ of 148.

He made twenty thousand dollars grow into seven hundred fifty thousand dollars in the stock market. One of the people who testified against him was his stockbroker —the broker said he made all of his own calls. He called the shots and came up with these winning stocks.

Heidnik, who drove a 1971 Rolls Royce, started the Philadelphia-based church in 1971 with just five followers and a fifteen hundred dollar investment. Ultimately, he raised more than five hundred thousand dollars for his cult. Heidnik was adept at manipulating and controlling his flocks. Soon, he began to kidnap women, chaining them in a cellar pit, a virtual chamber of horrors.

Heidnik used his victims as sex slaves and forced them to torture each other. He raped his victims, used electrical shock on them, and murdered two of them. He ground one of their bodies up, mixed it with dog food, and forced the other women to eat her flesh.

A Pennsylvania jury convicted him of first-degree murder, kidnapping, and rape in the slaying of two women and the imprisonment of four others in his basement torture chamber. He received a lethal injection on July 6, 1999, at the State Correctional Institution at Rockview. Heidnik was the last person to be executed in Pennsylvania.

Criminology research has proven that lawbreakers often attack soft targets or easy prey. In the academic book *The Psychology of Criminal and Antisocial Behavior: Victim and Offender Perspectives*: "Predators, irrespective of their end game, are exceptionally good at identifying the weak members of the herd." Heidnik sought out African-American females in their teens to mid-twenties. All were intellectually disabled, and all were influenced by money.

Watching horror films provides us with bizarre yet practical therapy. We use the outside monsters to conquer the internal ones—locked away in a repressed compartment of our design.

Horror films sling us onto a hell ride of blood-splattered walls and bullet-riddled corpses. We breathe in the thrill of an adrenalized cocktail. Rather than participate in the slaughter, we watch vicariously, safely, in the security of our living rooms and movie theatres—with no blood on our hands. Horror writer Stephen King crafted a stellar career based on that philosophy. In an interview with the Guardian, he said:

The world is a scary place, not just America. We're

in the spooky house – on the ghost train, if you
prefer – for life. The scares come and go, but
everyone likes make-believe monsters to stand in
for the real ones.

Terror seeps out from the inner corners of our minds as
spiders creeping across quaking flesh. We survive those
nightmares by placing our focus externally—whether in
horror films about monsters slithering under the bed or in
real-life boogiemen like Charles Whitman, Richard Speck,
and Gary Heidnik.

Chapter 4

The Sheppton
Convergence

Weird. Fantastic. Astounding. These words come to mind whenever the incomprehensible events of Sheppton, history's strangest mining disaster, are discussed.

Sheppton was a massive story for two long weeks in the waning days of August 1963. Over two hundred international newsmen, including reporters from the United Kingdom, Japan, and Germany, broadcasted from the scene. With an incongruency of supernatural, technological, and macabre elements, the world's attention was riveted on this remote Pennsylvania patch town for two impossible weeks.

The disaster created a "convergence" of improbable themes colliding atop one another—the miraculous with the supernatural, the punitive with the redemptive. Sheppton has been pronounced a "continuous, collective hallucination," an out-of-body experience, a miracle by Pope John XXIII, and proof of life after death. The Associated Press called Sheppton "one of the year's most significant" news stories. Three books and several documentaries have explored Sheppton, yet it remains virtually unknown to the masses.

Three coal miners were trapped for unimaginable minutes and hours in an accident that could have been prevented. Integral pillar structures had been robbed, and, ultimately, karma played its hand. The hoisting cable snapped, timbers exploded like toothpicks, and hundreds of tons of rock, dirt, and coal showered down upon the hapless miners.

Cannibalism

There was little hope for rescue, yet, after the extrication of survivors David Fellin and Henry Throne, allegations of cannibalism were raised. Many area residents believed the missing miner, Louis Bova, had been cannibalized. The 1971 song "Timothy," written by playwright Rupert Holmes and recorded by The Buoys, told the tale of cannibalism in a mine—and eerily paralleled Sheppton in a bizarre example of art imitating life.

J. Ronnie Sando and John Bova were the loudest voices accusing the miners of eating human flesh. Sando, a rescue team member, wrote about it in his book, *The Famous Sheppton Mine Rescue*. Bova, the son of the missing miner, sadly recounted the possibility of cannibalism. During an interview with the Hazleton *Standard-Speaker*'s Kelly Monitz, he said, "All my life, they said (Fellin and Throne) ate my father. To this day, I wonder if they ate him."

Rescue Technology

SHEPPTON MINE DISASTER AND RESCUE

On August 27, 1963, rescuers used a new technique to drill a borehole that successfully freed two coal miners trapped for nearly 2 weeks by a shaft cave-in 320 feet below ground. One miner was lost, and the incident gained national attention and prompted more stringent safety regulations for small independent mines. The borehole technique has been widely used for mine rescues worldwide, notably at Quecreek (2002) and Chile (2010).

PENNSYLVANIA HISTORICAL AND MUSEUM COMMISSION 2013

Few are aware of the rescue technology, which is another fragment of the mythology. One of the supporting characters was Houston billionaire Howard Hughes, who had tungsten carbide drill bits flown to the Hazleton airport to facilitate the rescue. Sheppton rescuers invented the borehole rescue technique, which was later used successfully in Quecreek, Pennsylvania, (2002) and Chile (2010). In Quecreek, PA, nine miners were trapped

245 feet below ground after they cut into an abandoned mine, releasing 150 million gallons of water into the mine. It was later discovered that the company had supplied them with outdated, inaccurate maps.

The Chilian disaster lasted sixty-nine days. Thirty-three copper miners had to endure high humidity and 95 degree Fahrenheit temperatures trapped 2,295 feet deep inside the San Jose gold and copper mine. Their rescue was documented in the film *The 33*.

Humanoid Creatures

Sheppton's black hell defined their existence. They suffered the inability to see movement or depth. It had been taken away. But despite their blindness, the miners could somehow see in the darkness. Fellin and Throne saw humanoids dressed in strange space suits with softly glowing lanterns attached to their helmets. They looked upon surreal blue doors linking them to what they thought was another dimension. Fellin recalled that happening for the *Philadelphia Inquirer:*

> We saw this door on the fourth or fifth day, although we had no light from above or our helmets. The door was covered in bright blue light. It was apparent, better than sunlight. Two ordinary-looking men, not miners, opened the door. We could see beautiful marble steps on the other side. We saw this for some time and then didn't see it.

Fellin looked into the darkness. An unearthly brightness met his view. He saw a Golden City, a massive gilded structure that stretched for miles in each direction. Fellin saw his relatives sitting in orderly groups on the steps, some near and others farther away. He recognized many of them, even strangers he instinctively sensed were related to him.

Fellin continued to tell his story. After Sheppton's first anniversary, Program Director Bill Schmeer of WAZL, a small radio station near Hazleton, approached Fellin and Throne for an interview. Schmeer's intention was not to explain the phenomenon but to report it as seen through the eyes of the survivors. His interview appeared in the March 1965 issue of *Fate Magazine* and was possibly the first Sheppton account marketed explicitly to the paranormal audience.

The recollections of the miners took a strange turn in their version of *The Twilight Zone*. Fellin told Schmeer that he saw three nonhuman creatures in the mine. He described them as "ruggedly handsome, about six feet, three inches tall, with bronze-colored skin and very slightly pointed ears." They had athletic builds, "like football players." He said they had thin lips and "normal eyes." They wore a wide headband, open at the top, to reveal dark, straight hair.

Interviewed separately, Throne's recollection of the humanoids offered a variation on the theme. He said the visitors had high cheekbones, Caucasian eyes, and thin lips. Their skin was darker on the hands and toes than on their faces. Their hair was ear length, combed back at the top but falling on the sides. The three wore green-gray garments similar to Japanese kimonos and had open sandals on their feet.

The Under-People

Sheppton took on a life of its own. Author Eric Norman's book *The Under-People* offered accounts of alien men and majestic stairways. Norman observed the recurrent theme of Fellin and Thorne, "who told of seeing a large door in the rock wall illuminated by blue light. The two miners claim to have watched the door open and seen a group of strange men dressed in 'weird outfits' standing on a beautiful marble stairway."

There has been much conjecture surrounding these paranormal occurrences. Connections between these events have been made, but what does it mean? Are the Sheppton events supernatural? Do they represent some incomprehensible spirit outside our normal scope of awareness? Herb Fox, an author and Richard Sharpe Shaver researcher, gathered together the loose threads of the Sheppton fabric, proclaiming:

> What makes the Sheppton Mine Disaster unique is its paranormal and mystical overtones, harkening back to the days of Hollow Earthers like John Cleves Symmes and Richard S. Shaver. Not only did the two trapped miners have—what were later described as—out-of-body experiences, but they

also had a guest: Pope John XXIII, recently deceased. He steadied their nerves during a mind-numbing 14 days of captivity. They were said to have been visited by the infamous Men in Black of UFO lore, witnessed a marble "stairway to heaven," and seen a shining city—300 feet underground.

American Journal of Psychiatry

This event's most intriguing aspect was that many believed the miners' strange accounts. Bill Schmeer provided a fitting epitaph to the supernatural event, observing that Sheppton was "unmatched in the annals of psychic research." Several psychiatrists from the University of Pennsylvania interviewed the miners. After publishing their results in the *American Journal of Psychiatry*, they concluded, "Neither man exhibited evidence of psychosis or marked mental abnormality when examined."

Dr. Richard Anderson, a US Navy medical doctor and psychiatrist, also interviewed them, determining that their account was truthful. Additional support came from Dr. Bruce Greyson, a psychiatrist at the University of Connecticut Health Center and editor for the *Journal of Near-Death Studies*. Greyson, citing the simultaneous paranormal experience, said:

> If they can corroborate each other's accounts, they could provide evidence for the reality of "The Other Side" beyond anything yet available.

In every instance, Fellin and Throne's collective experience was determined to be accurate. Assessments from the medical community deemed they were not the result of hallucination, trauma, or a miner's psychosis.

Finally, Daniel Rolph, writing for the *Historical Society of Pennsylvania*, observed that the ultimate deduction might lie not in the debate between miracles and hallucinations but the eye of the observer. His "Mines: Mysterious Discoveries & Miracles" intoned:

> The story of Throne and Fellin's survival and rescue were enough to captivate the world's attention. Still, it was what they claimed they saw and heard while entombed that fascinated the public, statements both men swore as to their authenticity, separately and publicly, emphatic declarations that they took to their graves. However, others believed they had simultaneously witnessed the same hallucinations.

The term "supernatural" denotes a force counter to scientific thought. In science, we connect the cause to the effect. Because of gravity, the apple drops. Because of evaporation, water from the earth rises, cools, and returns as rain. But in all the weird occurrences in Sheppton, we witness only the physical manifestations. We see strange things but can only guess the cause.

Writing in the *Skeptical Inquirer,* Investigative Files columnist Joe Nickell wrote:

Taken together, the different pieces of evidence demonstrate that the men's visionary experiences were, understandably, almost certainly hallucinations, delusions, and imaginings, shared through suggestion so that they eventually became more or less standardized between the two trapped miners. This probability is both plausible and corroborated by evidence. In contrast, the alternate explanation—that the visions were actual supernatural occurrences—loses out to the principle of Occam's razor, the scientific rule of thumb that suggests the hypothesis with the fewest assumptions is to be preferred. (Posting the supernatural requires assumptions not founded in science.)

This is not an unscholarly "debunking" attitude but rather an investigative one. I remain confident that an investigation leading to an explanation is the best approach. If something can be effectively explained, any needed debunking will take care of itself.

Publicity Seeker

It is essential to understand that Fellin did not approach the media to discuss his ordeal. He was merely responding to their voracious interview requests. It would be unfair to characterize him as a publicity seeker.

Also, Anna instructed her husband not to cooperate with the media; Fellin, in turn, instructed Throne to resist

these potential traps—something that the younger miner
failed to heed. Even so, Fellin must be given credit for
initially documenting his story. Fellin insisted on a
psychiatric examination upon his rescue. He also offered
to be polygraph tested after Bill Schmeer's 1964 *Fate
Magazine* interview.

Fellin fiercely defended his recollection that John XXIII
saved them, providing them resilience to endure. Trapped
for endless hours, they prayed for the impossible. They
prayed for sanity. If they gave up, they would go insane
and kill each other. Fellin, a devout Catholic, frequently
crossed himself. The centuries-old sign of the cross has
several meanings, including as a blessing and protection
from evil. For Fellin, it became a prayer for divine
intervention and rescue. Fellin's faith intermingled the
sacred with the supernatural. He was steeped in the
strewn philosophies of Jesus Christ and Mahatma
Gandhi. He prayed that the grace of God would protect
them. They prayed several times each day. It became
their religion.

Pray. Tap. Dig.

And then the miracle.

They saw things, encountering inexplicable beings. Pope
John XXIII and three humanlike creatures appeared.
Signs that they were going to be rescued. The stark
chamber holding them captive was filled with a bluish
luminance. A set of white marble stairs materialized.
Fellin thought it led to the Gates of Heaven and
described family members sitting on the stairway, giving

the miners hope. Days after his rescue, Fellin tried to explain the mystical aspects of their confinement to *Standard-Speaker* reporter Harrison M. Henritzy:

> There were two doors down there. Both of them were clearly visible. One was to the bright and glorious side, where our hearts told us to go, and one to the other side, that wasn't nearly as nice, and our hearts told us not to go there.

Fellin's recollections were detailed and lucid. He believed that what he experienced was a miracle. Fellin and Throne did not care if people thought they were crazy. They had heard worse. They knew what they had experienced. They held to that belief. Fellin and Throne granted the Associated Press an exclusive interview, discussing the weirdness they experienced. Upon their rescue, both miners were cross-examined by the Associated Press. Said Throne:

> There were times we saw people who weren't there and lights that weren't there, and doors that weren't there. Imagine seeing a regular house door down in the bottom of a mine. I'd sleep! I'd wake up. I'd see all kinds of lights and the actual figures of people. They now tell me these were hallucinations, but the crazy thing is that Davey would see the things the same as I did.

Fellin was reluctant to be interrogated and expressed an emotional outrage during his interview:

Now they're trying to tell me those things were hallucinations, that we imagined it all. We didn't! Our minds weren't playing tricks on us. I've been a practical, hard-headed miner all my life. My mind was clear down there in the mine. These things happened! I can't explain them. I'm almost afraid to think what might be the explanation.

Fellin left the mines and found employment driving a school bus. He died twenty-seven years after his rescue. He died in 1990 at age eighty-five. Throne continued to mine after the disaster. Later he worked on a bridge-building crew. Throne lived thirty-five years after his rescue. He died in 1998 at age sixty-three. The remains of Louis Bova have never been found.

Encompassing seemingly incongruous variables, Sheppton lies between the natural order and the supernatural. Some have inferred that Sheppton may be a portal to another dimension, another space-time continuum. We simply don't know.

We have no available language to articulate such themes of the supernatural. It's much easier—or perhaps more convenient—to write this off as a hallucination or miner's psychosis brought on by claustrophobic trauma. David Fellin had always been forthcoming with the media and candid about his disclosures. Nevertheless, there was something that he was holding back, something he refused to articulate.

There were vile things that he declined to discuss and things that would never be revealed. "I'm not going to tell you about them" were his cryptic words and perhaps his most significant clue. It was a revelation Fellin purposively took to the grave. The secret Fellin guarded could have unlocked the mystery of Sheppton and granted us the sweet salvation of closure. Alas, after reviewing the evidence and the convergence of themes, it remains the Coal Region's last remaining mystery.

Chapter 5

Alferd Packer's Flesh Eaters

According to playwright Rupert Holmes, the "Timothy" narrative eerily intersected with Tennessee Williams's *Suddenly Last Summer* and Tennessee Ernie Ford's 1955 hit "Sixteen Tons." Additionally, that gruesome song shares a possible connection to the cannibal mythology of Sheppton. But, after careful inspection, the alleged cannibalism is only that—"alleged."

Sheppton survivor Davie Fellon always contended that "Only evil men would ask such a question" when asked by the Chicago *Daily News* if he and Hank Throne had cannibalized their mate, Louis Bova. Still, rumors of flesh-eating persisted, fueled in part by books, including rescue team member Ronnie Sando's *The Famous Sheppton Mine Rescue: The Untold Story: The Blood and Sweat of the Rescue Team*.

The repulsive act of cannibalism permeates every culture and is found on most continents. It is vile, sordid, and unspeakable, and it is of little surprise that Sheppton shares a gruesome relationship with fellow Pennsylvanian Alferd Packer.

Many historians have unfortunately viewed Pennsylvania-born Alferd Griner Packer as "the Colorado Cannibal."

Alferd Griner Packer was born on January 21, 1842, in the lonely hills of Allegheny County. And just like Sheppton, his story is rooted in a concoction of myth and reality, getting larger with each retelling of the story. First, he became known as "Alferd" after misspelling his name and then, unfortunately, as "the Colorado Cannibal."

Packard was mustered out of the Minnesota Volunteer Infantry and the Iowa Volunteer Cavalry Regiment during the Civil War because of epileptic seizures. But in November 1873, he joined thousands of prospectors looking for gold in the rich Utah hills around Provo. Then on February 9, 1874, he and five others left their more extensive group of twenty-one, pushing on for the coveted Rocky Mountain gold.

Two months later, Packer arrived alone at the Los Pinos Indian Agency near Gunnison, Colorado. He confessed that he'd killed prospector Wilson Bell in self-defense after Bell killed the other men. Packer wrote that there was no food and inadequate provisions and that his only option was to survive by eating the flesh of the dead men. Authorities listed his victims as Frank "Butcher" Miller, Israel Swann, James Humphreys, George Noon, and Shannon Wilson Bell.

Convicted of manslaughter, he was sentenced to prison. Author and researcher Harold Schechter explores this western mystery in his book *Man-Eater: The Life and Legend of an American Cannibal*:

> It finally just seemed more plausible to say that Packer did kill those other guys. One of the things that I learned in my research is the incredible psychological effects of starvation, which reduce even the most civilized person to this very barbaric state. And, you know, Packer probably wasn't the most civilized person, to begin with.

Judge M. B. Gerry's famous quote that was uttered while handing down the sentence in Packer's first trial:

> Alfred Packer, the judgment of this court is that

you be removed from hence to the jail of Hinsdale
County and there confined until the 19th day of
May, AD 1883, and that on said 19th day of May
1883, you be taken from thence by the sheriff of
Hinsdale County to a place of execution prepared
for this purpose, at some point within the
corporate limits of the town of Lake City, in the
said country of Hinsdale, and between the hours of
10 A.M. and 3 P.M. of said day, you, then and there,
by said sheriff, be hung by the neck until you are
dead, dead, dead, and may God have mercy upon
your soul.

But Packer surreptitiously escaped from jail and went into
hiding in Cheyenne, Wyoming. He was returned to
Colorado, where he was tried and sentenced to death. In
1885, his bizarre tale continued when the Colorado
Supreme Court reversed his death sentence due to a
"grandfather's clause." However, he was retried and
sentenced to forty years in prison.

In January 1901, the governor granted Packer conditional
parole, and he was freed from prison but not allowed to
leave the state. Packer died on April 23, 1907, at the age
of sixty-five in Phillipsburg, Colorado. His story was told
in the 1980 film *The Legend of Alfred Packer*, and a folk
song, "Ballad of Alferd Packer," was written by Phil Ochs.

Dripping in ghoulish notoriety, Packer joins other real-life
cannibals Jeffrey Dahmer, Albert Fish, Armin Meiwes, and
Alexander Pearce in this aberrant forensic lineup. Serial
killer and sex offender Jeffrey Dahmer is easily

recognized as America's most famous cannibal. Dahmer, like a real-life Hannibal Lecter, murdered seventeen males between 1978 and 1991. Torture, necrophilia, and cannibalism were his modus operandi. Dahmer kept human body parts refrigerated so that he could feast on the flesh. A human head and three bags of organs, including two hearts, were stored in his refrigerator. In addition, three heads, a torso, and various internal organs were found inside a free-standing freezer.

Donner-Reed Party

The incidence of cannibalism isn't novel. In 1846, the Donner-Reed party attempted to reach California via wagon train using a presumed shorter route but became snowbound in the rugged Sierra Nevada Mountains.

To survive, the eighty-one pioneers ate bones, twigs, string, hides, and a concoction described as "glue." They also ate their family dog, Cash. Emigrant Virginia Reed Murphy wrote, "We ate his head and feet—hide—everything about him." One of the surviving forty-seven, Georgia Donner, claimed that human flesh was cooked for all party members but was given only to the children. Her claim has never been fully substantiated, but the legend persists.

Flight 571

Examples of cannibalism can easily be found. For example, the 1993 motion picture *Alive* portrayed the

October 13, 1972, crash of Uruguayan Air Force flight 571. Trapped in subzero cold 11,800 feet high in a remote area of the Andes, the sixteen survivors fed on the human flesh of dead passengers, preserved in the frozen snow.

In his 2006 book, *Miracles in the Andes: 72 Days on the Mountain and My Long Trek Home,* Nando Parrado reflected on his ordeal:

> ... again and again, we scoured the fuselage in search of crumbs and morsels. We tried to eat strips of leather torn from pieces of luggage, though we knew that the chemicals they'd been treated with would do us more harm than good. We ripped open seat cushions hoping to find straw but found only inedible upholstery foam. Again and again, I came to the same conclusion: unless we wanted to eat the clothes we were wearing, there was nothing here but aluminum, plastic, ice, and rock.

Researchers, including Piers Paul Read, who wrote *Alive: The Story of the Andes Survivors* (1974), concluded that because all passengers were Roman Catholic, they rationalized their act of cannibalism as morally correct and equivalent to Holy Communion or Eucharist. "Transubstantiation," the official Roman Catholic concept referring to the change that takes place during the sacrament of Holy Communion, maintains that the bread and wine are turned miraculously into the body and blood of Christ Himself.

The biblical verse in John 6:55, "For my flesh is meat indeed, and my blood is drink indeed," appeared to be the words that addressed their dilemma, while another, John 15:13, reads, "No man hath greater love than this: that he lay down his life for his friends."

Uncanny Similarities

In the Sheppton mining disaster of 1963, accusations of cannibalism were made after only two miners were rescued. Townspeople demanded to know what happened to the missing miner. The 1971 rock song "Timothy" seemed to parallel similar events at the Pennsylvania mine. Recorded seven years after the Pennsylvania incident, "Timothy" brought back memories many would rather forget.

A more recent incident, with uncanny similarities, occurred on August 5, 2010, when thirty-three Chilean coal miners became trapped 2,295 feet underground inside the San Jose Mine in the northern Atacama Desert.

The miners, trapped for sixty-nine days, were forced to conserve what little food stores they had. Each man received a ration of two teaspoonfuls of tuna, half a glass of milk, and half a cookie every forty-eight hours. They knew that at some point, the food supplies would be exhausted. In the early days of their ordeal, cannibalism was discussed as a means of survival.

Survivor Mario Sepulveda, interviewed by author
Jonathan Franklin, reflected:

> It was no joke, there was no more food. But how
> long before cannibalism became a very realistic
> option? I would say five or ten days. Food or no
> food, I was going to get out of there ... I had to
> think about which miner was going to collapse first
> and then started thinking about how I was going
> to eat him ... I wasn't embarrassed, I wasn't
> scared.

Another miner who survived the ordeal, Samuel Avalos,
explained to Chile's TVN public television network: "It
was kind of who died first, that's where we were, he who
died first ... the rest will go there, like the little animals,"
Avalos said of the possible actions.

Those celebrated thirty-three miners were rescued by
using rescue technology developed forty-seven years
earlier in Sheppton, Pennsylvania. A historical marker was
erected in 2015 by the Pennsylvania Historical and
Museum Commission on Schoolhouse Road, near
Sheppton, Pennsylvania, in Schuylkill County. It reads:

> On August 27, 1963, rescuers used a new
> technique to drill a borehole that successfully freed
> two coal miners trapped for nearly two weeks by a
> shaft cave-in 320 feet below ground. One miner
> was lost and the incident gained national attention

and prompted more stringent safety regulations for small independent mines. The borehole technique has been widely used for mine rescues worldwide, notably Quecreek (2002) and Chile (2010).

Nine Hundred -Day Siege

One of World War II's more sordid chapters involved cannibalism. The Siege of Leningrad, also known as the Nine hundred -Day Siege, began after German and Finnish forces surrounded the Soviet Union's second-largest city. All supply lines, including food rations, were cut off. After all pets, birds, and rats had been eaten, predatory gangs resorted to extreme measures. Unfortunate pedestrians were killed, and their flesh consumed. These gruesome acts were reported in the winter of 1941–1942, and as described by *History.com*:

> Residents burned books and furniture to stay warm and searched for food to supplement their scarce rations. Animals from the city zoo were consumed early in the siege, followed before long by household pets. Wallpaper paste made from potatoes was scraped off the wall, and leather was boiled to produce an edible jelly. Grass and weeds were cooked, and scientists worked to extract vitamins from pine needles and tobacco dust. Hundreds, perhaps thousands, resorted to cannibalizing the dead, and in a few cases, people were murdered for their flesh. The Leningrad

police struggled to keep order and formed a special division to combat cannibalism.

That special division uncovered human carcasses hung on meat hooks in gruesome-smelling frozen food lockers. More than one million Leningrad citizens and soldiers perished from the Nazi siege, lasting from 1941 to 1944, and over 260 Leningraders were imprisoned for the crime of cannibalism.

Autocannibalism

Cannibalism is erroneously relegated to our dark, primitive past. Nicholas D. Kristof, in his 2010 *New York Times* essay "The Grotesque Vocabulary in Congo," discussed the strange term "autocannibalism." Kristof says the word "describes what happens when a militia in eastern Congo's endless war cuts flesh from living victims and forces them to eat it."

That barbaric part of the world around Bukavu, Congo, maintains a system of control that incorporates autocannibalism and repeated rapes of the same person —all means of terrorizing and controlling the populace. Kristof concludes that autocannibalism is not "just mindless savagery" but wartime atrocities that are part of "a calculated military strategy." He argues that they are premeditated and deliberate, serving two main purposes.

First, these horrible acts terrorize entire populations, who then live in fear of future violence. They also create a bonding among the soldiers, often youths or teens employed by warlords. Kristof believes that once they participate in autocannibalism, they are more apt to identify with their military structure and not return to society, due in large part to the shame they experience over their barbaric behavior.

The Parable of Cannibalism

The parable of cannibalism has been articulated in American literature. Herman Melville's first book, *Typee*, was about cannibals, and American humorist Mark Twain wrote "Cannibalism in the Cars." Other similar projects include the diverse works of Poul Anderson, Max Brooks, Arthur C. Clarke, Bret Easton Ellis, Cormac McCarthy, and William Shakespeare.

Survivor Type, by horror master Stephen King, followed a shipwreck victim, stranded on a desolate island, who ate his own body parts to survive. The 1973 science fiction film *Soylent Green*, based on *Make Room! Make Room!*, Harry Harrison's 1966 novel, told of citizens being fed rations of small green wafers in response to a global food crisis. The wafers, advertised as being produced from "high energy plankton," were actually the processed remains of human corpses.

The Martian practice of eating one's dead comrade was viewed as an act of great respect in Robert A. Heinlein's *Stranger in a Strange Land* (1961), and similarly, Anne Rice's *The Queen of The Damned* (1988) depicted an ancient culture whose consumption of their loved ones signified a more appropriate funeral rite than burial or cremation.

Another example can be found in a popular motion picture adaptation. In Tennessee William's aforementioned *Suddenly Last Summer* (1959), the horrific scene when the homosexual Sebastian Venable is chased through the streets of Cabeza de Lobo and then eaten alive by a ravenous mob was meant, according to Williams, metaphorically and not literally.

Snuff Flick

The savage realism of Ruggero Deodato's *Cannibal Holocaust* (1980) blended fact with fiction and led to Deodato's arrest shortly after its Italian premiere. The graphic "Most Controversial Movie Ever Made" was purportedly banned in more than sixty countries.

But suspicious authorities believed that the bloody film was an authentic "snuff flick" and that Columbian actors were actually killed on-screen. Although found not guilty, Deodato was barred from making films in Italy for several years and his film banned. The filmmaker explained, "I make films that people call 'horror' because I want to make films about real things that happen in the world, and most real things aren't very nice." Shot with handheld cameras as a pseudo-documentary, the film is often cited as an influence on *The Blair Witch Project* (1999), one of the most successful independent movies of all time.

Despite violent and sadistic themes, a voracious appetite exists for these stories. Cannibalism, one of the few remaining taboos in our Judeo-Christian society, was explored in the television series *Hannibal*. The program, loosely based on Thomas Harris's *Red Dragon* (1981) and the classic *Silence of the Lambs* (1991), stoked public fascination. The series travels a much darker path than television offerings *CSI*, *Criminal Minds*, and *The Following*. In a representative episode, brilliant psychopath Hannibal Lecter delicately slices through a sautéed human leg before consuming it with "a nice Chianti."

Repugnant Myth

Some primitive cultures believed that by eating the flesh of their enemies, they would become more ferocious warriors. The Aghori of India, stigmatized as a "dark sect," distinguish themselves from other Hindu sects and priests by consuming raw corpses, believing that it gave them immortality and supernatural powers. The Wari tribes of Brazil ate their fallen enemies and also their own dead.

Wallace's excellent work *Indians in Pennsylvania* (1970) explored this shadowy theme:

> The Shawnees were famed fighters. "It is a tradition," said the Shawnee Prophet, "that The Shawnees have never been in the habit of suing

for peace themselves but of receiving the propositions of their enemies."

In war, they were ruthless. They survived among them, as indeed among most other Indians until the 18th century, the practice of ritual cannibalism. The eating of human flesh was in general abhorred by Indians, but cannibalism survived as a war custom because it was believed that the virtues of a brave enemy could be transformed by this means to his captors.

Art and Life

The intersection between art and life was evident in the persona of Richard Parker, the former mutineer in Edgar Allen Poe's *The Narrative of Arthur Gordon Pym of Nantucket*. To survive, the fictitious crew draws straws to determine which of them will be sacrificed to provide meat. Parker is stabbed to death after drawing that fateful straw.

Forty-six years later, a yacht named the *Mignonette* left England, headed toward Sydney, Australia. Unfortunately, the four-person crew didn't have enough provisions for survival. Stacy Conradt noted a bizarre connection to Poe's narrative:

One man, a seventeen-year-old named Richard Parker, fell overboard and then made the mistake of drinking seawater to attempt to quench his thirst. Parker started going downhill fast, and that's when his fellow survivors decided they would kill him to ensure their own survival. The men had considered drawing straws, but they figured Parker was so far gone they might as well kill him and drink his blood while it was fresh (instead of risking the contaminated blood that might occur if they just waited for him to die due to illness). After stabbing Parker in the throat with a penknife, the three men devoured him.

The rationale for cannibalism is fascinating in its variation: survival, empowerment, torture, control, respect, and psychosis. Although the name of "Richard Parker" is not as well-known as that of Alferd Packer , he represented the juncture where cannibalism became reality and truth stranger than fiction.

Chapter 6
The Third Man Factor

In 1963, the entire world was gripped by the human drama unfolding in a remote Pennsylvania coal mine.

After being rescued from the Sheppton tomb, Davey Fellin testified that Pope John XXIII had been with him and Hank Throne during their two-week ordeal. But what the miners saw has been at the center of ongoing controversy. The Pope's specter has been alternately described as a miracle, as attested by Vatican scholars, and a collective hallucination.

But could there be other theories to explain the Pope's ghostly visitation, and if so, what might those look like?

Did Sheppton's guardian angels take the form of three humanoid creatures? Researcher Martin Piechota attributed the Sheppton visitation as proof of eventual rescue:

Three men appeared to Fellin and Thorne with a

plaque. The men were six feet three inches tall,
with bronze-colored skin and slightly pointed ears.
They were dressed in green-gray garments with
open sandals on their feet.

One of the characters in the apparition seen by the two
miners was carrying a tablet or slate that had no writing
on it. This may have been a symbolic message that Pope
John XXIII had died. These men may have been sent to
promote Pope John XXIII, who passed away on June 3,
1963.

Piechota believed that the sixteen-inch-by-twenty-four-
inch blue triangular plaque was a sacrament the visitors
offered to the miners. Furthermore, he thought that the
heart-shaped plaque represented eventual rescue.

Martin Piechota regarded Sheppton as a "less known,
religious event" parallel to the 1917 Miracle at Fatima. He
believed that mysterious Men in Black, emissaries who
covertly contact human beings, visited Sheppton to offer
the miners a sign of probable liberation.

Paranormal Editor Deena West Budd believed that the
Pope's imagery provided much-needed spiritual
optimism:

> As both parties (Fellin and Throne) were
> interviewed separately yet reported the same
> story, I tend to believe it was NOT a hallucination.
> I think these men were not meant to die at that
> time and were visited by the spirit of Pope John

XXIII to bring them the hope and strength they
needed to get through those two weeks of horror.

That hope and strength, granted to the trapped miners by
the Pope, embodied the narrative known as the third man
factor. As described by researcher John Geiger, his book
The Third Man Factor: Surviving the Impossible explored
the human capacity to survive and transcend extreme
physiological conditions like Sheppton, *but with divine
help.*

Geiger's third man factor is a theory of how people, in
many critical situations or at the very edge of death,
often sense an unseen presence offering hope,
protection, and guidance. These spirit guardians
encourage individuals, under extreme circumstances, to
make a final effort to survive. In his book, Geiger lists a
number of similar accounts, such as Ernest Shackleton.

Shackleton

Explorer Sir Ernest Shackleton (1874–1922), CVO (1874–
1922), is regarded as the greatest of Antarctic explorers.
He was a member of Captain Scott's expedition to the
South Pole (1901–1903), and in 1907 was knighted for his
expedition on the whaler *Nimrod*. Shackleton sailed
within ninety-seven miles of the South Pole, as chronicled
in *The Heart of the Antarctic*.

Shackleton led three British expeditions during the
Heroic Age of the Antarctic Exploration period.
Shackleton's attempt to become the first person to cross

Maxim W. Furek

Antarctica failed, but his successful effort to reach help at a remote South Atlantic whaling station, leading his men to safety after being stranded for two years, is considered a heroic feat of endurance. Today, Shackleton is celebrated as one of England's greatest heroes for his actions during the ill-fated *Endurance* expedition.

His book, *South: The Endurance Expedition,* was one of the first recorded instances of the third man factor, John Geiger's bizarre psychological phenomenon. In the book, Shackleton recounted this third man factor (he called it the fourth presence) and described having "a sense of an unseen being who had joined them, the fourth presence":

> I know that during that long and racking march of thirty-six hours over the unnamed mountains and glaciers of South Georgia, it seemed to me often that we were four, not three. I said nothing to my companions on the point, but afterward, Worsley said to me, "Boss, I had a curious feeling on the march that there was another person with us." Crean confessed to the same idea.

Shackleton, Worsley, and Cream separately concluded that they were accompanied by an unknown fourth companion, a mysterious presence that appeared during their grueling journey.

But what was this mysterious presence? Shackleton admitted that, because of "the dearth of human words" and the difficulty in describing "things intangible," he felt obligated to include it in his book, *South.*

The Waste Land

The Church Army Gazette

WITH WHICH IS INCORPORATED THE CHURCH EVANGELIST.

WEEK ENDING FEBRUARY 5, 1920.

THREE MEN—

OR FOUR?

SIR ERNEST SHACKLETON
the great Antarctic Explorer says:
"I KNOW"

FOUR—NOT THREE.

The 192Ø *Church Army Gazette*
documented Sir Ernest Shackleton's
mysterious "third man factor."

According to paranormal researchers, the third man
factor has been experienced throughout history by
numerous traumatized adventurers, including lone sailors,
pilots, and explorers, sensing a guiding presence. Once it
became public knowledge, Shackleton's ordeal was
articulated by poet T. S. Eliot (1888–1965) in *The Waste
Land*, considered the twentieth century's most influential
poetic work. In part V, "What the Thunder Said," Eliot
addressed Shackleton's unseen fourth companion but
changed the number to three:

Who is the third who always walks beside you?
When I count, there are only you and I together.
But when I look ahead up the white road.
There is always another one walking beside you.
Gliding wrapt in a brown mantle, hooded
I do not know whether a man or a woman.
—But who is that on the other side of you?

Since then, Eliot's poetic license has taken root, and the phenomenon is now known among climbers and other explorers as the "third man factor" or sometimes "third man syndrome."

Shackleton's ship, *Endurance*, was discovered in 2022, one hundred years after he was buried. The vessel had been crushed ten thousand feet below the surface of the Weddell Sea, and the footage revealed the ship to be in excellent condition.

Guardian Angels

The third man factor asserts that spirit guardians appear during physical and psychological stress. Like Sheppton's Pope John XXIII and Shackelton's unknown fourth companion, spirit guardians provide comfort, support, and a deeper affirmation of our religious beliefs. They give us hope to move forward as we use free will to determine our direction.

Spiritual guardians, or angels, have been called "protectors" and are discussed in the Bible throughout the

Old and New Testaments. According to biblical scholars, guardian angels are divine agents of God sent to protect and aid humans in times of need. In *When Angels Appear*, Hope Macdonald interviewed numerous Christians claiming to have had real-life encounters with angels. She says, "while some believe their guardian angel takes the form of a human being to guide them through troubled times, many describe their angel as a soft glow of loving light that fills them with a feeling of great tenderness."

Guardian angels may take the form of apparitions, and for centuries, the Blessed Virgin Mary, Jesus' mother, has appeared to pious Christians. The Roman Catholic, Orthodox, and Anglican Churches have sanctioned more than a dozen of these metaphysical events, known as Marian apparitions or visions. They have been recognized as "worthy of belief" or bona fide miracles.

In 1858 she appeared before Bernadette Soubirius in Lourdes, France. The fortunate witness became Saint Bernadette. And in 1917, the Blessed Mother appeared in Fatima, Portugal. She revealed three secrets to a trio of young women, Lucia de Jesus Dos Santos, Francisco, and Jacinta Marto.

The most popular book of Jewish law, the Midrash Rabbah, revealed that God created a guardian angel for each person to help protect us from evil, and sent special angels to guide us. They have been described as having wings or radiating with marvelous bright light, described as God's beautiful and supportive "intercessors."

Prophecies foretold that the ultimate goal of an angel is for us to be with God one day:

> Angels are supernatural beings who stand in the presence of God and protect humans from the cosmic forces that threaten them. The Bible makes it clear that an individual's guardian angel is always watching over them and that God desires for all His children to be blessed with the presence of a guardian angel.

Some believe that guardian angels contact us through signs, such as numbers. At times, we may see specific number sequences. For example, maybe our attention is drawn to a clock or watch every day at precisely 1:11. Or perhaps we wake up with numbers dancing in our head, the same numbers each day. According to Sunny Dawn Johnson:

> Angel numbers are one of the more common ways angels communicate with us. Angel numbers are repetitive number sequences that appear seemingly randomly. When you see a redundant number, it's a sign that the angels are with you. However, they also have a deeper meaning. Repetitive numbers signify new beginnings.

New beginnings allow us to evolve, progress to a better place, and become better people.

Humans are interconnected through vibration, light, and Jung's "collective unconsciousness." We never travel alone. Our ancestors protect us along our journey in the form of mysterious apparitions. They watch as we navigate through inevitable human pain and suffering. Thucydides (c. 460–400 BC), Athenian historian and general, wisely observed:

> The bravest are indeed those with the clearest vision of what is before them, glory and danger alike, and yet notwithstanding, go out to meet it.

The third man factor has been explained as everything from hallucination to divine intervention. Consider, then, the concept of the doppelganger (as discussed in chapter 3). Suppose the doppelganger wields the ability to replicate one's whole self. In that case, the third man factor can be viewed as the manifestation of a benevolent phantom self—transforming one's whole self into a real outside presence. In other words, we may have the ability to become our own guardian angels. As the Buddha said, "No one saves us but ourselves. No one can, and no one may. We must walk the path."

Charles Lindbergh

There has been lingering debate over the actual definition of this phenomenon. Ghosthunter Charles J. Adams III, who has written extensively about the Pennsylvania Coal Region, observed:

> "Guardian Angels" stories in shafts and pits circulate any mining culture. While that is the moniker given to the apparitions by some miners, others simply cannot attribute their presence to anything necessarily "angelic" and recall them only as "apparitions."

Still, Adams's apparitions, or spiritual guardians, can be easily transposed to realms miles high above his native coal mines.

Charles Lindbergh was the first to complete a solo flight across menacing Atlantic wind currents and between two major international cities. His 1927 *Spirit of St. Lewis* flight from New York City to Paris took thirty-three and a half hours. He believed that spirit guardians helped him.

During his transatlantic flight, there were no automatic pilot devices. Lindbergh's most significant challenge was staying awake; at times, he flew ten feet above the ocean to avoid the blinding fog. After twenty-four hours into the journey, he became delirious. As documented by History.com, Lindbergh experienced ghostlike apparitions that spoke to him:

> He later wrote of mirage-like "fog islands" forming in the sea below and of seeing "vaguely outlined forms, transparent, moving, riding weightless with me in the plane."

After the hallucinations faded, the exhausted aviator landed in Paris with a crowd of more than 150,000 jubilant spectators. He had been awake for sixty straight hours.

Lindbergh later revealed his otherworldly secret in the books *The Spirit of St. Louis* (1953) and *Autobiography of Values* (1977). During his ordeal, he suffered from fatigue and an altered state of consciousness, pondering "the nearness of death" and "the longness of life."

Lindbergh became aware of humanlike, ghostly phantoms in the fuselage behind him. Lindbergh felt caught in some "unearthly age of time" as he viewed these apparitions:

> These phantoms speak with human voices— friendly, vaporlike shapes, without substance, able to vanish or appear at will, to pass in and out through the walls of the fuselage as though no walls were there. Now, many are crowded behind me. Currently, only a few remain. First, one and then another presses forward to my shoulder to speak above the engine's noise and then draws back among the group behind.

Lindbergh heard clear and familiar voices, "conversing and advising on my flight, discussing problems of my navigation, reassuring me, giving me messages of importance unattainable in ordinary life." He recalled that the voices gave him helpful advice and mystical wisdom that was "unattainable in ordinary life."

Lindbergh associated these spirit guardians with the dead and pondered whether he had crossed the boundary between life and death and was in the land of the dead. He offered a description of the spirit beings steeped in the fantastic and the paranormal:

> The spirits have no rigid bodies, yet they remain human in outline form—emanations from the experience of ages, inhabitants of a universe closed to mortal men. I'm on the borderline of life and a greater realm beyond, as though caught in the field of gravitation between two planets, acted on by forces I can't control, forces too weak to be measured by any means at my command, yet representing powers incomparably stronger than I've ever known.

All of these explorers—Fellin, Shackleton, and Lindbergh—are believed to have experienced visitations from spiritual guardians. The third man factor is more prevalent than previously documented, but what that phenomenon represents remains a matter of conjecture and personal faith.

Chapter 7
Roman Catholic Mysticism

The Good Pope

Angelo Giuseppe Roncalli (1881–1963) was elected Pope at the age of seventy-seven. As St. John XXIII, he led the Roman Catholic Church for a comparatively brief five-year reign. His reign was revolutionary, celebrated by Liberal Catholics and vilified by conservatives. One observer noted that St. John XXIII, "broke the mold" when he "brought the Church kicking and screaming into the twentieth century."

Upon his election, Roncalli was the first Pope in more than five hundred years to take the pontifical name of "John." With his simple, pastoral style, and because he was more accessible than his predecessors, Pope John XXIII became known as "the Good Pope."

He went out to meet his flock, visiting polio-afflicted children and prison inmates. He frequently attended parishes in Rome and was known to stroll around the city, by himself, at night, hence the Vatican's code name "Johnny Walker." True believers contend that the ostensible Sheppton visitation was in character with John's assertive personality.

The vision of Pope John XXIII appeared during the 1963 Sheppton mine disaster for two agonizing weeks. The rescued miners believed that "the Good Pope" had saved their lives, and Vatican scholars deemed Sheppton as one of the Pope's miracles.

On April 11, 1963, John's "Encyclical on Establishing Universal Peace in Truth, Justice, Charity, and Liberty" impacted the Civil Rights Movement of the 1960s. It read in part:

Today, on the contrary, the conviction is

widespread that all men are equal in natural dignity. So, on the doctrinal and theoretical level, at least, no form of approval is being given to racial discrimination. All this is of supreme significance for the formation of a human society animated by the principles we have mentioned above, for man's awareness of his rights must inevitably lead him to the recognition of his duties. The possession of rights involves the duty of implementing those rights, for they are the expression of a man's personal dignity. And the possession of rights also involves their recognition and respect by other people.

His policies were of openness to non-Catholic Christians and to the modern world. John's concern was for the world and for all humankind rather than solely for the Church. His most famous statement was, "We were all made in God's image, and thus, we are all Godly alike."

Vatican II

He opened the Second Vatican Council, or Vatican II, which took place from 1962 to 1965. It became his legacy, making the Catholic Church relevant again. Vatican II focused on matters of faith such as Liturgy and the use of languages other than Latin in prayer, the role of bishops, and matters of scripture, belief, and missionary activity. Vatican II changed how the Church related to the world and other religions. It remains controversial, and to this day, there are many individuals and groups who do not accept these teachings.

Pope John XXIII called the council because he felt the Church needed "updating" *(aggiornamento)*. He wanted to connect the church with the twentieth century, sensing that some of the Church's practices needed to be improved and presented in a more modern and understandable manner.

Cuban Missile Crisis

Upon convening Vatican II, John XXIII was immediately thrust into an international emergency—the Cuban Missile Crisis of 1962. American spy planes discovered that Cuba and the Soviet Union were constructing bases in Cuba for several medium-range and intermediate-range ballistic nuclear missiles with the ability to strike most of the continental United States. This event threatened to bring the world to the brink of nuclear war and mutually assured destruction.

Because the Pope had a dialogue with Soviet leader Nikita Khrushchev and United States President John F. Kennedy, he attempted to defuse the situation. On October 25, 1962, the Pope broadcast from Vatican Radio with a message titled "For Peace and Fraternity Among Mankind." He did not point fingers or invoke his papal authority. Instead, the pope simply gave voice to the fears of everyone following the developments off the coast of Cuba. He said:

May they, with hands on their chest, hear the anguished cry that rises up to the heavens from all corners of the earth, from innocent children and the elderly, individuals, and communities: peace, peace!

At the same time, a series of secret diplomatic communications took place between the Vatican and the warring parties. Agreements were made. The Cuban Missile Crisis ended within days, and a nuclear war was averted. Scholars agreed that the Pope's interventions gave the Soviet Union and the United States a graceful way out of the standoff. Seven months after the Cuban Missile Crisis, *Pacem in Terris* was published and addressed humanity with an encyclical on world peace.

Called "the Good Pope," John XXIII, who did much to modernize the church, is among history's greatest visionaries and peacemakers.

Sainthood

Pope Francis declared John XXIII a saint on July 5, 2013. A dual canonization was held in St. Peter's Square on April 27, 2014. John XXIII and John Paul II entered sainthood—canonized because of their profound holiness and because both were responsible for medical miracles.

John's canonization was viewed by over eight hundred thousand of the faithful. They came seeking healing and mercy, assuming a personal walk of faith. They paid homage to John's humanitarian legacy and prayed to a piece of his exhumed flesh. The canonization process is a lengthy one. Tradition had called for two authenticated miracles, but in 2013, Pope Francis opted to waive the requisite second miracle usually needed for non-martyrs to reach sainthood.

Nonetheless, Vatican academics have identified three miracles attributed to John XXIII. All of them inexplicably took place after his death and within the context of a predictable modus operandi.

The Miracles of Pope John XXIII

On August 13, 1963, three Pennsylvania coal miners, David Fellin, Henry Throne, and Louis Bova, were trapped more than three hundred feet beneath the earth. Many believe that a miracle saved their lives. During the Eternal Word Television Network (EWTN) coverage of Pope John XXIII's canonization, Franciscan Missionary Rev. Fr. Joseph Mary stated:

> They (Fellin and Throne) both witnessed the appearance of Pope John XXIII, who had just died ten weeks prior, and he was much younger, about half the age of which he died at eighty-one, dressed in a black cassock, with his arms crossed and smiling.

The 2014 EWTN Vatican broadcast concluded with Fr. Joseph Mary stating, "We are a part of the communion of the saints."

Punitive Existence

Sheppton forced them to question their punitive existence. *Why do bad things happen to good people? Why was their rescue taking longer than expected?* Angry and confused, Fellin questioned his Roman Catholic faith. He asked God why he was being persecuted. "What wrong had I done to deserve this punishment?" he asked.

My God, my God, God, why have you forsaken me?

He recalled that a short while later, three tiny bluish fireflies suddenly appeared in the darkness. They began expanding and swirling, filling the entire chamber with a bluish light. The light cast no shadow but provided perfect visibility, expanding the small confines of the mineshaft and enabling them to move around.

And it provided the gift of vision. Fellin testified that the bluish light enabled them to see Pope John XXIII in the distance. The Pope was visible only from the waist up. He was wearing a black cassock "like that of a poor parish priest," and he was grinning at them. His arms were folded in front of him. The Pope appeared to be much younger than his eighty-one years at his death.

Fellin said, "It wasn't a vision, and it wasn't a picture. It was him. Pope John! I'd have recognized him anywhere." Fellin said he hoped Throne wouldn't see the pope—fearing Hank would go insane if he realized a dead man was with them—but the younger man saw him, because he had pointed at the pontiff and excitedly asked, "Who's that fella? Who's that stranger?"

According to writer Nora V. Clemente-Arnaldo, because of the timing of the pope's death, the Sheppton incident was viewed as a miracle. She wrote:

Like St. John Vianney, Pope John XXIII is also credited with after-death appearances. The story was written by Madeline Pecora Nugent in the "Messenger of St. Anthony," which gives the documented testimony of two coal miners, David Fellini (sp) and Henry Throne, trapped 300 feet underground in Pennsylvania way back in August 1963, 10 weeks after the death of Pope John XXIII. This is what the two miners said:

> That they both saw the "Good Pope" in his black cassock grinning comfortingly and lovingly at them in the chamber while his body radiated the bluish light. That he was with them until their successful miraculous rescue on 27 August 1963.

Nora V. Clemente-Arnaldo concludes, "Clearly, the Lord answered Pope John XXIII's prayer by saving from death these two trapped miners given up for dead."

After their rescue, Fellin and Throne said that the Pope saved their lives. This was verified by several Vatican academics who cited Sheppton as one of the Pope's miracles. Fellin testified that Pope John stayed with them until they were hauled to the surface, wearing parachute harnesses and football helmets. Newspapermen from around the world, including Japan, Germany, and the UK, were gathered at the mine site to document the miraculous rescue, which many thought impossible.

Sister Caterina Capitani

Angelo Roncalli's miracle took place in May 1966. Sister Caterina Capitani of the Daughters of Charity, twenty-three, was from the Naples region. Sister Capitani, a nun from the Naples region, suffered multiple stomach ulcers and intestinal diseases. Capitani had endured fourteen surgeries for a gastric hemorrhage and other grave intestinal maladies. Sister Adele Labianca, director of Umberto I hospital in Fasano (southern Italy), recalled:

> Doctors discovered a gastric hemorrhage, and she underwent 14 operations. I looked after her for about a month, while she was in the hospital, I prayed the rosary in suffrage of Pope John, who had died in the odor of sanctity on June 3rd. Then she got worse. She suffered an unexpected collapse, and everyone feared her time had come.

She was readmitted and suffered further collapses. Sister Caterina looked like she was on the verge of death; she asked to profess her vows in *articulo mortis*. Everyone looked dismayed and lost, especially her father. But her death was to be denied. Sister Caterina recalled the exact details of her medical miracle that began on May 19, 1966:

I pronounced my vows, and I was immediately administered the Extreme Unction. On May 22nd a sister brought me a relic of Pope John's from Rome—a piece of the sheet upon which the Pope had died. I placed it on the perforation which had opened on my stomach. Since I was suffering quite a bit, I prayed to the Pope to take me to Heaven. I was slowly dying. I felt that my strength was leaving me. The temperature was very high. A sister guarded the room day and night.

On 25 May, at around 2.30 in the afternoon, I asked a sister who was guarding the room to close the window a little because the light bothered me. She did so and then left the room for a few minutes.

I drifted off to sleep. At a certain point, I felt a hand pressing the wound on my stomach and the voice of a man saying: Sister Caterina, Sister Caterina. I thought it was Professor Zannini who came to check on me occasionally. I turned towards the voice and saw Pope John standing beside my bed. He had the same smile as the image that had been given me. He was the one who was holding his hand on my wound. You prayed to me very much, he said with a calm voice. Many people have prayed to me, but especially one. You have really taken this miracle from my heart. But don't be afraid now, you are healed. Ring the bell, call the sisters who are in the chapel, and have them take your temperature and you will see that you will not have even the slightest temperature. Eat whatever you want, as you did before the sickness: I will hold my hand on your wound, and you will be healed. Go to the Professor, have him examine you. Have some X-rays done. Have it all written down because these things will be needed someday.

Hospital officials agreed that there was no medical explanation for the healing. "Miracle" was the only word that made any sense. Dr. Giuseppe Zannini said that it could not be humanly explained. Sister Caterina passed away in 2010 at the age of sixty-eight.

A Woman from Sicily

The following year, 1967, another miracle took place. It concerned a woman from Sicily who suffered from tubercular peritonitis and cardiac issues. She, too, was cured after experiencing what was called "a supernatural visitation" by the Good Pope.

His Death

The Pope died on June 3, 1963, in the chambers of the Vatican Palace. His death was caused by peritonitis brought on by a stomach tumor. All of his miracles came about after his death because, as told to this writer by a Roman Catholic nun, the Pope received the power to perform miracles only after entering heaven.

The Discovery Channel's *Spirit of Survival* produced a documentary about the disaster. Narrator Peter Thomas called Sheppton "scientific documentation of life after death" and a "passageway to the afterlife." The miracle was presented as spirituality within an authentic framework. In every instance, Fellin and Throne's collective experience was determined to be authentic, not the result of hallucination, trauma, or a miner's psychosis.

Chapter 8
St. Teresa of Ávila

Spanish Mystic

St. Teresa of Ávila (1515–1582) was a Spanish mystic, author, and worker of miracles. St. Teresa lived during a tumultuous time. She witnessed Martin Luther's Protestant Reformation that swept through Europe in the 1500s, directly contradicting the Catholic Church's teachings. She also experienced the expulsion of Muslims and Jews from Spain, and the notorious Spanish Inquisition (1478–1834), established to combat heresy in Spain through infamously brutal methods.

Despite her father's opposition, Teresa entered the Carmelite Convent of the Incarnation at Ávila, Spain. Within two years, she developed a malignant type of malaria. She was an invalid for three years, during which time she developed a love for mental prayer.

Spanish mystic St. Teresa, the self-described "wicked" girl, became one of the greatest saints in Church history. Her "Four Stages of Mystical Prayer" consisted of Meditation, the Prayer of Quiet, Union, and Rapture and may have played a role in the Sheppton mythology. (Painted by François Gérard [1770–1837], [public domain] via Creative Commons.)

After her recovery, St. Teresa underwent a religious awakening. As her devotion grew, she began to display more and more signs of her mystical side. She consulted with other members of the clergy for guidance. Some truly believed that she was blessed with divine visions, while others only thought she was insane. Still, she experienced a succession of extraordinary phenomena, including visions, locutions (the sense of Christ speaking to her), and rapture, a feeling of being wholly absorbed in God.

In 1558 Teresa began the restoration of Carmelite life, which restored the Carmelite life to its original primitive observance of austerity. Her reform required total withdrawal so that the nuns could meditate on divine law and, through a prayerful life of penance, exercise "vocation of reparation" for the sins of humankind.

According to *Catholic Miracles*, one of St. Teresa's most famous miracles was similar to the miracle of Jesus and Lazarus:

> The wall of a building fell on Teresa's young nephew, and he was crushed. Apparently dead, he was brought to Teresa. She held her little nephew in her arm and prayed deeply. Minutes later, the boy came back to life. This miracle, in fact, was presented at Teresa's canonization.

Many feel that St. Teresa's conversion was her greatest miracle. In her autobiography, she once said:

> The possession of virtuous parents who lived in the fear of God, together with those favors which I received from his Divine Majesty, might have made me good if I had not been so very wicked.

"Four Stages of Mystical Prayer"

St. Teresa, the self-described "wicked" girl, became one of the greatest saints in Church history. Her "Four Stages of Mystical Prayer" consisted of Meditation, the Prayer of

Quiet, Union, and Rapture. Meditation can be achieved, at least partly, by our efforts. That is in sharp contrast with all the stages that follow—the Prayer of Quiet, Union, and Rapture—because our individual efforts cannot achieve them. Meditation is an excellent and safe road until the Lord leads us to the following supernatural stages.

The Prayer of Quiet, the second stage of mystical prayer, is a prayer state that borders on the supernatural and places us in a state of quiet and recollectedness:

> It reveals grace more clearly and fills us with deep inner satisfaction. It never becomes wearisome. We are in union with God for as long as the Prayer of Quiet lasts. When we experience the Prayer of Quiet, it seems that no greater blessing is even possible. For that reason, few people go beyond it.

During the "Union stage," your faculties fall asleep, and you become absorbed in a union with God. The pleasure, sweetness, and delight you experience are incomparably greater than in the Prayer of Quiet—even your body shares in the soul's joy and delight.

Flight of the Spirit

The last and most dramatic stage is called Rapture. St. Teresa exchanged other words for Rapture, such as Elevation, Flight of the Spirit, Transport, and Ecstasy. The website *Explore the Faith* described St. Teresa's Rapture in the following manner:

> During Rapture, all your faculties fade away and are suspended. The Lord gathers up your soul. Your soul no longer seems to animate your body. Your hearing and thinking are dimmed. And you are carried away. Gently. Joyfully. Silently. Ecstatically.
>
> There is no power left in your body. Your eyes involuntarily close. Your breath diminishes. Your pulse slows. You can hardly move your hands without great effort. You feel such bliss and consolation that you would never abandon it. And we willingly go wherever we are carried away. Your soul soars upwards, far above itself and above all created things.

Some documentation described that, at times, the Rapture was so powerful that Teresa's body was lifted off the ground. Literally. Her fellow nuns held down her body. It was also noted that "Nobody will believe this without having experienced it."

Fellin and Throne

The "Four Stages of Mystical Prayer" are trance states believed to be the result of repetitive prayer and meditation—like the altered states experienced by Fellin and Throne. Although not documented by Ed Conrad or

Elizabeth Kubler-Ross, the Sheppton miners experienced St. Theresa's Rapture in the form of her "Flight of the Spirit."

The miners underwent an out-of-body episode. They rose above the mine and looked down upon hundreds of rescue workers and support personnel. Fellin told a Lancaster reporter that he could fly through the mountain of debris and rocket skyward, breaking out of the mine. He landed on firm earth, hearing the roar of cheering Sheppton residents. He rushed into the loving arms of his wife, Anna. Fellin experienced this out-of-body astral projection numerous times, but Throne said he only did it once.

Concerning his claims of having shared two out-of-body trips with Throne at his side, Fellin told Dr. Kubler-Ross, during a day-long conversation in her home in Headwaters, Virginia, that on two separate occasions, he and Throne had been out of their physical bodies at the same time. During those events, they were engaged in conversation. Dr. Kubler-Ross said she was sure this had taken place, calling them "very real, as I am happy to witness from my own life experiences."

Fellin wanted the world to know what had happened. Five years before his death, he left numerous notarized letters and audio and videotaped conversations vividly describing the supernatural events he experienced.

Fellin said he was certain he and Throne had been out of their physical bodies because, the first time it happened, they found themselves standing some forty to fifty feet from the refuge area with a crowd of normal-looking men on both sides. He said he looked over his shoulder and saw himself and Throne sitting back in the enclosure. Fellin said he needed additional proof that it wasn't a dream or a hallucination; therefore he extended his right hand in front of one of the men standing next to him to see if it would cast a shadow, which it did.

God's Awe

Father Svercheck, Fellin's parish priest, constantly offered comfort and prayers to Anna Fellin and her family while another man of the cloth intervened. A Roman Catholic missionary, Rev. Edmond Roman, brought a rosary and St. Christopher's medals to the rescue site. The Pope had blessed the religious items donated by a Hazleton family who had just returned from a trip to the Vatican. The medals were lowered to Fellin through the six-inch borehole, his spiritual lifeline.

Upon his rescue, it became apparent that Fellin's survival was based on some special belief he clung to during his darkest hour. Fellin's physician, Dr. Anthony Fidulla, described his patient as "a spiritual man" and "thinks it was a prime factor in coming through."

David Fellin attributed his rescue to faith, his belief in God, and Pope John XXIII's miracle. Fellin had figured it out by himself. While entombed, the miner told Rev. Roman and the rescue team, "I am praying. If you don't believe in God down here, you won't believe in Him anywhere." Fellin knew that in Christianity, the concept of faith is vital. And so too is acceptance of God's Awe. Upon being rescued, Fellin confessed, "If you don't believe in God, go through a thing like this. Then you'll know there's a God."

Religious Conversion

Hank Throne confessed that he experienced a religious conversion during that horrible two-week period. He discovered God and found religion. Upon his rescue, he stopped drinking and co-founded a nondenominational church in Hazleton, PA.

Throne continued to mine after the disaster. Later he worked on a bridge-building crew. Throne died in 1998, thirty-five years after his rescue. He was sixty-three years old.

David Fellin left the mines and found employment driving a school bus. He died in 1990, twenty-seven years after his rescue. He was eighty-five.

The remains of their comrade, Louis Bova, have never been found. While Fellin and Throne's account is one of faith and survival, the legacy of St. Teresa's is a story of love and devotion, as written by the Eternal Word Television Network.

St. Teresa was canonized in 1662. Her written works have appeared in uncounted Spanish editions and have been translated into many languages. An ever-spreading circle of readers through the centuries have found understanding and courage in the life and works of this nun of Castile, who is one of the glories of Spain and the church. Teresa's emblems are a heart, an arrow, and a book.

"Luminous Mystical Theology"

A prolific writer, St. Teresa developed a reputation as a great mystic due mainly to her three books "of luminous mystical theology." These included her autobiography, *The Way of Perfection,* an instruction manual on how to pray, proposing an almost stream-of-consciousness meditation on the importance of humility, charity, and nonattachment. *The Interior Castle*, considered her masterpiece, was based on a vision Teresa received of the human soul as being like a glittering castle carved from a single luminous diamond. In reading her book, St. Teresa guides the reader through seven mansions in the castle of the human soul, with the end goal being complete oneness with God. The book gives an overview of divine growth for spiritual pilgrims committed to giving themselves entirely to God.

The Book of Her Life, The Way of Perfection, and *The Interior Castle* offer holistic insight into her teaching. Author Carl McColman asserts that "these books have become crown jewels in the literature of western mysticism." Jesuits, Dominicans, and laypersons recognize the spiritual depth of St. Teresa's writings. One edition of *The Interior Castle* features commentary by a Redemptorist priest, Fr. Dennis Billy, observing at least nine dimensions of prayer that Teresa described, leading ultimately to degrees of mystical union with God. The blog site Caring Catholic Convert respectfully called her "the Original Flying Nun":

> Teresa's levitations occurred during times of deep prayer. She regarded her levitations as chastisement from God. When she would feel like God was going to levitate her body, she would lie down on the ground and ask her sister nuns to sit on her and hold her down. She continually begged God to stop causing her to levitate in public.

The levitations of St. Teresa, as described in *The Book of Her Life*, were witnessed repeatedly by many people. Although she preferred not to discuss such matters, she wrote her autobiography in obedience to her superior. She described how she resisted these raptures that sometimes led to levitation:

> These effects are very striking. One of them is the manifestation of the Lord's mighty power: as we are unable to resist His Majesty's will, either in soul or in body, and are not our own masters, we realize that, however irksome this truth may be, there is One stronger than ourselves, and that these favors are bestowed by Him, and that we, of ourselves, can do absolutely nothing. This imprints in us great humility. Indeed, I confess that in me, it produced great fear—at first, a terrible fear.

> One sees one's body being lifted up from the

ground; and although the spirit draws it after itself, and if no resistance is offered, does so very gently, one does not lose consciousness—at least, I myself have had sufficient to enable me to realize that I was being lifted up. The majesty of Him Who can do this is manifested in such a way that the hair stands on end, and there is produced a great fear of offending so great a God, but a fear overpowered by the deepest love, newly enkindled, for One Who, as we see, has so deep a love for so loathsome a worm that He seems not to be satisfied by literally drawing the soul to Himself, but will also have the body, mortal though it is, and befouled as is its clay by all the offenses it has committed.

Diego de Yepes, who wrote one of her early biographies, *Vida de Santa Teresa de Jesus* (Toledo, 1530), observed that St. Teresa was embarrassed and conflicted by these levitations:

There are similar anecdotes told by nuns who saw St. Teresa spontaneously levitate. After the events, she would order them to never to speak of it, but later, under obedience to higher authorities during the Church's investigation into her life, they described the incidents. For her part, St. Teresa was greatly embarrassed by her levitations and prayed that they would stop, and by all accounts, they decreased greatly in her later life.

In 1970, St. Teresa was declared a "Doctor of the Church" by Pope Paul VI. She was the first woman to be honored—indicating that the hierarchy considered her writings exemplary for all Catholics to study.

About ten years before she died, she experienced a sense of being spiritually married to Christ, leading to a deep abiding feeling of union with him. She was one of the greatest Christian mystics and was canonized as a saint forty years after her death.

One of her famous prayers represented her devotion to her Lord. It was titled A Love Song, and read:

> Majestic sovereign, timeless wisdom,
> your kindness melts my hard, cold soul.
> Handsome lover, selfless giver,
> your beauty fills my dull, sad eyes.
> I am yours, you made me.
> I am yours, you called me.
> I am yours, you saved me.
> I am yours, you loved me.
> I will never leave your presence.
> Give me death, give me life.
> Give me sickness, give me health.
> Give me honor, give me shame.
> Give me weakness, give me strength.
> I will have whatever you give.

Chapter 9

Ed & Lorraine Warren: Demonologists

Demonologists Ed and Lorraine Warren are known for being among the first to investigate suspected hauntings, including Rhode Island's Perron farmhouse and the infamous Amityville Horror. Perhaps through default, they became the paranormal's most recognized celebrities, investigating over ten thousand cases in the US and abroad. Writing for *Creepy Catalog*, Chrissy Stockton reflected on their legacy:

> The Warrens pioneered the field of paranormal investigation. Whatever you think about the couple, so much of modern horror culture has its roots in things the Warrens did. The New England Society of Psychic Research (NESPR), created by the Warrens, is the oldest ghost-hunting group in New England. Their investigations paved the way for the success of TV shows such as *Ghost Hunters*, *Ghost Adventures*, and even *Haunted*,

which has episodes on a number of cases the
Warrens worked on.

They warned a younger generation about demonic
possession, speaking at over seven hundred colleges.
Their strange profession triggered widespread interest in
the paranormal—they were frequent guests on *AM
America*, *In Search Of*, *PM Magazine*, *Mike Douglas*,
David Susskind, *Tom Snyder's Tomorrow*, and *To Tell the
Truth*.

Ed and Lorraine Warren with Barrett
Ravenhurst (center), owner of the
Victorian Palace Theatre, in the quaint
village of Jim Thorpe, Pennsylvania. The
Warrens were on a fifteen-city book tour
promoting their book *The Haunted,* about
the West Pittston Smurl haunting. (Maxim
W. Furek photograph.)

Among their published works are *Ghost Hunters* (1989),
Satan's Harvest (1990), *Graveyard* (1992), and *In a Dark
Place* (1992).

Like a shark frenzy, Hollywood picked up the scent of the highly marketable Warrens, producing a series of successful horror films—*The Conjuring* (2013), *Annabelle* (2014), *The Conjuring 2* (2016), *Annabelle: Creation* (2017), *The Nun* (2018), *Annabelle Comes Home* (2019), *The Curse of La Llorona* (2019), and *The Conjuring 3: The Devil Made Me Do It* (2021). Patrick Wilson and Vera Farmiga were cast as the infamous couple, as the *Conjuring* universe became a huge success. According to *Creepy Catalogue*, the *Conjuring* movies are the second highest-grossing horror franchise of all time, behind only *Godzilla*.

The Amityville Horror

Ed Warren approached his work from a Christian perspective. He used "religious provocation" to provoke dark spirits, such as his terrifying experience investigating High Hopes, the site of the Amityville murders. Warren recollected:

> I usually wander about a house like Amityville by myself, trying to provoke what is there. Well, I didn't have to wait very long. I used a crucifix and holy water in the name of Jesus Christ.
> The first thing I felt as I stood here in this room was a sensation of smothering. I felt (as though) a hot wet blanket had been dropped over my face, then a powerful force pushing me to the floor. At that point, I felt what I could only describe as numerous pinpoints of electricity hitting my body.

I knew what was happening. I was under a diabolical attack.

Warren said that what he had experienced in the house christened "High Hopes" was pure evil. He encountered demonic forces capable of possession, but the demonologist came prepared to do battle:

I then went into what we call "religious resistance" to ward off this attack. I envisioned myself being Christlike. I called on Christ, St. Michael the Archangel, and Padre Pio to help me. At this point, it lifted. I wasted no time getting out of there, for I knew exactly what was in that house then.

Although the Amityville Horror has been labeled as another psychic fraud, Ed Warren disputes that claim:

Nobody lives in the Amityville house to this day. The Cromartie family still owns it. They bought it for fifty thousand dollars from the Lutz family and hoped to sell it to American International Pictures for two hundred fifty thousand dollars. And they got stuck with a pig in a poke.
Now, if this is a hoax, how come there are six books written on it and nine investigators claiming it was a reality? If it's a hoax, why hasn't somebody bought that Amityville Horror for the meager price it's being sold for?

Ed Warren has some strong beliefs about potential sites for hauntings. He puts his money on New England and California:

> Because there are many old homes in New England, the older a house is, the more tragedies occur. Tragedies create the ghost syndrome.

He viewed California as a potential evil area "because they have such an influx of satanic rituals and witchcraft that they bring in these hauntings within the homes." California has had its share of satanic personalities—cult leader Charles Manson; Anton LaVey, founder of the Church of Satan and author of *The Satanic Bible*; and Richard Ramirez, the Night Stalker of Los Angeles:

> It's more prevalent today because more people are becoming involved with satanism and witchcraft and more interest in the occult, which we try to warn the public about, as you can see.

Was Ronald DeFeo Jr. possessed by demonic forces? One of the Amityville Killer judges called him the "devil incarnate." DeFeo claimed that he was controlled by an evil spirit that forced him to commit the crime. The defense entered an insanity plea—along with the evil-spirit-possession argument—none of those worked. De Feo received twenty-five-years-to-life sentences, for each of his victims, for his November 13, 1974, bloodletting.

The Smurl Haunting

One of the most horrific cases of purported demonic possession occurred in West Pittston, Pennsylvania, over thirteen years. The horror took root inside a ninety-two-year-old duplex dwelling at 328-330 Chase Street belonging to Jack, Janet Smurl, and Jack's parents.

From 1974 to 1987, the Smurls and their four daughters endured howls, bloodcurdling screams, pig grunts, kitchen appliances catching fire, and awful odors. Amorphous black clouds materialized inside the lodging. Janet was dragged out of bed by malevolent forces, and Jack was sexually assaulted by a succubus, a demon in female form.

Monsignor Francis Kane was the pastor of their Immaculate Conception parish. He went to the home and blessed every room. Then, after the spirits continued to torment them, he did this again. Monsignor Eugene J. Clark, rector of St. Pius X. Seminary, Dalton, PA, was directed by church officials to stay overnight on three occasions but observed nothing unusual.

Finally, after agonizing torment, they began to look outside the church for help, and paranormal researchers Ed (1926–2006) and Lorraine (1927–2019) Warren were called. Ed, a former police officer, described himself as a "religious demonologist" and Lorraine as a "sensitive clairvoyant" who can see that which seems to be invisible.

Jim Thorpe Presentation

Because of their knowledge of the occult, they were asked to co-author a book. As a result, St. Martin's Press published *The Haunted: One Family's Nightmare* (1988). It was written by Robert Curran, a reporter for the *Scrantonian-Tribune* and *Sunday Independent* newspapers. The Warrens and Jack and Janet Smurl were listed as co-authors. The book became a national bestseller with an initial press run of six hundred thousand copies. It sold for $16.95, was published in seventy-eight countries, and was serialized in *Redbook Magazine*.

Several years later, FOX TV presented *The Haunted*, a made-for-TV adaptation of the book starring Sally Kirkland, Jeffrey DeMunn, and Diana Baker. Directed by Robert Mandel, it aired on May 6, 1991.

To promote *The Haunted*, the Warrens began a fifteen-city book tour in the quaint village of Jim Thorpe, Pennsylvania, surrounded by Bear Mountain and the extended ridge of Mauch Chunk Mountain. They appeared at the Victorian Palace Theatre on July 19, 1988, presenting two slideshows with personal photographs of Amityville and other psychic investigations. It was hot and cramped, but electricity was in the air. Barrett Ravenhurst, the owner of the theatre, reflected on the Warrens' visit. He said:

> They were friendly people. I kept in touch with Lorraine, and we occasionally talked on the phone

throughout the years. She had a pet rooster, and every time I would speak to her, the rooster would be crowing in the background. She was, as I am, an animal lover.

As a researcher, I was fascinated by the Smurl haunting and read everything I could about the events in nearby West Pittston. I drove to 328-330 Chase Street, took photos, and spoke with several neighbors. The Smurls were avoiding the media then, but when I heard that the Warrens were going to be in Jim Thorpe, I contacted the owner of the Victorian Palace Theatre, requesting an interview. I conducted my interview with them on the sidewalks of Jim Thorpe. It was a hot July evening. Ed and Lorraine were friendly and highly knowledgeable. In addition, they professed their Christian faith, allowing me to photograph them on the street and tape their comments. At the time, Ed was sixty-two years old, and Lorraine was sixty-one.

Spirit World

Both the Smurls and Warrens were devout Catholics. The Warrens were well versed in Roman Catholic mysticism and believed literally in a spirit world encompassing heaven and hell, limbo and purgatory. They believed in lost souls and demonic entities. These abstract concepts fit neatly into the Roman Catholic tradition of a mid-place between the living and the dead, concepts spoken in muted voices by the curious and the faithful. It was in this murky realm that the Warrens lent their expertise.

The Catholic Church is typically reluctant to get involved with something that might be a hoax and bring about Vatican embarrassment or condemnation. The Church focuses on God's love, mercy, and forgiveness and avoids demonic themes, a subject they would rather not talk about. Around 1977, the Catholic Church quietly asked the Warrens to investigate the Hodgeson family's alleged poltergeist. This haunting took place in an Enfield, North London, council house. Writing for *The Catholic World Report,* film critic Nick Olszyk, in his "So I Married a Demonologist," concluded that the Warrens (investigating the Hodgeson home outside of London) had God on their side:

> The Warrens are able (to) withstand such tremendous evil because their strength comes from a covenant relationship that puts God at the center of their lives. This is the opposite of the Hodgeson family (whose London haunted house inspired *Conjuring 2*) and whose father recently left them for his mistress. It is implied that Janet and her sister got involved in the occult because of his absence.

Ed explained how he prepared himself for these paranormal encounters. To battle against demonic possession, he used weapons such as the Bible, a crucifix, and holy water. There were other options as well. Ed Warren called upon "religious provocation" to provoke spirits into action. He explained in *The Haunted* that he often used religious provocation:

> It works this way: You invoke the name of Jesus
> Christ and his sacred blood, and then you
> command the demon to reveal itself and be
> banished from the home.

Believing the Smurl home was possessed, the Warrens
brought in Rev. Bishop Robert McKenna, OP, from Our
Lady of the Rosary Chapel in Monroe, Connecticut.
Considered a "rogue" priest, McKenna is among the
traditional priests of the Catholic Church holding to her
ancient ritual for mass and the Sacraments because he
rejected Vatican II. Pope John XXIII was responsible for
the Vatican II Council that modernized the Catholic
Church, allowing the mass to be spoken in languages
other than Latin. The Pope, who had died several months
before the August 1963 Sheppton mining disaster, is
believed to have performed a miracle at that event and
was canonized in 2014.

McKenna attempted three unsuccessful exorcisms in
1986. Then, in June 1987, writing the book's introduction,
he described the Smurls' "treacherous and unending
torture." "Why has a demon chosen to infest the lives of
the Smurls, who are religious, hardworking, and sincere
people?" he asked:

> Further, I wish my attempts to exorcise their
> demon had been successful. But, though I've said
> mass in their home and have given the rites of
> exorcism three times, the demon always returns.

Psycho-Ergokinesis

Still, other supernatural forces could have been at work. For over fifty years, the public has been enculturated into forbidden themes of the occult through motion pictures such as *Children of the Damned* (1964), *Rosemary's Baby* (1968), *The Exorcist* (1973), *It's Alive* (1974), *The Omen* (1976), *Carrie* (1976), *Children of the Corn* (1984), and *Firestarter* (1984).

Although pure cinematic escapism, these films investigated children with preternatural abilities. One parapsychological theory espouses that latent telekinetic powers of female adolescents may cause "hauntings." These abilities were called psionics or psionic energy manipulation (also known as psycho-ergokinesis). The famous Stephen King thrillers *Carrie* and *Firestarter* utilized this premise. The Smurls did have a seventeen-year-old daughter, Dawn, who witnessed attacks by demons and dark shapes following her in the house.

In *The Haunted*, Lorraine Warren explained that the Smurl house was unique in several ways:

> Demonic spirits are often attracted to houses where young girls go through puberty. The spirits draw on the particular type of energy the girls emit, the emotional level being very high and ideal for the spirit to feed on.

Not everyone agreed. Amid a battle with unnamed demonic entities, the Warrens were suddenly attacked by a more human force. Researcher Paul Kurtz, chairman of the Committee for the Scientific Investigation of Claims of the Paranormal, concluded that the Smurl haunting resulted from "misperception" and the Smurls "projecting their fantasies into the house."

Critics also pointed to the appearances on *Sally Jessy Raphael*, *Geraldo Rivera*, *Larry King*, *Entertainment Tonight*, and *A Current Affair* as proof that the Smurls had, in some way, sold out for financial gain. That part of the narrative was accurate. The Smurls, the Warrens, and Robert Curran all hit the road, embracing the media, as they told their varied stories to a public hungering to learn more about the bizarre incident. It didn't matter what the critics charged. The Warrens stuck to their original claims that the Smurl hauntings were real and that their investigation was of the highest order, as Lorraine Warren explained to this researcher:

> Our motivation is most positive. We think from a Christian standpoint and ask only for Christian protection in our work.

Inside the Smurl house, Ed Warren brought "relics of the saints and true pieces of the cross." He played religious music and prayed to "frustrate the devil." Then he experienced cold spots and temperatures below freezing, and dark shadows were moving across the bedroom; the words *You filthy bastard. Get out of this house* were suddenly etched upon a mirror. Yet, as a true believer, he remained steadfast in his Catholic faith and conviction:

I learned long ago that everything we speak about is in the Bible—apparitions, ghosts, demonic spirits, levitations. Who would the victims go to if nobody in the Catholic Church were to become knowledgeable about these forces? So, this is my job, to recognize it, bring in the church's authority, and bring in the exorcist.

The Smurl horror ended after Bishop James Clifford Timlin intervened. When bishops feel they don't have a qualified exorcist in their diocese, they're allowed to look elsewhere. So Timlin summoned Father Alphonsus Trabold, a priest-exorcist from the Diocese of New York and St. Bonaventure University, "with authority to do whatever is necessary." Trabold was an exorcist, professor, and paranormal expert. But unfortunately, it took a fourth exorcism before the family would find peace. The Smurls had moved to Wilkes-Barre in 1987, and in 1989 Trabold's church-sanctioned exorcism ended the haunting. Subsequent tenants at the West Pittston Chase Street home reported no disturbances.

Several incongruous themes appeared in *The Haunted*, the 1988 project co-authored by *Sunday Independent* reporter Robert Curran, Ed and Lorraine Warren, and Jack and Janet Smurl. Unfortunately, because the book was published before his involvement, Father Trabolt is not recognized as having performed the final and most successful exorcism. And, too, the book contends that the church did not cooperate with the Smurls during their ordeal, while supplemental data shows a pattern of the church being involved and helpful from the beginning. Thus, *The Haunted* told some stories but did not tell them all.

Questions and accusations followed the family like a curse. Did they make it all up? Was it a hoax? But ultimately, why would the Smurls subject themselves to a nonstop media circus, invasion of privacy, personal humiliation, and castigation? Knowing their character and spiritual foundation, it is difficult to believe they would devise a hoax involving their children. No amount of money or notoriety would be worth it.

Warning that the Smurl hauntings were real, the Warrens cautioned about a coexisting demon world. Lorraine concluded that four spirits haunted the family: a harmless older woman, an older man who had died at the house, a young and violent girl, and a malevolent demon that turned the other spirits against the Smurls, driving them to the brink of madness. There are many things residing outside the laws of science. The Smurl incident is among them.

Chapter 10

Fr. Alphonsus Trabold &
the Smurl Haunting

In 2014, Pope Francis declared two of his predecessors, John Paul II and John XXIII, saints of the Roman Catholic church, in an unprecedented double-canonization mass in St Peter's Square. Many believed Pope John XXIII performed a miracle during the Sheppton mining disaster, but Pope John Paul II was recognized for something of a different nature.

Pope John Paul II (1920–2005) was an exorcist. He said Satan, a fallen angel, "has the skill in the world to induce people to deny his existence." During his papacy, he reintroduced the ancient rite of exorcism that continued after his death.

Until the beginning of his pontificate, exorcisms were considered a "medieval" practice that was disappearing in the face of scientific advances and technology. In 1998, the pope approved an updated form of the Rite of Exorcism, nearly four hundred years after the previous version. He had already performed the rite of exorcism inside the walls of the Vatican. Pope John Paul II said:

> In the inner heart of every person, the voice of God and the insidious voice of the Evil can be heard. The latter seeks to deceive the human person, seducing him with the prospect of false goods, to lead him away from the real good that consists precisely in fulfilling the divine will.

The purpose of exorcism is the expulsion of demons or liberation from demonic possession, performed by a priest with the bishop's permission. During this rite, the Catholic Church asks authoritatively, in the name of Jesus Christ that a person or object be protected against the power of the Evil One and withdrawn from his dominion.

In July 2014, the Congregation for Clergy, with the blessing of Pope Francis, granted juridical recognition to the International Association of Exorcists (IAE), a group training 250 priests in thirty countries, exorcists fighting against demonic possession.

Archbishop Ron Feyl-Enright, chief exorcist at the Order of Exorcists, the Sacred Order of St. Michael the Archangel in Ontario, California, believes:

> Not everyone can be an Exorcist or an Investigator. We believe it's important that you have a "calling" from God to do this type of ministry.

Priests can find the ancient liturgy of prayers and exhortations used to exorcise demons and devils in the last paragraphs of the *Rituale Romanum*, the Catholic Rite of Exorcism:

> The priest delegated by the Ordinary to perform this office should first go to confession or at least elicit an act of contrition, and, if convenient, offer the Holy Sacrifice of the Mass, and implore God's help in other fervent prayers. He vests in surplice and purple stole. Having before him the person possessed (who should be bound if there is any danger), he traces the sign of the cross over him, over himself, and the bystanders, and then sprinkles all of them with holy water. After this, he kneels and says the Litany of the Saints, exclusive of the prayers which follow it.

The *Rituale Romanum* also contains prayers and rites administered by the priest, including liturgies for the sick and the deceased.

Father Gabriele Amorth

One of the most celebrated exorcists was Father Gabriele Amorth (1925–2016), the official exorcist of Vatican City in the archdiocese of Rome. In Amorth's book, *The Devil is Afraid of Me: The Life and Work of the World's Most Famous Exorcist,* he claimed to have personally handled more than thirty thousand exorcisms during his career, at a pace of seventeen per day.

He dedicated his life to abolishing Satanic evil and taught that ghosts were not real, but demons were. An article written by Rosemary Ellen Guiley stated that Amorth believed demonic possession could happen in one of four ways:

> Through a curse by another, by continuing a life of sin, by practicing occultism, and as a test of the victim's faith, most usually the trials endured by the saints that prove their holiness. The possessed person invites Satan into their life by choosing the paths of sin and occultism; the two ways are foisted upon the unwary.

Fr. Alphonsus Trabold, OFM, Exorcist

Another famed exorcist was Fr. Alphonsus Trabold, OFM, (1925–2005), who straddled the line between ghost busting and academia. Trabold graduated from St. Boniface School and Aquinas Institute. He taught theology and a popular parapsychology course called Religion and the Paranormal at St. Bonaventure University. He had a personal interest in the paranormal, demonic possessions, and connecting with those who had crossed over before him. Trabold was an authority on exorcism. According to *St. Bonaventure University: A Haunted History*:

> Fr. Alphonsus Trabold was not only well-known for his strange hobbies and interests, but for the class, he offered on campus, nicknamed "Spooks."

Fr. Alphonsus taught students about the paranormal, discussing ghosts, demons, and ESP. In every class he taught, he left the front row of desks open for any "visitors from the other side" that might want to join them for the day.

Fr. Alphonsus Trabold is acknowledged for performing a series of successful exorcisms that ended the West Pittston Smurl hauntings. Because Bishop James Timlin's diocese did not have a qualified exorcist, they summoned Trabold "with authority to do whatever was necessary." It took four exorcisms to drive the demons out. (Photo: archives.sbu.edu)

Trabold, a Franciscan Friar, grew up with a keen interest in the paranormal. In a 2003 interview, he said:

I suppose all kids kind of have an interest in the scary and the occult. I've been interested in magic and witchcraft and the occult, both from the point of view of the paranormal powers and history.

Trabold was known internationally in the paranormal field and wrote numerous articles on the subject. He contributed to Robert Pelton's *In My Name Shall They Cast Out Devils* and consulted on numerous cases, including events that inspired the 1979 movie *The Amityville Horror.*

Buffalo Rising author Mason Winfield paid Trabold the highest of compliments:

Demonic possession may strike us as something out of the Middle Ages; out of Gothic fiction and film; or, too sadly, out of TV-style ghost hunting and sensationalism. The matter is indeed far from the daily work of the Church; but on those rare occasions that someone calls for help with a problem that might be supernatural, someone is needed to sort things out, to tell the psychological from the psychic, and the ordinarily psychic from that which is serious. A holy person can be needed to deal with the unholy. For Western New York, Father Alphonsus was the one.

And, as clarified by writer Winfield, it is crucial to ascertain that one is dealing with the presence of the Evil One and not a mental illness. Graham C. L. Davey, writing in *Psychology Today,* said that in Western societies, witchcraft and demonic possession were common explanations for psychopathology until the eighteenth century:

> Demonic or spirit possession is still a common explanation for mental health problems in some less developed areas of the world—especially where witchcraft and voodoo are still important features of the local culture, such as Haiti and some areas of Western Africa.

Davey believes that, unfortunately, exorcism has been used to treat individuals with a known history of diagnosed psychotic symptoms.

The Haunted Hinsdale House

Trabold is most famously known for performing the exorcism of the Dandy home, now known as the Haunted Hinsdale House. Clara and Phil Dandy were plagued by strange occurrences involving poltergeist activity, such as flickering lights, which soon became more threatening. Objects would fly off of shelves, and knives were hurled across the room. The Dandys' two young children heard screams and chanting sounds and suffered bruises and scratches. In addition, they saw shadowy, nonhuman apparitions.

In 1974, the family contacted Father Alphonsus to perform an exorcism. On April 13, 1974, noted psychic

Alex Tanous, a film crew of NYU students, and Fr. Trabold ventured to the home to attempt to "de-psyche" or cleanse the property, but the haunting became more extreme. Immediately, the house began shaking violently, accompanied by a screaming noise. Reluctantly, Father Alphonsus told the family they were in danger and needed to evacuate their home:

> Some ground is just bad, no one knows why. So just leave as soon as you can and take only your things with you. Don't discuss your plans inside the house. This place is just a hole to Hell.

Another of his infamous cases was that of a young woman in her twenties who reportedly sold her soul to the devil. She told the priest she wanted revenge on a family member and began worshipping the devil. Trabold was unable to calm the woman down and sprinkled her with holy water. Then he commanded the demon to leave in the name of Jesus Christ, the Blessed Trinity, St. Michael, and Our Lady of the Immaculate Conception. The woman threw herself on the floor and began crawling around the room. The priest repeated his commands for the next thirty minutes before she relaxed. Finally, something ugly and vile began to lift away. The grateful woman told him that this was the first time she felt happy in years.

Trabold is acknowledged for performing a series of successful exorcisms ending the West Pittston Smurl hauntings that previously involved demonologists Ed and Lorraine Warren. Because Bishop James Timlin's diocese did not have a qualified exorcist, they summoned Trabold "with authority to do whatever was necessary." But, unfortunately, it took four exorcisms to drive the demons out.

Trabold never felt any contradiction between his passion for his religion and parapsychology and sought to integrate them, as he told *BonAdventure* writer Jim Miller:

> Any power that we have has to ultimately come from God. That's to be understood. Otherwise, it just wouldn't be there. Very often, you will find that people associate any kind of paranormal ability—for instance, ESP—(with) something evil. I've had certain groups of clergymen of certain denominations condemn these things. They say, "It's the devil." No! No, it isn't. It's just things we don't understand.

In 2001, Rev. Alphonsus Trabold, OFM, celebrated the fiftieth anniversary of his ordination at the Holy Ghost Church in Gates, New York. Trabold died in 2005 at the age of eighty, recognized as one of the most accomplished in the realm of exorcism.

Chapter 11
Centralia: Gateway to Hell

Some believe that a curse has been placed upon Centralia, which lies on the remote fringes of the Pennsylvania Coal Region. It is a virtual ghost town with broken sidewalks, obsolete street signs, and only a few remaining individuals . A feeling of foreboding greets those passing through the village, and there have been various accounts of strange shadow figures and apparitions lurking around the abandoned structures.

The road leading to Centralia can be easily mistaken for the Gateway to Hell because, for decades, a massive underground fire has raged beneath the deserted city streets, spewing toxic carbon monoxide and other gasses. Of this, a modern-day Hades, writer Katie Machado observed:

> On some days, a trip into Centralia might mean seeing smoke rising from the cracks in the highway's asphalt, while on other days, it might

mean an eerie gray fog that claims the town after a rainy morning.

Immersed in isolation and superstition, the Coal Region remains a place of desolate stretches of culm, things that go bump in the night, and dead silence. Here are things that people do not discuss. An unspoken protocol is evident, as strange occurrences are whispered in guarded tones while other topics are pushed deeper into a repressed consciousness.

Father Daniel Ignatius McDermott

As the least-populated municipality in Pennsylvania, the town has conjured bizarre tourism fostered by individuals drawn to its surreal madness. Centralia, called the "creepiest place in the United States," had more people buried in its three cemeteries—Saint Ignatius, Saints Peter and Paul Orthodox, and Assumption of the Blessed Virgin Mary—than are alive in the town today. Only a handful of people still reside in Centralia. From 1981 to 2013, its population dwindled from over a thousand to less than ten, driven out by governmental intervention, hysteria, and, some say, the curse of an enraged priest.

Father Daniel Ignatius McDermott was only twenty-five years old when he began working in Centralia, celebrating two Masses in a schoolhouse, having been ordained as a priest only ten months earlier. But in 1868, Centralia's founder, Alexander Rea, was found murdered while riding in his horse-drawn buggy. According to Canadian researcher Bruce Forsyth, this became the catalyst for a series of fateful events:

> Father McDermott, suspecting the killers were members of his congregation, began denouncing the Molly Maguires from the pulpit. On a night in 1869, a group of men attacked Father McDermott in the church cemetery in retaliation. According to the legend, Father McDermott made his way back to the church after being assaulted and rang the church bell to summon the townsfolk, after which he pronounced a curse on the town.

McDermott said that there would be a day when the St. Ignatius Roman Catholic Church would be Centralia's only remaining structure and prophesied that the town would be erased from the face of the earth.

McDermott directed his anger at the townspeople for supporting the Mollies, but his prophecy proved only partially accurate . Saint Ignatius was not the last remaining structure. The stately church continued to hold mass until its final service on June 25, 1995. It was razed in 1997 due to the fire.

A group of Irish Catholics accused of being members of the Molly Maguire secret society was convicted by James McParland, an undercover Pinkerton detective, and Frank Gower, the Schuylkill County district attorney, in a courtroom trial that many believed reeked of injustice

Believed to have participated in the murder, three alleged members of the Molly Maguires were convicted and sentenced to death by hanging.

Molly Maguires

The Mollies were draped in mystery and mistrust, viewed as folk heroes by some and villains by others. Some believed they never existed but were a fictional propaganda tool used by ruthless mine owners who wanted to instill fear and dislike for the Irish.Others believed that the Mollies were Irish Catholics seeking retribution for unfair treatment by the mine owners and landlords. As an example, the coal barons were exploiting the Irish, paying them low wages. Hundreds were killed in mining accidents, leaving their families indigent.

The alleged Molly Maguires gathered secretly under the cover of peaceful organizations such as the Ancient Order of Hibernians.

Frank Gowen, president of the Reading and Philadelphia Railroad, covertly bought up mines to gain industry control. He hired the Pinkerton Detective Agency to infiltrate the Mollies and quash any resistance or unionization attempts from the miners.

One can easily trace the paranormal breadcrumbs from Centralia to other locales in the haunted Coal Region. In nearby Carbon County, another Molly haunts the old Jim Thorpe jail. The ancient two-story lockup has a prisoner's macabre handprint outlined on the wall of prison cell 17.

The inmate, Alexander Campbell, vowed that the handprint would forever remain on the wall as proof of his innocence. On June 21, 1877, on "the Day of the Rope," four Mollies, including Campbell, were sent to the gallows for murder, underscoring a dark chapter in America's early labor movement. According to the Old Jail Museum "History" site:

> Before their hanging, the men proclaimed their innocence, and today historians believe many of the condemned men were falsely accused of murder. Before his hanging, one man put his hand on the dirty floor of his cell and then placed it firmly on the wall, proclaiming, "This handprint will remain as proof of my innocence." That handprint is visible today for everyone to view, even though past wardens tried to eradicate it by washing it, painting it, and even taking down part of the wall and re-plastering it. The handprint was initially thought to be Alexander Campbell's, but after research, it is now believed to be Thomas Fisher's.

Coal Region Mythology

There's some evil in the hills, some weirdness that has infected the area. Coincidence? Probably not! Centralia is fifteen miles from Sheppton, the 1963 mining disaster site that netted international attention and claimed one miner's life. The missing miner's body led to rumors of cannibalization that continue to this day. Sheppton, one of the Coal Region's last paranormal anomalies, harbor stories of supernatural humanoid creatures and additional high strangeness.

Silent Hill

Centralia has inspired countless books, horror films, and documentaries. *Strange Highways* is Dean Koontz's short story about an alcoholic returning home to attend his father's funeral. He takes the highway to Coal Valley, whose residents "lived above a subterranean fire that churned relentlessly through a network of abandoned mines, eating away at untapped veins of anthracite ..." Coal Valley is based on Centralia, not far from Koontz's Everett, Pennsylvania, birthplace.

In 2004, director Christophe Gans and screenwriter Roger Avary began writing a script that would be the first in a series of *Silent Hill* films. The 2006 psychological horror film was an adaptation of Konami's 1999 video game *Silent Hill*. The film follows Rose, who takes her adopted daughter, Sharon, to the town of Silent Hill and awakens to find Sharon missing. While searching for her daughter, she fights a local cult and discovers Sharon's connection to the town's dark past.

Director Gans described the Silent Hill concept of the town's connection to the child Alessa and the cult: "It's a town of people trapped in dark dreams, and she inflicts onto the town what those people did to her body. That is, to me, the meaning of the darkness. The appearance of the town is corrupted in the way that her flesh was wounded."

Avary used Centralia as his inspiration for the town of Silent Hill, modeled after its unique features, including its gothic-style church. He explained that his father, a mining engineer, had told him stories about a raging underground fire that released toxic gases, forcing the residents to abandon their town.

The "Devil's Fire"

Centralia's history has been ripped from the pages of a horror novel. An underground mine inferno has burned under the tiny community for more than fifty years. It started in 1962 in an abandoned mining pit used to get rid of the town's garbage. Soon, a seam of coal running under the town was ignited by the flames. That event may or may not have been the cause, according to writer Bill Clawser:

> There are various opinions as to how the mine fire got started. Some think it was the result of burning trash at the landfill. Whatever the case, when smoke and fumes began billowing from the ground, action had to be taken. The US Congress allocated millions of dollars for family relocation. Most people accepted the offer and moved out, after which their homes were destroyed.

Nothing has been able to extinguish the fire. Workers attempted to blast and excavate the inferno and later drilled boreholes, pouring in concrete, wet sand, and fly ash to suffocate the fire. Workers dug a vast containment trench as a last resort to stop the fire's progress. That failed as well.

In his article "I Live in Centralia, PA: It's America's Creepiest Ghost Town," writer Evan V. Symon explained:

> Underneath Centralia, the endless fire has created an environment as deadly as the surface of Saturn. While the gases aren't lethal up above, they still play hell with the residents' health. Poison gas has even built up in some citizens' basements. One guy explained how that all simply became part of the weather in Centralia. "We always had the smoke, and my wife felt sick if she was near it. We stay away from it. It's bad news. Only the tourists go into the damn thing."

The village, a once-bustling boomtown, had seven churches and a tight-knit community of over 2,500. Fourteen anthracite-rich mines provided employment. But all that changed around 1984, when almost all residents relocated, accepting the government's buyout offers. Most of the houses were bought and torn down as part of a federal relocation program, although a few residents remained in protest, refusing to leave their lifelong homes despite the toxic fumes.

In 1992, Bob Casey, then governor of Pennsylvania, declared eminent domain, condemning all buildings and appropriating the town. The residents were bought out. Most inhabitants agreed to the government program, purging the village of human presence. The US Congress allocated forty two million dollars in 1984 to relocate homes and businesses in the town to safer ground. Massive bulldozers demolished over five hundred homes, and the remaining structures were condemned. Conspiracy theories spewed rumors that the government and the coal companies wanted to drive out the citizens and claim the rich anthracite veins below.

The dwindling residents unsuccessfully fought back in court. In 2002, the US Postal service revoked Centralia's zip code, 17927, forcing the locals to receive mail via post office box. The final act in this tragedy occurred in 2009 when Governor Ed Rendell began formally evicting the remaining citizens.

Graffiti Highway

Route 61 once ran through the town. In 1993, it was closed and rerouted after the road surface shifted and buckled from decades of intense heat from below. Cracks ripped across the paved asphalt road, and hot blasts of steam shot through the highway. The residents choked on fumes of carbon monoxide and acrid smoke.

"Graffiti Highway," an abandoned stretch of Route 61 attracting horror fans and curiosity seekers, has achieved cult status. It became an unofficial tourist attraction and possibly the state's sixth-most-visited attraction. The road was closed and rerouted in 1993. In 2020 approximately four hundred loads of dirt mounds were dumped on the abandoned stretch of road, ending Centralia's most bizarre attraction. (David Karchner photograph.)

The Transportation Department abandoned a three-quarter-mile section of Route 61 that eventually became known as the Graffiti Highway. Over the years, the road had attracted gawkers and curiosity seekers who wanted to see the smoldering and abandoned mountainside or spray-paint the graffiti-strewn roadway. It had become an unofficial tourist attraction. Writing for *Atlas Obscura*, reporter Julie Knutson observed that the abandoned three-quarter-mile stretch of road:

> ... had achieved cult status in the first decade of the 2000s. After years of disuse, it took on new life as an artistic commons adorned with

everything from pineapple-carapaced turtles to less-than-family-friendly fare, often of the male anatomical variety. By 2017, it was anecdotally cited by some locals as the sixth-most-visited attraction in the state.

Knutson wrote that Centralia was a magnet for horror fans, ghost hunters, and the generally curious and that the Graffiti Highway is—in the words of playwright and Kutztown University professor Deryl Johnson—really an "epilogue" to the story of Centralia itself.

In 2017, the Commonwealth of Pennsylvania began to target curious onlookers, citing trespassers. In April 2020, the Fox Coal Company dumped rows of dirt mounds on the abandoned stretch of road— approximately four hundred loads of material. This was the final attempt to chase away the swarms of tourists, mainly curious college students, who gathered at the site by the thousands. The now-abandoned stretch of road is now private property.

Considering all of the bizarre, seemingly paranormal elements, an article titled "Is Centralia Haunted?" offers an exciting conclusion:

> With any strange or unusual occurrence comes rumors and stories. Centralia is no different in that respect. Walking amid the ruins of this modern-day ghost town gives one the feeling of supernatural forces working underfoot. From visitors to the town, stories arose from these

ashes. Some were stories from visitors who left in fear after thinking they saw a person or thing, heard odd sounds, and felt they were being watched. Others go as far as to say Centralia is the gateway to Hell. Imaginations can run wild. As Centralia becomes a modern-day ghost town and the fire encroaches upon the graveyards of the abandoned village, rumors have circulated that Centralia is haunted.

And perhaps it is. Today Centralia is a weed-strewn ghost town where only a handful remain, living above the persistent nightmare of an underground fire that refuses to burn itself out. How long this buried inferno will blaze, the devil only knows.

Chapter 12

TWA Flight 800

On July 17, 1996, Trans World Airlines flight 800 took off from New York's Kennedy International Airport in the twilight dusk of sunset. The two hundred and thirty people aboard were on their way to Paris, France.

Flight 800 flew at a lower altitude than usual because of another approaching jet. After receiving clearance to climb to cruise altitude, the Boeing 747 jetliner leveled off at 13,700 feet above sea level. Then, twelve minutes after takeoff, the plane exploded without warning. Thousands of pounds of kerosene were dumped from the plane's center, and wing tanks vaporized and ignited. An orange fireball burned along the coastline as sections of the 747 plunged into the Atlantic Ocean, south of Long Island.

Twenty-one passengers were from Montoursville, Pennsylvania, heading for a once-in-a-lifetime trip to the City of Light. Sixteen were members of the Montoursville

Area High School French Club, accompanied by five chaperones. There were no survivors.

On a flight to Paris, TWA flight 800's Boeing 747 jetliner exploded. It had eighteen crew members, including four pilots and fourteen flight attendants. Twenty-one passengers were from Montoursville, Pennsylvania. Sixteen were members of the Montoursville Area High School French Club, accompanied by five chaperones. There were no survivors of the 230 people on board.

Further Explanations

As a result, investigators began to look into the safety record of the twenty-five-year-old plane. The Boeing 747 had been manufactured in November 1971 and had accumulated about 93,303 flight hours and 16,869 cycles. The airplane had eighteen crew members, including four pilots and fourteen flight attendants. However, there was no documentation of the flight crew reporting a problem to air traffic control.

Although some believed that the 747 went down because of a malfunction, the National Transportation Safety Board's (NTSB) official report, issued four years after the crash, concluded an electrical spark ignited fuel vapors in the center fuel tank and was the probable cause of the explosion.

Questions remained about flight 800, now regarded as the first conspiracy of the Internet Age, as the debate was far from over. Further explanations came from politicians, engineers, and conspiracy theorists. For example, Pierre Salinger, former press secretary for Presidents Kennedy and Johnson, proclaimed that a Navy missile caused the crash. Next, software engineer Michael E. Davias wrote a fifty-one-page thesis titled "Flight 800 Meteorite Interface Hypothesis—A Hypothetical Solution to the T.W.A. Flight 800 Paradox?" Finally, J. K. Henderson, a retired instrument engineer, offered that a pressure issue may have caused the explosion.

Other theories suggested that the plane's front cargo door blew off, while another believed that laser rays emitted from Long Island destroyed the aircraft. Ball lightning was still another of the unproven theories. Finally, a different view was that a bolide, a giant meteor, exploded in Earth's atmosphere and sent one of its fragments into the fuselage of flight 800.

Maxim W. Furek

The Missile Theory

Conspiracy theorists rallied around the possibility that a missile shot the jetliner down. And several comprehensive reports appeared to support those claims. The Associated Press detailed on June 19, 1996, that "Radar detected a blip merging with the jet shortly before the explosion, something that could indicate a missile hit." In its story of September 22, 1996, the *New York Post* reported, "Law-enforcement sources said the hardest evidence gathered so far overwhelmingly suggests a surface-to-air missile."

Investigators identified one hundred and eighty-three eyewitnesses who saw something rising from the ocean and strike flight 800. They saw an explosion and the plane's wreckage dropping into the Atlantic Ocean.

The missile theory continued to resonate. An Associated Press article, published on March 10, 1997, read:

The report said "compelling testimony" indicated a missile hit the plane on the right side, forward of the wing, passing through the fuselage without exploding. This is consistent with a test missile with a dummy warhead.

Some charged that the Federal Bureau of Investigation (FBI) misled the public. The FBI did not believe the eyewitnesses were accurate in their testimonies and disregarded their accounts. According to MilitaryCorruption.com writer David Smallwood:

A massive cover-up ensued, with the FBI suppressing the truth in an effort to save Bill Clinton's 1996 re-election chances. A surface-to-air missile that blasted the 747-100 right out of the sky, killing two hundred and thirty people, becoming the third-deadliest aviation accident in US history.

Books and Documentaries

Several books and documentaries have investigated the crash. For example, *TWA 800: The Crash, the Cover-Up, and the Conspiracy*, written by investigative reporter Jack Cashill, claimed that the official explanation for the explosion was slanted, concluding that the FBI, CIA, and President Bill Clinton were involved in a cover-up. Although many agreed with him, others criticized Cashill for his partisan ranting about Benghazi and other right-wing themes with little connection to flight 800.

Author James Sanders's book, *The Downing Of TWA Flight 800*, revealed that a TWA employee gave Sanders two samples of cloth from seats from TWA 800, requesting that an outside, non-government-linked laboratory test them. The seat fabric samples contained a bright red residue that had stained three rows of seats in the aircraft. Sanders claimed tests on the first sample revealed elements that experts confirmed were consistent with the combustion byproducts of a military solid-fuel rocket motor of the powdered aluminum and perchlorate type.

Sanders gave his last sample to CBS news to have tested, but CBS returned the sample to the government, who declared that the red residue was seat glue.

Another argument came from airline veteran Andrew Danziger, one of the pilots to fly Barack Obama during his 2008 presidential campaign. Danziger wrote an article in the *New York Daily News* titled "TWA Flight 800 was not blown up by a faulty fuel tank; it was shot down. I'll always believe that, and here's why." He wrote:

> Jets do not explode in midair. If they do, it's usually because they've been shot down or bombed. There's little to suggest that there was a bomb on board, but there is ample evidence that a missile of some sort detonated in the air very close to the plane and brought it down.

The flight 800 crash was the first conspiracy theory to surface on the budding World Wide Web and the first conspiracy of the Internet Age. Conspiracy theorists began spreading misinformation and conjecture through chat rooms that were widely circulated. David M. Zimmer, writing in *USA Today,* observed:

> One early version posted online alleged the crash resulted from an attack designed to kill former US Secretary of State Henry Kissinger, who was, in fact, not on board. Another claimed the friendly fire was designed to kill former Arkansas state

troopers once assigned to then-President Bill Clinton's security detail.

Aftermath

Ignoring that conspiracy theory, President Clinton addressed the crash, vowing to take "immediate steps to improve airline safety and security." However, he asked the public to not "jump to conclusions" and theorized that either mechanical failure or sabotage caused the crash.

The tragedy prompted one of the most extensive and expensive aviation investigations in history. The NTSB eventually deemed it an accident and found no evidence of foul play. Former NTSB board member John Goglia, who spent four years investigating the crash, addressed "the TWA 800 Project," a group of petitioners who wanted the NTBS to reopen the crash investigation, claiming that a "detonation or high-velocity explosion" caused the crash. Goglia wrote in *Forbes* in July 2014 that eyewitness accounts of a "flash" in the sky just before the airplane blew up were not supported by radar evidence. The fuselage wreckage also did not show any evidence of an explosion next to the plane, he concluded:

> At the end of the day, "damage patterns within the airplane were consistent with a center wing tank explosion." In addition, the debris pattern was consistent with a fuel-air explosion in the center wing tank. The NTSB concluded that the

petitioners had not introduced any evidence which would warrant overturning the Board's prior conclusions or determination of probable cause.

Investigators concluded the streak observed by hundreds of witnesses was burning fuel streaming from the plane's wing tank. NTSB investigators recovered more than ninety-five percent of the aircraft. A ninety-three-foot segment of the aircraft fuselage was reconstructed and then moved to a thirty-thousand-square-foot hangar in Ashburn, Virginia. The reconstructed plane was used in accident investigation training for nearly twenty years. It was decommissioned and destroyed in July 2021.

The NTSB finding led to regulations requiring a system that pumps inert gas into empty fuel tanks, and Boeing was required to replace the brittle wiring on other 747s and redesign their air-conditioning packs.

The remains of all passengers were recovered, and all two hundred and thirty names were etched into the TWA Flight 800 International Memorial at Smith Point County Park on Long Island. The memorial was dedicated in July 2004 and included flags from the thirteen countries of the victims.

We will never conclusively know what happened to flight 800, and over twenty years later, questions linger about one of the worst airline crashes in history and what would become the Internet Age's first conspiracy.

Chapter 13
Unidentified Aerial Phenomenon

They were initially called "foo fighters," mysterious flying objects that harassed and mystified soldiers during World War II. The term was used by World War II Allied aircraft pilots to describe what they believed to be UFOs or any other unexplained aerial phenomena. These sightings began around November 1944 and were seen in the skies over both the European and Pacific theaters. Witnesses assumed that the "foo fighters" were secret weapons employed by the Axis powers.

But that wasn't true, according to the Robertson Panel.

The postwar Robertson Panel concluded that "foo fighters" were not, in fact, threatening. The panel looked for other probable explanations. One such possibility that they offered was electrostatic phenomena similar to St. Elmo's fire, electromagnetic phenomena, or simply reflections of light from ice crystals. Three years later, "foo fighters" would reappear, but in another curious variation.

Kenneth Arnold

It was June 24, 1947, a date forever galvanized in the annals of ufology. That was when pilot Kenneth Arnold, thirty-two, was returning home from a business trip, flying his private light plane. The CallAir A-2 was a three-place single-engine land ship and an extremely high-performance airplane. It was made for high-altitude mountain work and was designed and manufactured in nearby Afton, Wyoming.

Approaching Mount Rainier, Washington, on a clear summer's day, Arnold saw something that would give him the title of "the man who started it all." Arnold saw a formation of nine unidentified objects fly at high speed in front of his plane. He estimated their speed at about 1,200 miles an hour. He described them as crescent-shaped, silvery and shiny, and flying in a V formation. They had no tails. Another individual, a prospector named Fred Johnson, witnessed the same aerial formation and verified Arnold's account.

The term "flying saucer" was coined not by Arnold but by a reporter. Arnold stated that the objects flew "erratic like a saucer would if you skipped it across the water." *East Oregonian* newspaper reporter Bill Bequette paraphrased Arnold's statement when he placed the story on the AP news wire. Arnold's term "saucer-like" became "flying saucers."

Operation Sign

Such a post-war event had never been experienced before. The public response to Arnold's flying discs and the Roswell crash, one month later, was one of controlled hysteria. The government felt compelled to take action, organizing a Pentagon summit only a few days after the Roswell crash. According to UFO Database:

> On the 7th of July, a meeting was held at the Pentagon in the office of General Schulgen, Chief of the Air Forces' Air Intelligence Requirements Division. It was decided that reports from "more qualified observers of flying discs" should be selected for follow-up investigation, and Project Sign was born.

Operation Sign was the government's response to the widespread interest in the Arnold episode, increased UFO sightings, and the incident at Roswell, New Mexico, the "flap" that wouldn't go away. After official sources claimed that they had confiscated a crashed flying saucer, the Roswell stories grew, assuming a mythological life of its own. A new subculture of "ufology" was born.

Some of our nation's most remarkable minds took a hard look at the evidence. Initial theories proposed were that the sightings were sophisticated Soviet aircraft, possible variations of their Sukhoi Su-7 or Tupolev Tu-28. Others speculated that they were possible extraterrestrial spacecraft but later concluded that there was no evidence of beings from other planets visiting Earth.

The twenty-one-year US Air Force UFO investigation was abandoned in 1969. The programs had included Project Sign (1947–1948), Project Grudge (1949–1951), and Project Blue Book (1952–1969). Of the 12,097 UFO sightings investigated, 90 percent were explained as planes, satellites, balloons, or various natural phenomena. But the remaining ten percent would dominate the ongoing debate and prove to be the most vexing. Although many sightings are explainable as natural or artificial phenomena, some are not.

Over the decades, millions of people have reported seeing unidentifiable things. More than 3,500 documented sightings of "unidentified aerial phenomena"—the new Pentagon designation for UFOs— by pilots, have been recorded by the National Aviation Reporting Center on Anomalous Phenomena (NARCAP).

Dismiss and Ridicule

The US Air Force investigators deemed Kenneth Arnold and Fred Johnson "credible witnesses" but concluded that they saw a mirage and not actual flying crafts.

This was one example of an overall strategy to dismiss and ridicule UFO sightings. Over the years, there have been countless sightings where empirical data has been mischaracterized by government agencies and ignored by scientific research. These cases are typically written off as hallucinations, swamp gas, reflections from the planet Venus, or deliberate hoaxes. Witnesses to these unexplained events are often viewed as odd and histrionic kooks.

Although dismissed by the scientific community, unidentified flying objects became a popular theme for motion pictures. They were relegated to pop culture and cinematic fantasy. A horde of movies depicting Hollywood's wide-screen version of the UFO included popular films such as *The Day the Earth Stood Still* (1951), *War of the Worlds* (1953), *This Island Earth* (1955), and *Earth vs. the Flying Saucers* (1956).

There exists a thin line between truth and fiction, reality and conjecture. In her article titled "UFOs—Visitors from Outer Space," American cultural anthropologist Margaret Mead (1901–1978) argued that the UFO phenomena represented a tangible entity, not some abstract construct demanding our unwavering faith. Dismissing the question, "Do you believe in UFOs?" she wrote:

> Belief has to do with matters of faith. It has nothing to do with the kind of knowledge that is based on scientific inquiry. We should not bracket UFOs with angels and archangels, devils, and demons. But this is just what we are doing when we ask whether people "believe" in UFOs—as if their existence were an article of faith. Do people believe in the sun or the moon or the changing seasons or the chairs they are sitting on?

Mead argued that most people continue to frame the UFO question around their personal belief system rather than looking to the scientific community for answers to this phenomenon.

Dr. Helen Sharman

One British cosmonaut would be quick to agree with Mead. Dr. Helen Sharman completed an eight-day space mission aboard Mir's Russian space station in 1991. At twenty-seven, she became the first British cosmonaut in space and a national hero. Dr. Sharman told *Observer Magazine* that it is without a doubt that "all sorts of forms of life are alive in the universe—but perhaps they are so different from humanity." She added:

> Aliens exist, there's no two ways about it … there are so many billions of stars out there in the universe that there must be all sorts of forms of life … Will they be like you and me, made up of carbon and nitrogen? Maybe not. It's possible

they're right here right now, and we simply can't see them.

Sharman's theory may be bolstered by the scientific observations of NASA's Kepler Space Telescope, opening the door to exciting possibilities. The thirteen-billion-year-old Milky Way galaxy may be home to many potentially habitable planets. Estimates are that close to 20 percent of the galaxies two hundred billion stars may have ideal conditions where liquid surface water and other conditions could support lifeforms.

For example, the Kepler Space Telescope has discovered Kepler-186f, the first Earth-size planet orbiting a star in the "habitable zone." The discovery confirms that planets the size of Earth exist in the habitable zone of stars other than our sun.

The UFO Renaissance

The UFO renaissance began in 2017 after the *New York Times* reported on the Pentagon's Advanced Aerospace Threat Identification Program. The Pentagon had been secretly investigating UAPs for years. In 2019, the Navy began formulating new guidelines for its pilots to report UFO sightings, signaling a move to destigmatize them.

Everything changed in 2019. That was when the US government, perhaps bending to public pressure, began to view this phenomenon as something of substance and not the stuff of urban legend.

The US Navy updated its protocols for pilots and other officials to report sightings of "unidentified aircraft." In a statement to *Politico*, the Navy stated:

> There have been a number of reports of unauthorized and/or unidentified aircraft entering various military-controlled ranges and designated air space in recent years. For safety and security concerns, the Navy and the [US Air Force] takes these reports very seriously and investigates each and every report.
>
> As part of this effort, the Navy is updating and formalizing the process by which reports of any such suspected incursions can be made to the cognizant authorities. A new message to the fleet that will detail the steps for reporting is in draft.

Although the Navy did not acknowledge the existence of alien life, they did conclude that these unexplained sightings should be investigated.

NASA Panel

NASA's inquiry is separate from the Pentagon-based investigation of UAPs. A 2021 Pentagon report found insufficient data to determine the nature of more than 140 credible sightings documented by Navy personnel since 2004. Senior defense and intelligence officials testified before Congress that the list of cataloged UAP sightings had since grown to 400, but many remain beyond explanation.

This is not hard science, and the number of UAP sightings varies. Peter Davenport, seventy-four, of Harrington, Washington, estimates he's meticulously logged 180,000 UFO reports over the past twenty-eight years. He took over the site in 1994 from the late Bob Gribble, a Seattle firefighter and UFO enthusiast. He runs his one-man center seven days a week. According to *Seattle Times'* staff reporter Erik Lacitis:

> Davenport's site is referenced in stories that have run in the *New York Times,* the *Washington Post,* and the *Wall Street Journal*. It is his site that the Federal Aviation Administration recommends for reporting UFOs.

A recent report proclaimed Washington the No. 1 state in the country for UFO sightings, based on two years of UFO reports from Davenport's site. Washington reported 88.03 sightings per 100,000 residents, about twice the national average of 44.95.

> In 2022, NASA formed a sixteen-member panel to investigate UAPs. The study, focused on sightings collected from civilian government and commercial sectors, included experts from scientific fields ranging from physics to astrobiology.

The *New York Times* reported over one thousand UAP sightings in April 2020. However, that report's significance was confusing because it happened during the chaos and uncertainty of the Covid-19 pandemic. Still, there were other things of significance, according to Steve Gorman, writing for *Reuters*:

> The parallel NASA and Pentagon efforts highlight a turning point for the US government after spending decades deflecting, debunking, and discrediting observations of unidentified flying objects, or UFOs, dating back to the 1940s.

Politico reported that Rep. Mark Walker, the ranking member of the Intelligence and Counterterrorism

Subcommittee, wrote a letter to Navy Secretary Richard Spencer. The July 16, 2019, letter requested more information about the source of the UAP. Walker was concerned that the Pentagon wasn't sufficiently investigating the strange sightings regularly reported by Navy pilots.

Based on pilot accounts, sightings of UAPs often entail complex flight patterns and advanced maneuvering. The UAP technology appears to use revolutionary advances in quantum mechanics, nuclear science, electromagnetics, and thermodynamics. Walker expressed concern that the UAPs might result from significant advances in Chinese aeronautical engineering technology. Discussing his concerns on Fox News's *Tucker Carlson Tonight* program, Walker asked:

> Is this something that's a defense mechanism from another country? We do know that China is looking at hypersonic missiles, that's 25,000 [kilometers per hour] or to break it down into our language that's getting from DC, where I'm at, to LA in about nine minutes ... If the accounts are true, the unidentified crafts could pose a serious security risk to our military personnel and defense apparatus.

The debate between true believers and nonbelievers continues. In August 2000, the *Fortean Times*' cover headline was "UFO? The shocking truth about the first flying saucers." Writer James Easton suggested that

Kenneth Arnold's UFO sighting of possible extraterrestrial craft was actually American white pelicans, a theory quickly criticized and dismissed by many in the paranormal community.

Alien Abductions

As reported in "The Gate to Strange Phenomena," Luis Elizondo revealed in an interview with the *Sun* that our military has experienced alien abductions and implants. He also admitted that there is much we do not know:

> There's something in our skies, we don't know what they are, we don't know how they work, we don't fully know what they can do, we don't know who's behind the wheel. We also don't know their intentions, and there's nothing we can do about it.

Elizondo worked in the Pentagon's secret UFO program from 2007 to 2012 and was interviewed by journalist Baptiste Friscourt.

Then, in 2020, the Navy formally released three UFO videos, first made public by the *Times* and former Blink-182 front man Tom DeLonge's "To the Stars Academy"—self-described as "a public benefit corporation that was established in 2017 as a revolutionary collaboration between academia, industry and pop culture to advance society's understanding of scientific phenomena and its technological implications."

Videos released by the Pentagon show unknown objects demonstrating speed and maneuverability exceeding known aviation expertise. The Pentagon concluded these UAPs are either advanced earthly technologies, atmospherics, or something alien. Traditional theories are being challenged. If UAPs prove to be extraterrestrial, academics, theologists, and scientists will have to rethink outdated mindsets and accept new possibilities.

The UFO Clown Show

After Kenneth Arnold's sighting and the Roswell crash, it was off to the races. Just as America was memorizing the letters UFO, the predictable clown show arrived—narcissists hovering around the flying saucer storyline like flies swarming over dog crap. Their sole intent was to rip away a piece of notoriety and exploit it for personal gain.

The list of con artists is long and sordid—Adamski, Corso, and Lazar come to mind. There were others, and their stories all have a kernel of truth or maybe not.

After Kenneth Arnold's sighting, George Adamski saw a fleet of 184 spacecraft. Four years later, the self-styled professor of oriental mysticism communicated telepathically with Orthon, an alien from Venus, warning us to stop using atomic weapons. Truman Bethurum was also a member of the clown show. He flew aboard a flying saucer with Captain Aura Rhanes, a gorgeous female from the planet Clarion. The Space People gave Van Tassel instructions to construct the "Integratron," a four-story-high domed machine. George King had his Aetherians, and Ruth Norman, aka Uriel, her Unarius Foundation. Phillip Corso and Bob Lazar participated in secret government programs that reverse-engineered extraterrestrial spaceship technology, leading to the Strategic Defense Initiative (SDI), or "Star Wars."

These bogus claims were all lies and deceit that sullied legitimate research. It gave a bad name to ufology. The realm of ufology has always been endemic with government disinformation and conspiracy tales. The truth is hard to come by. Science writer Sarah Scoles has cautioned against what an *Atlantic* headline termed "The UFO Trap," where media outlets display less skepticism or rigor when it comes to UFO reporting. Still, a Gallup poll shows that the number of Americans who think UFOs could be literal alien craft from outer space has substantially increased, especially among people with college educations.

Everything has evolved. UFOs are now called UAPs, and their descriptions have radically changed. UAPs no longer project the traditional bulky flying saucer appearance. They are now often described as orbs of light or other unexplained aerial-propelled objects. UAPs are no longer mere physical crafts but can be mystery lights or energy vehicles that appear to us in the form of craft, as suggested by Rosemary Ellen Guiley. The descriptions, across the globe, tend to be consistent. UAPs in Philadelphia look much like those in Bombay.

After World War II, and the dropping of atomic bombs on Hiroshima and Nagasaki, sightings of UFOs began to frequently appear. Something had triggered this phenomenon, and since that time, it has not dissipated. What has changed are the varied shapes; cigar, triangle, tic-tac, but what remains is the familiar and nagging question — what exactly are they?

Chapter 14

The Kecksburg UFO Incident

It came out of the sky in what has emerged as one of the most bizarre accounts in modern ufology. On December 9, 1965, a fireball streaked across northeastern North America with sightings reported as far apart as Indiana, New York, Virginia, and Ontario. The mysterious anomaly, believed to have been a UFO, spread debris over parts of Michigan, Ohio and Pennsylvania, touching off numerous fires. Flying at an estimated speed of one thousand miles per hour, the object created a sonic boom that could be heard as far away as Canada. As flaming debris fell, the thing crashed in the small western Pennsylvania town of Kecksburg in Westmoreland County. Kecksburg is located along PA Route 982 in a heavily wooded area about thirty miles southeast of Pittsburgh, with an elevation of 1,209 feet.

At that point, things transpired with blurred military precision. First, the US Army stepped in, and the area was tightly roped off in almost martial law fashion. Next, armed soldiers turned back citizens who came out into the woods to investigate. They were instructed to never discuss anything about what they may have seen. It became clear that this was more than just a crashed meteorite. The day after the event, the Greensburg *Tribune-Review*'s "Unidentified Flying Object Falls near Kecksburg—Army Ropes off Area" proclaimed it a UFO.

A life-size replica of Kecksburg's UFO was constructed for the 1990 documentary *Unsolved Mysteries*. The cryptic UFO, known as Pennsylvania's Roswell, was reported to have been an acorn-shaped, copper-colored spacecraft. It was fifteen feet long and encircled by a band of writing like Egyptian hieroglyphics. (Maxim Furek photograph.)

The area where the object landed was immediately sealed off on the order of U.S. Army and State Police officials, reportedly in anticipation of a "close inspection" of whatever may have fallen ... State Police officials there ordered the area roped off to await the expected arrival of both U.S. Army engineers and possibly, civilian scientists

US Army

The US Army reported that, after investigating the woods around Kecksburg, nothing was found. But years later, numerous witnesses disputed this claim. For example, a group of volunteer firefighters saw the object in the woods when they responded to what they thought was a plane crash. Instead, they discovered a suspected extraterrestrial craft buried in the ground and covered in hieroglyphics.

Paranormal researcher Stan Gordon (Pennsylvania Association for the Study of the Unexplained) interviewed James Romansky, who was an eighteen-year-old firefighter at the time. Romansky was called out after numerous reports of a possible downed aircraft in Mount Pleasant Township, just off Kuhn Lane.

Romansky described the object as bronze colored and shaped like an acorn-some twelve feet long and ten feet in diameter; it had a slightly

> raised "blunt" end and strange markings:
> It had writing on it, not like your average writing,
> but more like ancient Egyptian hieroglyphics. It
> had sort of a bumper on it, like a ribbon about six
> to 10 inches wide, and it stood out. It was elliptical
> the whole way around, and the writing was on this
> bumper. It's nothing like I've ever seen, and I'm an
> avid reader. I read a lot of books on Egypt, the
> Incas, Peruvians, Russians, and I've never to this
> day come across anything that looked like that.

Romansky told Gordon that the solid bronze-gold object was large enough for a man to stand inside it. He said it "looked as though it was constructed from liquid metal that had been poured into an acorn-shaped mold."

Bill Bulebush believes that he was the first person to observe the object. He saw the object as it was streaking overhead and immediately drove out past Kune Lane to the highest point overlooking the crash site. In his book *The Kecksburg UFO Incident*, author George Dudding documented witness Bill Bulebush's recollections:

> It was about ten or twelve feet long and was making a crackling sound with sparks flying off its surface and it was giving off a burned sulfur smell. It was a burnt orange or gold colored object and was shaped like an acorn. Around the widest part of the acorn at its base, was a band of metal which wrapped around the craft and it displayed strange symbols or markings similar to Egyptian hieroglyphics.

Lockbourne Air Force Base

According to Stan Gordon's investigation, the military set up a nearby command post. There, two military flatbed tractor-trailers retrieved and then transported a conical-shaped object, about the size of a Volkswagen Beetle, concealed under a large tarpaulin. The transport vehicles, including military jeeps and personnel carriers, drove to

Lockbourne Air Force Base near Columbus, Ohio. the convoy then continued to Wright Patterson Air Force Base, where, according to UFO mythology, the Roswell humanoids are clandestinely stored. Micheal Rambacher, a security officer for the Air Force, claimed to have guarded the Kecksburg object and believed it was extraterrestrial.

Gordon later produced a ninety-two-minute documentary video, *Kecksburg: The Untold Story*. Often referred to as "Pennsylvania's Roswell," Kecksburg has been a favorite topic among UFO researchers. Some believe it is one of the most compelling cases for extraterrestrial existence in US history.

It is still hotly debated, and while some are convinced that an alien craft crashed in the woods outside of town, others find the story ridiculous and the media attention to their town intrusive.

Freedom of Information

Researcher Ray Boeche filed a Freedom of Information request for more data on the incident. In 1985, thirty pages of vague data were procured. A memo stated that a three-man team had been dispatched to Acme, PA, to pick up the object that started the fire. In 2003, a lawsuit was filed against NASA to release the documents from the military investigation. A NASA spokesperson told the Associated Press that a Russian satellite had been discovered on the site. However, this possibility was ruled out conclusively. The study of the orbital analysis of all known man-made crafts orbiting at the time was conducted by one of NASA's scientists.

While some believed this was, in fact, an optical illusion and that the object could not have landed in the Kecksburg area, others claimed that there was a Kecksburg cover-up. According to Los Angeles-based writer Jacob Shelton, the Freedom of Information Act lawsuit did not produce the anticipated NASA data:

> Steve McConnell, NASA's public liaison officer, testified that two boxes of papers from the Kecksburg investigation were lost, but he argued that this isn't strange because NASA often misplaces information.

Still, the Pennsylvania UFO enigma shares uncanny similarity to Roswell's alleged government cover-up. Kecksburg expert Stan Gordon stated, "I have no doubt the government knows a lot more about this than it has revealed to the public."

With widespread conspiracy theories and lack of official documentation, deciphering the Kecksburg incident has only gotten more confusing. Everyone seems to have their own opinion as to what actually happened. Local WHJB radio station news director John Murphy produced a radio documentary titled *Object in the Woods*. And although he claimed to be the first to actually see the object, that has not been authenticated.

Numerous attempts have been made to decipher the Kecksburg enigma. In 1990, the Kecksburg Incident was explored in a segment of *Unsolved Mysteries*. In addition, the Sci-Fi Channel filmed a documentary titled *The New Roswell: Kecksburg Exposed*, hosted by Bryant Gumbel, former host of *Today* and *The Early Show*. And in 2011, the Discovery Channel's *Ancient Aliens* investigated the incident.

None of the shows provided conclusive proof of extraterrestrial activity. To date, no definitive explanation has been determined, although the Air Force official statement concluded that the hysteria surrounding the glowing object was actually caused by a meteor. Other, less conventional attempts have been made to explain what crashed outside Kecksburg, Pennsylvania.

Kosmos 96

Some speculated that it was a meteorite that flew over Canada and the three American states. However, another theory is that the object was the Kosmos 96, a crashed Soviet Union Venus space probe. In the early days of Soviet space exploration, Russian launches were shrouded in secrecy. The Kosmos 96 was a Soviet spacecraft intended to make a flyby of Venus. The failed mission is believed to have crashed shortly after launch on December 9, 1965, and has been speculated by some as the cause of the Kecksburg UFO incident. Because it contained heat shield technology, it could survive reentry into the Earth's atmosphere and not burn up. Kosmos 96 could maneuver while landing on Venus and may have attempted those movements over Kecksburg, giving the impression of a controlled UFO.

Some of the most bizarre explanations conclude that the object was either an extraterrestrial UFO or a Nazi Bell. The Nazi Bell, or *Die Glocke*, was a secret weapon Germany developed during World War II. According to researcher George Dudding, it used high levels of radiation to affect the space-time fabric, allowing an alteration in the flow of time. It was believed to be able to freeze time and allow stormtroopers to suddenly materialize, using the element of surprise against their opponent.

(L-R) Bigfoot and UFO expert Stan Gordon and paranormal researcher Maxim Furek at the 2022 Kecksburg UFO Festival. Gordon is the author of *Silent Invasion* and several other paranormal books. (Patricia A. Furek photograph.)

But not everything mandates an extraterrestrial or science-fiction origin. According to researcher Stan Gordon, writing in his book *Silent Invasion*:

Many UFO sightings were artificial or natural objects that looked strange under certain conditions. Many flying saucers or UFO reports were just bright meteors, planets, stars, satellites, and sometimes just lights reflecting off meandering birds and insects. Other strange events quite often could be explained as well.

In respect to Kecksburg, the theories continue to manifest in the wake of newly uncovered evidence. According to John Ventre of MUFON and Shafton native Owen Eichler, their investigations have led them to speculate that the object that reportedly landed in Kecksburg was of earthly origin. They submit that a General Electric Mark 2 Re-entry Vehicle that had been launched by the Air Force as a spy satellite, had fell out of orbit.

Kecksburg hosts an annual Old Fashion Days and UFO Festival, now a lasting part of the town's culture. In 2005, a UFO Store was opened. A replica of the acorn-shaped object, constructed as part of a documentary several years earlier, was mounted in front of the local fire station. After the 2010 UFO Festival, the *Daily Courier* reported that a new location for the town's annual celebration was needed because of the large crowds.

Chapter 15
The Bigfoot Enigma

Does an unknown species of man-ape, known to some as "Bigfoot," really exist?

The recorded history of Bigfoot goes back over two hundred years. Rumors of a humanoid-like creature first jarred the public's awareness in the early 1950s after Himalayan Mountain climbers brought back stories of giant footprints discovered in the snow on remote mountain trails. The climbers believed the tracks had been made by a creature the natives called yeti.

The creature is called *Almieta* in Russian and the abominable snowman or yeti in the Himalayas. The natives of Tibet and Nepal fear the yeti, and some believe it is fateful to even gaze upon the beast. Writer Ray Robertson has suggested even more:

He has no name. But people at various times and in other parts of the world have tried to describe him. They call him *Seeahtik*, Creek Devil, *Dsonoqua,* or *Buk was*. He is known as the "Abominable Snowman" in the Himalayas. The Indians of the Pacific Northwest call him Sasquatch, and lately, he goes by the name of Bigfoot—due to the gigantic footprints he leaves all over the place.

Sasquatch or Omah ("Devil of the Ridges") is Bigfoot's name in the Huppa Indian tongue and what Native Americans call him in the Pacific Northwest. Sasquatch was an Anglicization of *sasq'ets*, or *sésquac*, a word from the Halq-emeylem language of the First Nations peoples in parts of southwestern British Columbia.

Asia's yeti is believed to be smaller than the North American Omah-Bigfoot. One popular theory is that Bigfoot migrated to Alaska and the Pacific Northwest by crossing the Bering Straits. Depictions often portray them as a missing link between humans and human ancestors or other great apes. Another theory is that the yeti is the missing link from the Ice Age and an ancestor of the Neanderthal man. The remains of *Gigantopithecus*, found in the Himalayan foothills, may be a possible ancestral candidate.

Numerous hypotheses have attempted to explain the origins of this creature. Michael Newton, writing in his book *Strange Pennsylvania Monsters*, offers his theory about the beast:

Among cryptozoologists, the hands-down favorite Bigfoot candidate is *Gigantopithecus,* a prehistoric ape known from fossil teeth and mandibles found in Asia since 1935. While no complete skeletons have been recovered, paleontologists using modern apes as models estimate that "Giganto" stood approximately ten feet tall and weighed 1,200 pounds.

Gigantopithecus, believed to have lived half a million years ago, closely resembles eyewitness descriptions of the yeti in size and shape.

Others, searching for proof, look at the Bible. A biblical theory traces the Sasquatch back to the Nephilim, an antediluvian race of giants produced by the union of fallen angels and human women (Genesis 6:4). Some see the Sasquatch as a remnant of the Nephilim, or perhaps a new breed of gorilla produced the same way.

North American Bigfoot

An interesting history of Bigfoot can be cobbled together from various documented sources. Over a century ago, the Kwakiutl Indians of Canada carved figures of the Sasquatch with pouted "whistling lips."

Sasquatch is believed to be hairy and upright-walking apelike creatures who dwell in the wilderness and leave behind giant footprints.

People who claim to have seen it describe Bigfoot as a large, muscular, bipedal apelike creature around seven feet tall and covered with black, dark brown, or dark reddish hair. They are quick and elusive, fleeing when they encounter humans. Their stride is consistently described as "gliding." The first white man's record of this creature dates from 1811, after a Canadian exploring party found fourteen-inch footprints. The men thought the print was too large to be a bear. Countless sightings have been reported in North America since that time.

In 1924, a group of miners encamped near Washington's Mount St. Helen were attacked by a horde of giant apelike creatures. One of the creatures was shot and fell into what came to be known as "Ape Canyon," while the others were scared away. This was the first verified sighting of what some have called the "Abominable Snowman of California."

In 1951 Eric Shipton took fresh and clear photographs of giant, manlike tracks frozen in the snow. Afterward, Shipton recalled, "Here one was in the presence of something quite unknown." The tracks had no claw marks, and the prints were larger than that of known apes. In 2014, Christie's auction house in London capitalized on the worldwide interest in the yeti and sold the original photo for nearly five thousand dollars.

Chestnut Ridge

The Travel Channel determined that Pennsylvania is the No. 3 state for reported Bigfoot sightings. Their analysis found 2,032 reported sightings in Washington, 1,697 in California, and 1,340 in Pennsylvania. Additional sightings have been reported from the wooded-areas of the Pacific Northwest, British Columbia, New Jersey, Ohio, and Illinois.

Bigfoot has been around longer than UFOs, even though Pennsylvania researcher Stan Gordon claims there is a recent trend of seeing both entities simultaneously. Gordon is a former electronics salesman from Greensburg. He operates the Pennsylvania Association for the Study of the Unexplained and is listed in the 1988 edition of *Who's Who in UFOlogy*.

In Pennsylvania, Bigfoot sightings are most prevalent in the southwestern region. More reports emanate from Chestnut Ridge than any other area in Pennsylvania or West Virginia. Chestnut Ridge is a hundred-mile stretch that runs from West Virginia up through Pennsylvania's Westmoreland, Fayette, and Indiana Counties, in the Allegheny Mountain foothills. The Ridge also extends into Preston County, West Virginia, and Morgantown. According to Stan Gordon:

> I was told about UFO sightings, encounters with Bigfoot, underground sounds, ghostly apparitions, and even something like a doorway that supposedly opened and closed in the side of the mountain. A lot of this activity seemed to be taking place around the Derry Township section of the Chestnut Ridge.

Gordon claims that the Westmoreland and Fayette County sections of the ridge seem to be the most active as far as bizarre sightings:

> There have been close encounters with Bigfoot, Thunderbirds, Black panthers, strange entities, low-level UFO sightings, encounters with small balls of light, mysterious loud vocalizations and mystery booms, unusual footprints in the snow, falls from the sky, and many other very strange incidents.

The ridge is approximately two miles wide and a hundred miles long. Its highest elevation rises to only 2,650 feet above sea level. Close to forty caves are located in the area, frequently explored by weekend adventurers hiking through the poplars and white birch. But something weird is happening in these hills—Pennsylvania's Twilight Zone is the epicenter of numerous Bigfoot and UFO sightings.

Eric Altman, also from Western Pennsylvania, heads up the Pennsylvania Bigfoot Society, an all-volunteer research and investigation organization founded in 1998. Membership consists of individuals with diverse skill sets, experiences, and occupations, including current and ex-law enforcement, military, scientists, private investigators, paramedics, first responders, hunters, fishermen, hikers, and outdoors people. PBS's mission statement:

> To objectively investigate, research, and collect data on the Bigfoot phenomenon in Pennsylvania.

We collect data from sighting reports, encounters, and field expeditions using the latest technology.

Eric Altman is the president of the Pennsylvania Bigfoot Society, the largest volunteer organization in the state. (Maxim W. Furek photograph.)

Another researcher, Rosemary Ellen Guiley, American paranormal writer and host of *Exploring Unexplained Phenomena*, believed that Bigfoot possesses special abilities:

We have what would be called a "bilocation," or rapid transport, and that's the ability to be here and then suddenly there without visual means of getting there. That has been described on many occasions where people will see a being in front of them, and then suddenly it's behind them, and they

171

don't see it go behind them—how did it get there? It's just suddenly there ... If a Bigfoot seems to want to be material and tangible, it seems to have the ability to do that and then to turn itself into something intangible, as though it's going through an interdimensional doorway.

The Patterson-Gimlin Film

Most researchers point to a short strip of motion picture film shot in 1967 by ranchers Roger Patterson and Robert Gimlin as the most significant evidence to date. Patterson had searched for the creature for eight years. His motion picture consisted of eighteen seconds of film and was shot in Bluff Creek, north of Eureka, California, from atop a horse.

Even though the Patterson film is jumpy and unfocused, it is the only photograph believed to be of a Bigfoot creature. It shows a shaggy dark-haired, long-legged creature walking upright. The fur was described as reddish-brown with protruding hindquarters. The female animal has well-defined breasts and turns to look toward the rancher. Patterson described the beast as weighing about five hundred pounds and standing eight feet tall. The head crest is male-like. There was also an overwhelming stench from the creature, which seems to be a common element with Bigfoot sightings. Sasquatch means "smelly ape" in a Native American dialect.

Peter C. R. Byrne, head of the Byrne Bigfoot Expedition, has been searching for proof of Bigfoot for years. When he asked Patterson how he happened to be carrying a sixteen mm camera, Patterson responded that he had spent the last eight years looking for the creature and, "When we met, I was damned well ready."

Numerous researchers from the international scientific community have studied the film. Writer Marco Margaritoff noted:

> Perhaps the most famous sighting remains in the Patterson-Gimlin film of 1967. It spans less than a minute and shows an ape-like (female) walking on two legs along the banks of a remote riverbed in Washington state. Although the video is considered a clear hoax to most, numerous experts have deemed the musculature and limb ratios of the beast too precise to be forged.

Patterson's film is the only known photograph of the creature. The sixteen mm film was examined frame by frame by a studio specializing in animation. Another expert, Dr. Donald W. Grieve, an anatomist studying the human gait, was consulted at the Royal Free School of Medicine in London. Grieve wrote that his impressions:

> Oscillated between total acceptance of the Sasquatch to irrational rejection based on emotional response to the possibility that the Sasquatch exists.

After an exhausting review of the data, all investigating parties concluded that the film was that of an animal, not a human in a fur suit.

Tim Renner, illustrator, author, folk musician, is one of Pennsylvania's foremost Bigfoot experts. He is the creator of *Strange Familiars*, a podcast concerning the paranormal, weird history, folklore and the occult. He has written *Where the Footprints End: High Strangeness and the Bigfoot Phenomenon* and *Bigfoot in Pennsylvania*. (Maxim W. Furek photograph.)

Among those was Bigfoot expert Timothy Renner, who believes that the film is authentic for several reasons:

> Whatever the Patterson-Gimlin footage shows, it is unlikely costume designers in 1967 would have been capable of making such a convincing fake. The locomotion of the creature is very unusual, and its proportions do not seem to match those of a human. To reinforce this argument, the contemporary "Gold Standard" for ape-man effects was used in the motion picture *Planet of the Apes*, released the following year. Even modern attempts to reproduce the film have fallen short.

Hoaxes

Most scientists have historically discounted Bigfoot's existence, considering it a combination of folklore, misidentification, and hoax. Bigfoot hoaxes date back to 1884 after a British Columbia newspaper reported an apelike creature had been captured. Just before the report's author was to see the beast, it was announced that there was no captive Bigfoot.

Ray L. Wallace

On November 26, 2002, Ray L. Wallace, eighty-four, died of heart failure at a Washington state nursing home. He is the original Bigfoot hoaxer who partially created the ongoing hullabaloo.

Two of his construction company workers reported seeing a series of giant footprints and a huge, hairy animal cross a Bluff Creek logging road in August 1958. This "evidence" was seen in the same region where the infamous Patterson-Gimlin Bigfoot video would later be filmed.

But on October 15, 1958, the Eureka, California, *Humboldt Standard* published the idea of a homegrown version of the Himalayan yeti, coining the term "Bigfoot." June Beal, the widow of longtime *Humboldt Standard* editor "Scoop" Beal, later revealed that her husband was in on the hoax from the beginning but said it was just supposed to be a short-lived, fun thing, but "the fun thing got out of hand."

After his death, Wallace's nephew, Dale Lee Wallace, admitted that his uncle had fabricated large wooden carved feet and photographed his wife wearing a hairy ape suit with the giant feet. Cryptozoologist Loren Coleman has issues with the media's soft treatment of Wallace, such as Steve Young's article "Lovable Trickster Created a Monster with Bigfoot Hoax," published in the *Seattle Times*:

> For the media to state with a straight face that there was a grand conspiracy on the ground in Bluff Creek during 1958, which included the local newspaper office, must be viewed as skeptically as some of Wallace's old yarns about Bigfoot guarding gold mines or that he had seen UFOs a total of 2000 times. Indeed, the gullibility and journalistic hoax about Wallace being the "father

of Bigfoot" continued globally long after it should have, into the present, is downright remarkable.

Wallace, true to form, was quick to insert himself into the controversy and may have had a "degree of involvement" with Patterson. He said:

> I felt sorry for Roger Patterson. He told me he had cancer of the lymph glands and he was desperately broke, and he wanted to try to get something where he could have a little income. Well, he went down there exactly where I told him. I told him, "You go down there and hang around on that bank. Stay up there and watch that spot."

Most researchers, including Loren Coleman, believe Wallace, a publicity-seeking opportunist, had nothing to do with Patterson's film. Coleman also argued that "the international media inappropriately confused the Wallace films of the 1970s with the Patterson-Gimlin 1967 film."

> Still, even though some in the media are intent on turning Wallace into a "Father of Bigfoot" celebrity, it seems reasonable that editor "Scoop" Beal was involved in this regionalized hoax. The real issue is that some view Wallace's exploits as creative and ingenious rather than shameful and dishonest. These hoaxers need to be called out for what they are.

As a fitting endnote, Coleman wrote, "Fakery not revealed is a lie that lives on into the future."

Rick Dyer

Rick Dyer, who once proclaimed he'd "go down in history as the best Bigfoot tracker in the world," will go down as history's most prolific Bigfoot hoaxer. In 2012, Dyer claimed he killed an eight-foot-tall Bigfoot-like creature near San Antonio, Texas, and that an unnamed university, through DNA analysis, determined that the animal was an unknown species. Dyer planned to take the beast on a national tour and charge people to see it. His proposed tour encountered problems from the start, such as a lack of venues willing to let him display the creature and Dyer's refusal to release the alleged genetic "test results."

Eventually, it was discovered that the "body" was a manufactured prop made by Twisted Toy Box. The hoax gave Dyer about sixty thousand dollars from a gullible public who paid to see his fake Bigfoot. Dyer confessed in a Facebook post that his purported Bigfoot was a fake:

> Coming clean about everything is necessary for a new start. From this moment (on), I will speak the truth! No more lies, tall tales, or wild goose chases to mess with the haters!

Dyer and others have clouded the Bigfoot Mystery with fraud and confusion, replacing scientific research with selfish interests. Dyer admitted how he easily duped vulnerable individuals:

> There's no more evidence for Bigfoot than the Tooth Fairy or the Easter Bunny. And that's what people have to get through their heads. I have taken people out to hunt for Bigfoot, and all the time, I was thinking in my head, "Why would someone pay to go out to hunt for something that does not exist?" But people do.

An interesting, coordinated hoax began to appear in Pennsylvania state trails and parks in late 2022. Printed on what seemed to be an official Department of Conservation and Natural Resources letterhead, the signs read:

> Due to encounters in the area of a creature resembling "Bigfoot," we are instructing all park visitors to observe elevated park etiquette, be cautious of your surroundings, and keep the location of any small children/pets within a tighter scope of awareness. Do not approach the creature.

DCNR officials had spotted the flyers for months, but they denied having circulated the leaflets, stating, "Bigfoot is not real."

Some people also assumed the "Bigfoot" creature in the Patterson-Gimlin film was another hoax, while others believed in the possibility. Writing for *Psychology Today*, in an article called "Why I Believe in Bigfoot," author William Irwin says:

> It could turn out that Bigfoot is another example of a creature that was believed to be a myth but turned out to be a reality. The giant squid, the platypus, and the okapi are examples. Why not one more?

> I admit, of course, that the evidence in favor of Bigfoot's existence is not good. There have been lots of hoaxes and very little credible documentation. Yet many people sincerely believe they have witnessed Sasquatch, and, according to the shows I've seen, hairs have been found that don't belong to any known species. This is enough to keep my hope alive.

Bigfoot and the FBI

In 1976, FBI Director Peter Byrne of the Bigfoot Information Center and Exhibition in Dalles, Oregon, sent the FBI "about fifteen hairs attached to a tiny piece of skin," believed to be an unknown animal.

Byrne's organization couldn't identify what kind of animal it came from and asked the FBI to analyze it. He also asked if the FBI had analyzed suspected Bigfoot hair before, and, if so, what the bureau's conclusion was.

Jay Cochran Jr., assistant director of the FBI's scientific and technical services division, found that the hair didn't belong to Bigfoot. In early 1977, he sent the hair back to Byrne with his scientific conclusion: "the hairs are of deer family origin." Four decades later, the bureau declassified its "Bigfoot file" about this analysis.

Where's the Evidence?

Primatologists as renowned as Jane Goodall are open to Bigfoot's existence, yet the only evidence consists of thousands of footprints, many cast in plaster, and hundreds of reported sightings. It remains controversial. You either believe, or you don't. We have no solid evidence for the existence of Bigfoot. What we do have, however, is based solely on anecdotes and hearsay—and some footprints, which are easily counterfeited. One example of forensic evidence offers potential hope for Bigfoot advocates. According to an article in *National Geographic*, Investigator Jimmy Chilcutt of the Conroe, Texas, Police Department has analyzed over one hundred and fifty casts of Bigfoot prints. Chilcutt says one footprint found in 1987 in Walla Walla, Washington, has convinced him that Bigfoot is real:

> The ridge flow pattern and the texture was completely different from anything I've ever seen. It certainly wasn't human and of no known primate that I've examined. The print ridges flowed lengthwise along the foot, unlike human prints, which flow across. The texture of the ridges was about twice the thickness of a human, which indicated that this animal has a real thick skin.

According to Pennsylvania Bigfoot researcher Tim Renner, there is a common thread that has been detected over the years:

> Witness accounts of Bigfoot display a consistent pattern of appearance and behavior manifesting in stories across centuries. Some of the newspaper "wildman" reports from the 1800s read very much like modern Bigfoot accounts, for instance.

Still, in the hundreds of years that people have been hunting the Sasquatch in Asia and North America, no one has ever captured one, dead or alive. Many have claimed to have shot Bigfoot, yet a carcass has never been found.

There have been numerous attempts to bring a conclusion to this anthropological mystery. In 1958 Russian ethnologist Prof. Boris F. Porshnev launched "Project Snowman." With two million dollars in government funding, his group attempted to find conclusive evidence of the yeti.

In 1995, thirty Chinese scientists began a yearlong expedition investigating reports of a seven-foot Bigfoot wandering the wilderness. They were set to explore the Shennongjia Nature Reserve in central China, where, for centuries, residents have reported sightings of a creature believed to be half man and half ape. Scientists expected to find an undiscovered species of ape, but, to date, have had little success.

Conclusions

There is much that man does not know. Mining excavations in northern Italy from 1871–1958 uncovered some fifty individual skeletons of a primitive apelike creature referred to as *Oreopithecus bambolii* or as "the swamp ape" or "the hill ape." *Oreopithecus bambolii* was believed to possess a hand capable of a precision grip like that of humans. Comparisons of *Oreopithecus* with humans, apes, and Old World monkeys revealed that *Oreopithecus* had an essentially apelike hand that emphasized apelike power grasping over humanlike precision grasping. The ape came from the late Miocene of Italy and is believed to have existed over five million years ago.

As recently as 1903, Germany's Von Beringe astonished zoologists by discovering a completely unknown mountain gorilla at volcanic heights of twelve thousand feet.

And in 1911, Ishi, a wild man, walked into the little town of Oroville, California. Anthropologists believed that he was a descendant of the state's primitive natives.

China's giant pandas, located between the China-Tibet border, were suspected to exist and had been hunted for nearly a hundred years. They were not discovered until 1937.

Mainstream tales of the mysterious yeti began in the late nineteenth century, but reports of the yeti have come from the Himalayas for over two hundred years. Villagers and explorers related similar eyewitness reports of these creatures. The first westerner to have published an account of the yeti was B. H. Hodgson in 1832.

Theories abound. Bigfoot advocates believe at least two thousand ape men are walking in the woods and mountains of North America. An adult male is said to be at least eight feet (2.4 meters) tall, weigh eight hundred pounds (360 kilograms), and have feet twice the size of a human. The creatures are described as shy and nocturnal, and their diets consist mostly of berries and fruits. One standard theory is that Bigfoot is the offspring of an Asian ape that migrated to North America during the Ice Age.

Nevertheless, some mountain climbers are quick to point out that the high altitudes and lack of oxygen can delude a person's mind and cause his imagination to loosen at sixteen thousand feet or higher—the yeti's equivalent argument to the familiar UFO refrain of marsh gas, reflections from Venus, and collective hallucinations.

People have seen bipedal monsters for centuries, as documented by early newspaper accounts. These creatures have been called various names, such as "wild men," "gorillas," "ape-men," and "hairy giants." The controversy will continue, as will the possibility of someday discovering incontrovertible evidence of Bigfoot's existence. Writing for the *Atlantic Monthly*, scientist and explorer Edward W. Cronin Jr. concluded:

Though I am intrigued with the *yeti,* I would be

deeply saddened to see it captured. We would
gain another possession, another ragged exhibit in
the concrete world of the zoological park, another
Latin name to enter on our scientific ledgers. But
what about the wild creature that now roams free
in the forests of the Himalayas? Every time man
asserts his mastery over nature, he gains
something in knowledge but loses something in
the spirit.

Chapter 16
The Bigfoot Hypothesis

1. The Bigfoot and UFO Connection

The Bigfoot-UFO connection remains one of the most controversial aspects of the paranormal world. The website Gaia, "Seeking Truth, Paranormal & Unexplained, and Cryptozoology" reports "that at least twenty percent of Bigfoot sightings coincide with UFO events."

Writing in *Mysterious Universe,* researcher Nick Redfern says:

> Indeed, I have seen so many Bigfoot researchers fume and rant when the matter of UFOs are brought into the domain of Bigfoot research. Too bad. The fact is there are more than a few reports of strange lights seen in the sky in the same location, and at the same time, that the Bigfoot creatures have been seen. Like it or not, there is a mystery to be resolved when it comes to the UFO angle of Bigfoot. Unfortunately, it's a mystery that is often ignored and deliberately. I choose not to ignore it.

A number of Bigfoot-UFO sightings have been documented in the southwestern corner of Pennsylvania. Bigfoot sightings are sometimes accompanied by other phenomena, according to Bigfoot researcher Tim Renner:

> Most often, this takes the form of mystery lights— be it orbs, will-o-the-wisps, spook lights, or UFOs. It isn't always lights, though—you also get ghosts, black dogs, anomalous animals, even other cryptid creatures such as dogmen, goatmen, and the like.

The theories are finite and continue to evolve into a convoluted mass. Dr. Franklin Ruehl, PhD and host of *Mysteries From Beyond the Other Dimension*, has offered numerous theories explaining the sightings:

Perhaps the Bigfoot creatures are UFO pilots, landing on Earth for exploratory purposes. Or, conceivably, higher level ETs are leaving behind some specimens as "guinea pigs" to test our environment for long-term survival. Or, possibly, these Bigfoots are criminal entities being deposited on Earth as a form of cosmic deportation!

Alan Megargle, director of *The Bigfoot Alien Connection Revealed*, explained his documentary's premise:

We are not alone in the universe. Alien life is here right now, contacting us in the form of Bigfoot, UFOs, orbs, and other inter-dimensional paranormal phenomena. These experiences are changing human nature as we have known it. Learn how researchers have identified locations where portals are opening to reveal many forms of nonhuman intelligence—intelligent lifeforms that are being kept secret.

2. Bigfoot as Ultra-Terrestrials

Stan Gordon, writing in *Silent Invasion*, recounts the varied manifestations of Bigfoot:

The information that we uncovered during the 1970's creature encounters suggested, in some cases, that we might be dealing with an entity that has a physical and non-physical component to its existence. For example, a Bigfoot observed from a short distance away appeared to be a solid physical animal, yet when shot at, sometimes just visibly vanished in front of the observer's disbelieving eyes.

The Bigfoot Phenomenon in Pennsylvania, by Dr. Paul G. Johnson, suggests that Bigfoot creatures possess certain abilities, perhaps the ability to access some portion of quantum physics, to "shapeshift" to various locations, avoiding capture.

Johnson is not alone as numerous reports have observed Bigfoot creatures behaving in ways that defy our fundamental understanding of quantum mechanics. They seem to vanish and then reappear in another location and they seem to be impervious to gunshots. In his definitive book *Silent Invasion*, Stan Gordon documents:

> There was the one well-documented case where the creature was fired upon at point blank range with a shotgun, and the creature reportedly dematerialized in a flash of light. In one 1973 Ohiopyle (A borough in Fayette County with a 2020 census of 38 people) incident, the creature was fired upon and apparently hit, then vanished in front of the shooter's eyes. The startled man could hear it running off but could not see the creature.

In this modern age, why haven't researchers been able to photograph these creatures? Some believe Bigfoot creatures have an uncanny ability to detect and avoid hidden trail cameras —technology that has used infrared photography to see other nocturnal animals.

Rosemary Ellen Guiley gave her final interview on January 27, 2019, for the feature documentary film *The Bigfoot Alien Connection*. Guiley believed that Bigfoot were interdimensional with the ability to cloak themselves, rendering them invisible.

> I always believed in the paraphysical nature of Bigfoot. The phenomena associated with their manifestations defies natural explanation. I think that we must turn to paraphysical or interdimensional considerations if we're going to fully understand their presence on Earth and their interactions with humans.

Guiley believed that Bigfoot creatures are large and muscular, possessing supernormal strength.

> They are intelligent beings that possess telepathic communications and often contact humans but also regard human beings with a lot of distrust. They are often described as gliding without the benefit of running or walking. They may possess the ability of bilocation or rapid transport where footprints come from nowhere and end nowhere, suggesting a possible interdimensional doorway. There are no known animals that share Bigfoot's attributes.

Maxim W. Furek

John Keel, the prominent ufologist and paranormal researcher famous for *The Mothman Prophecies*, once proposed the idea that there are "window areas" throughout the world, connecting our reality with parallel dimensions. These areas, Keel imagined, may help elucidate some unexplained reports of entities that are too fleeting or confusing to later detail or prove. He mused, with the increasing plausibility of the multiverse theory and infinite neighboring universes, maybe we should be asking ourselves, are UFOs and Bigfoot interdimensional travelers, and could there be a connection between the two?

Does Bigfoot have the ability to travel between parallel dimensions? Jack Cary, a cryptozoologist who has studied Bigfoot for decades, ascribes to the idea that something called the Mach effect could explain the possibility of interdimensional travel. The Mach effect, which is actually a sound principle in physics being tested by NASA, employs fluctuations created by a body of mass as it accelerates, which are, in turn, used to generate thrust.

Cary says he believes the Earth's fluctuations can create momentary tears in the electromagnetic membrane separating our universe from a parallel one and allowing extra-dimensional entities access into this dimension.

Jacques Vallee is also of the mindset that something extra-dimensional may be going on, sharing a similar sentiment to Keel when speaking about the UFO phenomenon. Vallee believes there is more than the traditional explanation of an extraterrestrial race visiting Earth, instead believing in a possible window to another dimension.

> We are dealing with a yet unrecognized level of consciousness, independent of man but closely linked to the Earth … I do not believe anymore that UFOs are simply the spacecraft of some race of extraterrestrial visitors. This notion is too simplistic to explain their appearance, the frequency of their manifestations through recorded history, and the structure of the information exchanged during contact.

Author Paul G. Johnson, a longtime UFO and Bigfoot researcher, believes that Bigfoot is not a flesh-and-blood "ape in the woods" but may be an interdimensional being with astonishing abilities.

For twenty years, Paul G. Johnson spent thousands of hours in field research in Pennsylvania, interviewing eyewitnesses who describe how Bigfoot appears and disappears in an instant, makes no tracks in the snow, passes through solid matter, teleports itself, glides instead of walks, becomes transparent and even invisible, and more.

Johnson's startling conclusion: Bigfoot "evolves from an alternate reality and conforms to the rules of what we know as the quantum world."

Or should we entertain the bizarre possibility that there are entities from another dimension operating in higher realms of existence here on Earth?Is there an invisible goblin universe that co-exists next to us? Michael Newton, in his book *Strange Pennsylvania Monsters*, says:

> Some researchers suggest that we live in close proximity to other realms—parallel times, dimensions, universes, take your pick—that may be breached from time to time, allowing denizens from haunted nether-worlds to drop in on our own. Most "flesh and blood" cryptozoologists rejects such theories of a Goblin Universe—a name coined by Colin Wilson and Ted Holiday in 1986— but who can say with any certainty?

What is the answer to the Bigfoot question?Stan Gordon, like other researchers, can only look at the murky possibilities :

> As reluctant as I am to say this, based on other nationwide reports that have come to my attention, if some of these creatures can disappear and have the ability to change physical form, then how can we be sure what we are dealing with? I surely don't have the answers, but will keep an open mind to all possibilities until the Bigfoot mystery is solved.

Writing for *Saga Magazine*, famed paranormal researcher Timothy Green Beckley (1952-2021), in his article "America's Abominable Swampman," concluded:

> Until the time comes when a Yeti can be captured and studied, the mysteries surrounding the creature will continue to provoke all kinds of speculation. Some will have open minds, others will scoff. We can only hope that the answers we seek come through scientific research and not through the barrel of a gun.

3. Bigfoot as Jung's Collective Unconsciousness

Do Bigfoot creatures represent Karl Jung's idea of the collective unconsciousness? Are they archetypal figures, deeply embedded into our DNA and shared by mankind? If so, these creatures may be the result of real terrors experienced by man over thousands of centuries, based on alarms or subliminal warnings from our psyche.

4. Bigfoot as Cannibals

Renowned Bigfoot hunter Bill Brock raised the idea about multidimensional portals. Brock referenced a recent NASA announcement that magnetic portals may be real. Brock said he came to believe in them when he travelled to West Virginia to study the Mothman case, popularized by John Keel in his 1975 book, The Mothman Prophecies.

Brock, however, is not convinced. He believes in the orbs, since he believes the description of Mothman's giant, glowing red eyes and ability to fly is more descriptive of an alien encounter than a Bigfoot encounter. But he has his theory on the origin of Bigfoot. He believes the creatures are the prehistoric human rivals, the Neanderthals.

"It's a known fact that human beings and Neanderthals were battling pretty heavy 35,000 years ago," he said. "I believe they split at that time and went off into the woods."

Under Brock's theory, Neanderthals developed as a species parallel to human beings. But while humans were developing technology and cities, Neanderthals were learning to live in the forests and hide from their enemies.

Like the portal theory, Brock notes that his more Earthbound beliefs can answer the questions raised by skeptics. Bigfoot has been able to remain concealed from man due to tens of thousands of years of experience with camouflage, he explains:.

> Like us, they became masters of their domain, but their domain was the forest. They know how to hide. They actually went beyond being masters of their domain.

And why are the remains of Bigfoot creatures so hard to find? Brock believes hunters cannot find Bigfoot remains because the creatures are cannibals.

> By eating their bodies, they do two things. First, they feed themselves. Second, they dispose of the bodies.

5. Bigfoot as the New Religion

On the Rolling Stones' 1972 *Exile on Main Street* album, Keith Richard states, "I Just Wanna See His Face." His song posed what many of us, maybe all of us, have asked. "Where is proof that God exists?"

Many spiritual leaders would respond by saying that we can never fully understand the existence of God. This is because of God's Awe. He is unknowable. The best we can do is believe and have faith in his presence.

Bigfoot, too, falls into that category. Seekers of the truth have searched for over two hundred years for defining proof of his existence. Yet despite the lack of evidence, true believers demonstrate continued faith in his existence.

They believe that Bigfoot lives! In a twisted but appropriate example, Rick Dyer explained how easy it was for him to fool people with his Bigfoot hoax:

> It's really easy to trick people. People that believe in Bigfoot are not idiots—they're just really naïve,

and they're missing something in their lives, so
they want to believe in something that they know
deep down inside does not exist.

But discredited hoaxer Rick Dyer should not be allowed
to render the last word on something far beyond his
comprehension.

Since the dawn of time, humans have searched for
meaning, seeking answers to unanswerable questions.
Bigfoot has now become an inexplicable part of that
quest. Although there is no doubt about the existence of
Bigfoot, cryptozoologists, in the shadow of Bernard
Heuvelmans and Ivan T. Sanderson, need to determine
conclusively if this elusive creature exists in a physical,
metaphysical, or spiritual dimension.

The answer will be revealed in one of them.

Chapter 17

Nick Adams: The Cursed Rebel

On February 6, 1968, actor Nick Adams (1931–1968) was found dead in his Los Angeles Coldwater Canyon home.

Adams was thirty-six years old at the time of his mysterious death, another sacrifice on the Boulevard of Broken Dreams. Immediately, there were speculations about his death. Adams's obituary, published in *Variety*, read:

> Death was attributed to an overdose of a drug used to treat nervous disorders and alcoholism, an autopsy established. "Immediate cause" of death, according to Dr. J. Wallace Graham, deputy county medical examiner, was "paraldehyde intoxication." Adams swallowed the drug in liquid form. The coroner's office reported no alcohol was found in [the] actor's bloodstream."

After the actor failed to show up for a dinner date, his attorney, Ervin "Tip" Roeder (1921–1981), drove to Adams's home. The attorney, an ex-LAPD officer, broke a window and climbed inside. Adams's body was slumped up against the bedroom wall, dressed in jeans, a shirt, and boots. A phone was well within reach.

Nick Adams as Johnny Yuma, star of ABC-TV's *The Rebel* and one of the "cursed" actors in the film *Rebel Without a Cause*. Adams is buried in Berwick, Pennsylvania, birthplace of the infamous Richard Sharpe Shaver. (This work is in the public domain in the United States because it was published in the United States between 1927 and 1977, inclusive, without a copyright notice.)

Crime Magazine writer Peter L. Winkler disclosed that Adams had been dead between twenty-four and thirty-six hours. His fully clothed body was found in a sitting position beside his bed:

> There was no indication as to the cause of death. No weapons or sleeping pills were found. Adams' lawyer told Det. Verne Jones he arrived at the fifty four thousand Cape Cod style home bordering Beverly Hills about 8 p.m. When no one answered the doorbell, Roeder crawled through a window and discovered the body.

Ervin "Tip" Roeder

Things immediately took a strange turn. Roeder discovered several documents that he thought needed safekeeping and took them home. The mystery grew as, about a month later, Roeder and his wife, actress Jenny Maxwell, were murdered in the driveway of their condo during a robbery attempt. Roeder was fifty-nine.

The murder of "Tip" Roeder provided another bizarre twist. Roeder lived his final moments on his hands and knees on his Beverly Grove sidewalk, screaming for help after being shot in the stomach. His actress wife, Jennifer, was also killed, as reported in *Los Angeles Magazine*:

> There was more horror to be discovered on that sunny June afternoon in 1981. Sprawled in the lobby of the condo building, half her head blown away, was thirty-nine -year-old Jennifer Roeder,

Tip's soon to be ex-wife. In a former life, many tequila sunrises ago, she'd been known to the world as Jenny Maxwell, a successful, blond starlet with wide-set eyes and a thin, mischievous smile.

A rising starlet, Jenny Maxwell appeared in thirty television shows, including *The Twilight Zone, My Three Sons,* and *Bonanza*, and shared the bill with Elvis in the 1961 comedy *Blue Hawaii*. The *Los Angeles Times* reported that the murder had probably been an attempted robbery gone wrong. Still, one of Jenny Maxwell's relatives, Buddy Moorehouse, suspected there was more to the story. In his exposé, *Murder of an Elvis Girl: Solving the Jenny Maxwell Case,* Moorehouse interviewed Detective Mike Thies, who believed Maxwell's husband was behind the killing:

> Despite the conclusions drawn at the time, Detective Thies says it's his belief the burglary theory was bunk. Nothing had been stolen from the Roeders, and rounds of the rare ammo used to kill them were found in Tip Roeder's Lincoln Continental. Thies believes that Tip had probably hired a hitman to murder his expensive, estranged wife.

The book concluded that Maxwell was killed so that Roeder would avoid paying spousal support and theorizes that Roeder was an accidental victim of a hitman. Still, more than one have theorized that if Roeder did have his wife killed, did Nick Adams receive

the same treatment? Allyson Adams believes her
father's death was suspicious and that his attorney was
involved:

> Yes, I believe his death was made to look like a
> suicide. I don't believe Tip Roeder's alibi or how
> he found my dad.

Roeder claimed to have found Nick Adam's body on a
Wednesday, after presumedly being dead for three days.
No drugs were found in the home. The doors had been
locked. Theories about Adams's death are numerous. And
despite the "accidental suicide" ruling, the case remains
inconclusive for many.

Paraldehyde

In the aftermath, there remained many unanswered
questions. Adams had reportedly taken an overdose of
paraldehyde, a sleep-inducing drug once popular as a
sedative. This sedative, archaic by today's standards, was
the precursor to such medications as Thorazine and
Mellaril. A second tranquilizer—promazine—was also
found in the body.

Paraldehyde was commonly used to induce sleep in
sufferers from alcohol withdrawal or delirium tremens. It
was believed to be one of the safest hypnotics, regularly
given at bedtime in psychiatric hospitals and geriatric
wards up to the 1960s. The clear, colorless liquid can be
administered orally, intravenously, intramuscularly, or

rectally to control extreme excitement, delirium, mania, or convulsions.

Information on the archaic drug is difficult to find because paraldehyde is not currently in use. It cannot be found in the *Physicians' Desk Reference*, the Bible of the medical industry. Nevertheless, lecturer and pharmacologist Ken Dickinson immediately detected a recognizable pattern of abuse:

> One could say paraldehyde is the granddaddy of Propofol, a drug that many are currently familiar with when it comes to fatal overdoses and similar pharmaco-dynamics. Both have a small window between the therapeutic dose and the fatal dose. Unfortunately, overdoses are very frequent, even with experienced users and prescribers. Paraldehyde took the life of Nick Adams, similarly as Propofol took the life of Michael Jackson fifty years later, most probably an accidental overdose with a highly toxic substance.

Because up to thirty percent of paraldehyde is excreted via the lungs, it leaves a lingering bad taste. Adams often complained about the drug's unpleasant taste and odor. Since then, it has been replaced by other drugs with fewer adverse side effects.

During the autopsy, Dr. Thomas Noguchi found enough paraldehyde, sedatives, and other drugs in the body "to cause instant unconsciousness." The death certificate lists "paraldehyde and promazine intoxication" as the immediate cause of death along with the notation accident; suicide; undetermined. There were no needle marks. During the 1960s, drug interaction warnings were not as prominent as they later were. However, the American Medical Association has warned that these two types of drugs should never be taken together.

Antipsychotic Drug

Promazine (Sparine) is an older medication used to treat schizophrenia. Promazine has been described in medical literature as "an antipsychotic drug of low potency used to treat disorganized and psychotic thinking. Also used to help treat false perceptions (e.g., hallucinations or delusions) with fewer movement side effects."

Allyson Adams explained her father's ongoing struggle with alcohol and that he was trying to stop drinking:

> The divorce (from actress Carol Nugent) and his career were very stressful. My father was someone who couldn't drink, meaning he would have a few on an empty stomach and pass out. His drug of choice was diet pills, and then I think he needed something to bring him down. He had a problem with his weight, being so short and all. He had a brother, Andrew Adamshock, a surgeon, who prescribed him drugs.

The Curse of *Rebel Without a Cause*

Some believe a curse was placed on Nick Adams after signing on to play one of the gang members in 1955's *Rebel Without a Cause*. This was director Nicholas Ray's teen angst movie and groundbreaking attempt to portray the moral decay of American youth. The famous film echoed a special post-World War II United Nations report warning of a massive "invasion" by degenerate street gangs.

The U.N. report called them "juvenile delinquents," teenage thugs who got their kicks from drugs and violence. Simultaneously, juvenile crime rose to alarming levels in every corner of the globe (according to the report). Gang rapes, sexual attacks, and sexual deviations were reported. Widespread vandalism, property damage, and organized rioting reached epidemic proportions. In addition, the abuse of intoxicants, including alcohol, "giggles" (marijuana), and pills, appeared to be rampant.

Something strange was happening in America's back alleys and mean streets, and Hollywood was quick to smell the money. And something weird was going on with the movie, based on Robert M. Lindner's book *Rebel Without a Cause: The Hypnoanalysis of a Criminal Psychopath*. Years after its release, *Rebel Without a Cause*, shot in the style of *Blackboard Jungle*, created additional controversy when film critics charged that a curse had been fixed on the actors. That curse, hovered over one of the most influential American films of the twentieth century, resulted in an undeniable bloody covenant.

Ray's film boasted an exceptional cast, with Adams surrounded by an explosive nucleus of talent. The group, known as the original Hollywood Brat Pack, included his pal James Dean, Natalie Wood, Sal Mineo, and Dennis Hopper. Adams and Dean represented an elite clique of Hollywood nonconformists. After the premiere of *Rebel*, the group celebrated by dining at Googies, the in spot on Sunset and Crescent Heights, were photographed and interviewed by hordes of paparazzi, and were idolized in numerous movie magazines and pictorials.

Dennis Hopper, a notable exception, escaped the film's so-called curse. Still, his early career days were marred with rebellion that branded him a pariah, but led to *Easy Rider*, the definitive counterculture blockbuster, as described in the Criterion Collection:

> The down-and-dirty directorial debut of former clean-cut teen star Dennis Hopper, *Easy Rider* heralded the arrival of a new voice in film, one pitched angrily against the mainstream. After the film's cross-country journey—with its radical, New Wave–style editing, outsider-rock soundtrack, revelatory performance by a young Jack Nicholson, and explosive ending—the American road trip would never be the same.

And other than Hopper, the rest of the cast were struck down, one after the other, like bowling pins. Los Angeles-

Maxim W. Furek

based writer Jacob Shelton connected the murky, heartbreaking dots:

> While *Rebel Without a Cause* was a landmark film, it also carries a history of being "cursed." Each of the film's leads passed away before the age of forty-five, and all of them were under tragic or mysterious circumstances. James Dean, Natalie Wood, Sal Mineo, and Nick Adams each went their separate ways after the film, with Dean passing away following a head-on collision while driving his Porsche Spyder, "Little Bastard," on September 30, 1955.

Others made the same connection. Writing for the *Orlando Sentinel*, Crosby Day observed:

> In retrospect, *Rebel Without a Cause* had an aura of doom. Three other cast members died unnatural deaths. Nick Adams, who played gang member Moose, died of a drug overdose in 1968.

In addition to Adams, Day listed the deaths of Sal Mineo, Rebel's "Plato," who was murdered in an alley in 1976, and Natalie Wood, who played girlfriend "Judy." Child star Mineo projected an attitude of youthful vulnerability begging to be nurtured. He became one of the youngest nominees in the Academy Awards history, being nominated for Best Supporting Actor in *Rebel*. Mineo died from a single stab wound that had perforated his heart, causing a massive hemorrhage.

Wood drowned in November 1981 off California's Catalina Island. Wood was on her yacht, accompanied by her husband, Robert Wagner. They had also invited Wood's co-star, Christopher Walken, as reported by Richie Maria Jacob:

> Wood was found dead near a dinghy quite a distance away from their boat, *Splendour*. The case over the years has seen various kinds of allegations, predominantly those raised against Robert Wagner. In the myriad of theories, one is the alleged romantic relationship between Walken and Wood.

Walken and Wood were working on a science fiction thriller titled *Brainstorm* and became close friends. As rumors continued about the cause of her death, Walken refused to discuss the matter, which is still considered unsolved.

James Dean

James Dean, who starred in only three films—*East of Eden, Rebel Without a Cause,* and *Giant*—was "the first rebel." He imbibed the fifties' Beat Generation and was crowned one of the first teen icons. After the *Rebel Without a Cause* release, Dean said in a press release that he considered costars Natalie Wood, Sal Mineo, and Nick Adams "the only friends I have in this town."

Adams had a close relationship with James Dean (and later with Elvis Presley). With strikingly similar background chronologies, both in their early twenties, they became roommates, sharing an apartment. After *Rebel*, they worked up a comedy routine that was critically acclaimed, even before it got off the ground. Soon approached by a Las Vegas promoter to take the show on the road, the duo rejected the proposal to concentrate on their acting.

Still, in *The Death of James Dean*, author Warren Newton Beath casts some negative light on Adams after the premiere of a documentary on the life of Dean, released after his death. Co-directed by Robert Altman, *The James Dean Story* (1957) reviewed Dean's life through little-seen photographs, narration by Martin Gabel, and interviews with family members. It was a poorly made, immediately criticized film, but in his book, Beath had another target in mind:

> The young Nick Adams, his head antlike and rapacious, was present in the lobby at the Indiana premiere, passing out photos of a car he claimed he and Jimmy had been working on before Jimmy had died. The film flopped.

It seems unfair criticism of Adams because everyone was climbing aboard the James Dean bandwagon, attempting to grasp any dying embers of his flame. Robert Conrad became friends with Adams when he majored in theater arts at Northwestern University. Adams helped Conrad get cast in *Juvenile Jungle* (1958), which TCM calls a "plodding crime caper with hep-cat punk," and also appeared in *Thundering Jets* (1958). Conrad, who slightly resembled Dean, stood outside movie theaters "to get buzz" for the 1956 film *Giant*.

Adams could imitate famous voices. For example, after Dean's car accident, Adams's voice was dubbed onto the end of the soundtrack of the final scenes in *Giant* because James Dean had mumbled the original take.

His Only True Success

Like Valentino, Monroe, and Elvis, James Dean was not allowed to be buried and forgotten. On the contrary, fans refused to accept his mortality as his myth only grew larger.

After Dean's accident, Adams received countless requests for articles of clothing that Dean had worn and even for strips of wallpaper that he had touched. Funerals were a part of the James Dean and Nick Adams mystique. When James Dean died on September 30, 1955, Nick Adams, the faithful friend, traveled to Fairmount, Indiana, to attend his funeral. Still, when Adams died in 1968, few of Hollywood's inner circle made the trip to McGraw's Funeral Home in Berwick, Pennsylvania, to pay their respects.

James Dean famously said, "If a man can bridge the gap between life and death, if he can live after he's died, then maybe he was a great man. Immortality is the only true success." James Dean, the Rebel Without a Cause, died at age twenty-four, frozen on the silver screen and resurrected as his "only true success."

In the same novel, Adams and Dean were characters sharing similar hopes and dreams. Both died young, in senseless deaths. The world, always looking for heroes, morned the promise of their talents—two cursed rebels searching for a cause.

Twilight of Honor

Adams lived a short yet exciting life, immersed in struggle and hardship. Born Nicholas Aloysius Adamshock in Nanticoke, PA, he hitchhiked to Hollywood, boasting, "Some men bet on horses and dogs. I gambled on myself." He was molded in the image of the smoldering male '50s icons, like James Dean, Elvis Presley, Dennis Hopper, and countless others, grunting and swaggering through life, creating a template for hungering youth, rebels without a cause—"rebels" being the operative word.

After numerous rejections, he joined the US Coast Guard, winning a small part in *Mister Roberts*, and, after discharge, he successfully starred as Andy Griffith's sidekick in *No Time for Sergeants*. However, Adams was notorious as a brash Hollywood renegade, especially after his frequent talk show appearances. Many found him arrogant and rude. One talk show host asked him politely to "shut up."

His highest professional recognition came later. Adams was nominated for an Academy Award in 1963 for Best Supporting Actor for his role in *Twilight of Honor* with Richard Chamberlain and Joey Heatherton. After that, he appeared in around thirty films, including *Picnic, Pillow Talk, Young Dillinger, Our Miss Brooks, Strange Lady in Town, The FBI Story*, and *Fury at Showdown*.

Johnny Yuma, *The Rebel*

The most critical role that Nick Adams played was as Johnny Yuma. *The Rebel* was a seventy-six-episode series on ABC TV that ran successfully from October 4, 1959, until September 24, 1962. The show was set in the post-Civil War west and featured the exploits of an embittered young Confederate soldier who searched the west seeking self-identity.

The short-lived *Saints and Sinners* followed, from 1962 to 1963, but without *The Rebel*'s popularity or success. With an eighteen-episode run, *Saints and Sinners* presented Adams as newspaper investigative reporter Nick Alexander. Adams also had a role in the 1967 Walt Disney Production *Mosby's Marauders*, a look at the Civil War through the eyes of a young Confederate scout who befriends a Yankee soldier.

And then it was over. His last TV part was the "Apache Kid," a poorly made segment of *Hondo,* completed two months before he died. Adams wore heavy pancake makeup and performed with a series of eye movements and menacing gestures for his role. He had no dialogue.

Fever Heat and *Mission Mars* were his final motion pictures. *Fever Heat* was released on May 10, 1968, after his death, although shot the previous year.

Mission Mars (1968), directed by Nicholas Webster, was filmed in Miami and starred Darren McGavin, George De Vries, and Nick Adams. The film's plot featured three American astronauts who landed on Mars and discovered the body of a frozen Russian cosmonaut. The film was poorly received, described as bland and having "dated clothing and clunky props, and special effects with a spaceship that looks like a Campbell's soup can." *Mission Mars* was made to resemble a 1950s sci-fi movie, although made in 1968.

Today *Fever Heat* and *Mission Mars* are obscure fragments of cinematic artwork, much like the life and times of Nick Adams.

Nick Adams's saga portrays another attempt at storming the fortress and climbing the treacherous rungs of the Hollywood ladder. Adams will always be remembered for his role in *The Rebel*, but his most successful role may have been his contrived "bad boy" image and his walk on the dark side of life in the fast lane.

At his death, surviving family members included his widow; two children, Allyson Lee and Jeb Stuart Adams; grandchildren Madison and Elijah Adams; parents, Mr. and Mrs. Peter Adamshock, Berwick, PA; and brother, Dr. Andrew P. Adams of Kankakee, IL.

Adams's body was transported from the airport in Charlie Robsock's 1947 V8 Cadillac hearse. It had a stick shift, a massive grille, and about thirty thousand miles on the odometer. Some two thousand mourners attended his funeral, where he was given a military funeral due to his Coast Guard service. The actor was buried at Saints Cyril and Methodius Ukrainian Cemetery in Berwick.

And, too, his death serves as a cautionary tale about the dangers of substance abuse, an unfortunate reality that is never far from our awareness. Sadly, his death was not mourned in silence. A voyeuristic public luxuriated in all the gruesome details, including his physical appearance and sordid speculations of what happened. In another example of celebrity blood voyeurism, it became the final performance of Nicholas Aloysius Adamshock.

Actors suffer for their craft with dashed hopes, broken dreams, and a million slivers of heartbreak—any part of this horror capable of destroying the strongest wills. For every megastar, there are scores who end up making commercials, taking bit parts, or waiting tables. Actors are cursed with the dream of success and the nightmare of fame. Unfortunately, that curse hung over Nick Adams, as it did over so many others.

Chapter 18

Die, Monster, Die!

A 1960s remake of a classic H. P. Lovecraft tale placed Nick Adams and famed horror master Boris Karloff together, but for Adams, his entrance into science fiction had already taken place earlier.

The Outer Limits

Adams appeared on *The Outer Limits* television program in a segment titled "Fun and Games," broadcast on March 30, 1964. Adams wasn't the first choice for this episode. Three other actors, Clu Gulager, George Segal, and Rip Torn, were initially selected for the role, only to turn it down. The fourth choice, or the last choice in this case, was Nick Adams, who was running out of options and didn't have any other choice than to say yes.

In "Fun and Games," originally titled "Natural Selection," Adams played the Brandoesque role of Mike Benson, an ex-boxer and small-time hood who, along with divorcee

Laura Hanley (Nancy Malone), is electro ported to the planet, Andera. There the Earthling pair are pitted against alien primitives from the Calco Galaxy in a battle of survival. The winner's prize: the survival of the homeland of the combatants.

Horror actor Boris Karloff co-starred with Nick Adams in the 1965 classic *Die, Monster, Die!*, a loose adaptation of H. P. Lovecraft's *The Colour Out of Space.* American International Pictures released the film as a double feature with *Planet of the Vampires.* (Pixabay image marked as public domain or CCO.)

Die, Monster, Die! (1965)

Adams's entrance into sci-fi garnered enough attention to ensure that he would become a frequent visitor to the land of monsters and evil geniuses. At that point, he was introduced to the undisputed master of the craft.

Nick Adams and Boris Karloff were at the end of their careers. Both struggled to find roles, and although the film *Die, Monster, Die!*, directed by Daniel Haller, was a poor adaptation of H. P. Lovecraft's *The Colour Out of Space*, it represented one of Karloff's last horror films as it opened doors for Adams.

In the plot, American scientist Stephen Reinhart (Adams) takes the train to Arkham, now located in the rugged hills of England. Replete with trench coat, suitcase, and Brooklyn swagger, Adams has crossed the Atlantic to continue romancing gal friend Susan Witley, daughter of the mysterious scientist Nahum Witley (Karloff). Karloff, who was badly crippled by arthritis and emphysema, appeared in a wheelchair for most of his scenes. Adams played the role with a confident bravado and with outbursts of impulsive overacting, blending sci-fi with gothic camp.

This British-made horror film, also billed as *Monster of Terror*, transplanted Lovecraft's original New England Arkham County to the UK, where Reinhart discovers that radiation from a glowing meteorite has mutated the vegetation. This is Haller's (Roger Corman's former production designer) initial attempt in directing. The same story was adapted in 1987, retitled *The Curse*.

Toho Pictures

Adams found work wherever he could, even at the risk of sabotaging his career. After appearing in several low-budget Japanese monster movies, *Frankenstein*

Conquers the World and *Godzilla Vs. Monster Zero*, he was mocked. His critics were quick to pounce. *Mad Magazine* joked, "The Japanese have their monsters, and Hollywood has its monster, Nick Adams."

Still, making Japanese monster movies kept him working, successfully incorporating his compulsive drive and work ethic. Unlike many other Hollywood stars, Nick Adams was drawing a paycheck, and according to Brian Camp's Film and Anime Blog, "Nick Adams was the first American star to go to Japan to appear in Japanese films that would get significant distribution in the US."

Henry G. Saperstein was also heading to Japan. Saperstein was the head of United Productions of America, a production outfit primarily known for animated shorts (*Mr. Magoo*; *Gay Purr-ee*). Saperstein was looking for science fiction movies to distribute, and approached the Japanese Toho Pictures. Toho agreed to projects that resulted in *Frankenstein Conquers the World, Godzilla Vs. Monster Zero,* and *the War of the Gargantuas,* all directed by Ishiro Honda and featuring obscure American stars.

They were like Major League Baseball athletes playing Japanese winter ball for the Hiroshima Carp, Chunichi Dragons, or Osaka Kintetsu Buffalos. American actors had appeared in earlier Japanese *Godzilla* films, typically in scenes that were separately shot and then inserted into the American versions.

Godzilla, King of the Monsters (1956) featured scenes of Raymond Burr as American reporter Steve Martin. The original Japanese film, *Gojira* (1954), had been released two years earlier. Another similar offering was *King Kong Vs. Godzilla* (1963), where American stars Les Tremayne, Michael Keith, and Harry Holcombe were added to the reworked US version.

Frankenstein Conquers the World (1965)

Nick Adams played the part of Dr. James Bowen in his venture into Japanese cinema. *Frankenstein Vs. Baragon* was the film's subtitle, and it was among the "kaiju" subgenre, which features an endless lineup of giant monsters, many born of atomic bomb experiments and powerful radiation. This Japanese sci-fi film, directed by Ishiro Honda, featured the first appearance of the kaiju creature Baragon, with Adams and Kumi Mizuno sharing the stage.

The film premiered in the United States on July 8, 1966, and adhered to the Toho Company Ltd. and American International Pictures' kaiju formula of gigantic reptilian creatures—Hedora, Kumonga, and Gabara—all lining up to battle Godzilla. The motion picture was filmed in widescreen Toho Scope with English subtitles and a ready-made demographic of drooling fans.

The plot involved the heart of the original Frankenstein monster, recovered by Japanese soldiers during World War II and exposed to radiation, creating a new body for the beast. Years later, this perpetually mutating man-monster is discovered wandering the streets of Hiroshima, where it is provided shelter by two benevolent scientists.

The monster ultimately escapes, grows to gargantuan size, and then fights the beast known as Baragon.

Godzilla Vs. Monster Zero (1970)

In the Japanese-American co-production *Monster Zero*, Nick Adams's astronaut character Glen (no last name) shared the billing with Godzilla and Rodan and Japanese astronaut Fuji (Akira Takarada). The astronauts are heading to a mysterious planet hidden behind Jupiter, seated in a two-person rocket sent by the World Space Authority. In the film, aliens plead with humanity to borrow Godzilla and Rodan to defeat King Ghidorah, only to betray the humans and unleash the monsters on the Earth. *Monster Zero* was directed by Ishiro Honda and was the sixth film in the *Godzilla* franchise.

The original US title was *Monster Zero,* but the official English title, as suggested by Toho Pictures, was *Invasion of Astro-Monster*. The original Japanese title, *Kaiju Daisenso*, translated as *The Great Monster War*.

Maron Films released the double bill of *Monster Zero* and *The War of the Gargantuas* in the United States on July 29, 1970.

Both Japanese monster films were produced by Saperstein using American actors Russ Tamblyn, Kipp Hamiton, and Nick Adams. Unfortunately, they were not released in the US until five years after final production and two years after Nick Adams's death.

Very Cooperative

Despite his image as a rebellious and ill-mannered star, Nick Adams earned the reputation as a hardworking actor and was well liked by the Japanese cast and crew. In John Rocco Roberto's interview with Saperstein, the producer offered Adams praise:

> Nick Adams was terrific, a real professional. Very cooperative, always on time, ready with his lines, available, totally cooperative. He loved being there. He stayed on after we left. He fell in love with a Japanese actress. He enjoyed the whole Japanese experience and being with her, so he worked in pictures there, including *The Killing Bottle*. An actor works in pictures any place.

Saperstein had as much disdain for Russ Tamblyn as he had respect for Nick Adams and Kipp Hamilton. Calling Tamblyn "a prima donna pain in the ass," Saperstein complained that he "had to re-shoot and re-record almost everything Russ Tamblyn did. He wasn't a Nick Adams, and I don't want to pursue that any further!"

Adams's last film in Japan, *The Killing Bottle* (1967), was an obscure detective comedy and one of a series of James Bond-inspired spy films. *The Killing Bottle* combined gadgets, dangerous traps, and slapstick humor with Adams at his chest-baring comedic best. Unfortunately, it was never released in the US, although, according to IMDB, it was dubbed into English. One Letterboxd reviewer wrote:

> Nick Adams is the best of the American actors who had a shot to work in Japan during the heyday of international co-productions. Unlike his lost, wooden counterparts who always felt awkwardly shoehorned into the narrative, Adams arrives as if he belongs there and has such rapport with the other leads he fits right in.

Greatest Social Commentary

In retrospect, the works of Nick Adams and Boris Karloff were culturally significant. As their stars dimmed, Adams and Karloff met at the twilight of their careers. Karloff had established himself as a star, but Adams was only at the beginning of his journey, merely a traveler, seeking his way and a place at the table. Adams died at age thirty-six, and Karloff, a year later, at age eighty-one.

Die, Monster, Die! was their cinematic intersection. Although Rotten Tomatoes gave that film a seventy-one percent Tomatometer approval rating, more importantly, it allowed Nick Adams, the student, to sit and learn at the master's feet.

Adams's earlier work, *The Rebel*, was about survival, revenge, and self-discovery. He portrayed Johnny Yuma, a soldier wandering through a violent and lawless world—a story of retribution, not forgiveness. In the plot, an outlaw gang murders Yuma's father. Yuma vows to exact revenge, clutching his father's double-barrel sawed-off shotgun while proudly wearing the cap of a defeated Confederate soldier. He keeps a journal of his adventures.

Nick Adams and Boris Karloff shared in a unique bond. The death of Adams took place during the turmoil of 1968, depicted in race riots, burning cities, and the anarchy of *Night of the Living Dead,* but Karloff's most significant social commentary, a warning to the world about impending danger, was yet to come.

Chapter 19

Roger Corman and
Charles Whitman's Ghost

"We have met the enemy, and he is us."
Walt Kelly, cartoonist (1913–1973)

Film director Roger Corman was a futurist. His exploitation film *Targets,* based on one of America's first mass killings, allowed us to gaze deep into the unsettling prophecy of his crystal ball.

Corman was also a genius, recreating the works of horror master Edgar Allen Poe, adapting them to the new CinemaScope screen. Between 1960 and 1964, Corman made eight film adaptations from the works of Poe, seven starring Vincent Price. Corman's "Poe cycle" included *House of Usher* (1960), *The Pit and the Pendulum* (1961), *Premature Burial* (1961), *Tales of Terror* (1962), and his 1964 masterpiece, *The Mask of the Red Death*. Corman's final installment in his homage to Poe was *The Tomb of Ligeia* (1964).

Corman's low-budget thrillers were culturally significant. American International Pictures developed *House of Usher* for only two hundred seventy thousand dollars, the most they had ever spent for a film up to that time. It was a calculated gamble that paid off many times over. Although most horror films play to a well-defined and limited audience, AIP's *House of Usher* ranked in the top five box office hits of 1960 and was a huge commercial and critical success. The public loved it and hungered for more.

Corman had tapped into something with macabre scenes of torture presented as romanticized Gothic melodrama. His vibrant colors and surreal stage sets painted death as an elegant art form. Although an enthusiastic box office applauded his achievements, Corman's most controversial film was yet to come.

Charles Whitman

Targets was based on the narrative of Charles Joseph Whitman, an ex-Marine sniper raised in an upper-middle-class family in Lake Worth, Florida. Charles excelled at academics, was an Eagle Scout, an accomplished pianist, and was well-liked by his classmates and neighbors. His father, Charles Adolph Whitman, owned a successful plumbing contract business.

In 1966, Charles Whitman climbed to the Clock Tower, the University of Texas's highest structure. From there, the former Marine shot sixteen students and wounded thirty-two others—inspiring the exploitation film *Targets*.

Charles appeared to be the boy most likely to succeed and did not fit the profile of a mass murderer. But hidden from the world, underneath layers of scarred synapses, festered a tortured, dark soul. His secrets, revealed later, painted a portrait of a family in crisis. The Whitman family was unraveling following years of verbal and physical trauma. Charles Adolph admitted to beating his wife, Margaret. He said:

> I did, on many occasions, beat my wife, but I loved her. I did and do have an awful temper, but my

Maxim W. Furek

wife was awful stubborn, and because of my
temper, I knocked her around.

The psychological damage had destroyed her love and
trust, so Margaret left and filed for divorce. She moved to
Austin to be close to her son, Charles, who had enrolled
at the University of Texas as a mechanical engineering
student. But Charles, too, was unravelling, battling
repressed fantasies of anger. At 6:45 p.m. on July 31,
1966, he typed a suicide note that referenced his
psychiatric interventions with university psychiatrist Dr.
M. D. Heatly:

> I do not understand myself these days. I am
> supposed to be an average, reasonable and
> intelligent young man. However, lately (I cannot
> recall when it started), I have been a victim of
> many unusual and irrational thoughts. After one
> session, I never saw the Doctor again. Since then,
> I have been fighting my mental turmoil alone,
> seemingly to no avail. After my death, I wish that
> an autopsy would be performed on me to see if
> there is any physical disorder.

His actions were calculated. He stabbed his wife, Kathy,
as she slept, and then choked and stabbed his mother,
explaining in a gruesome letter, "I have just taken my
mother's life. I am very upset over having done it. I am
truly sorry that this is the only way I could see to relieve
her sufferings, but I think it was best." Whitman's
psychotic thoughts were detailed in his letter:

230

I don't quite understand what it is that compels
me to type this letter. Perhaps it is to leave some
vague reason for the actions I have recently
performed. It was after much thought that I
decided to kill my wife, Kathy, tonight after I pick
her up from work at the telephone company. The
prominent reason in my mind is that I truly do not
consider this world worth living in and am
prepared to die. I do not want to leave her to
suffer alone in it. Similar reasons provoked me to
take my mother's life also.

His madness continued into the dawn of August 1, 1966.
Dressed in blue coveralls, he climbed to the twenty-
eighth floor of the University of Texas Administration
Building. He reached the Clock Tower, the university's
highest structure. At his feet were a .35-caliber
Remington rifle, a scoped 6 mm Remington rifle, a Smith
& Wesson .357 Magnum revolver, a 9 mm Luger pistol,
and a Galesi-Brescia .25 ACP pistol. Viperlike, he
methodically scanned the courtyard, tracking the moving
dots below. His mission was to kill as many as possible.
There would be little doubt about the outcome as he shot
"almost unimpeded" for ninety-six minutes. For the
targets, there was no place to hide, according to writer
Marlee Macleod:

> The Tower afforded Whitman a nearly unassailable
> vantage point from which he could select and
> dispatch victims. It was as if it had been built for
> his purpose. In fact, in previous years, Charlie had

remarked offhandedly to various people that a sniper could do quite a bit of damage from the Tower.

Looking down from the 307-foot Clock Tower's observation deck, he shot sixteen students and wounded thirty-two others as they walked to class. The ex-Marine sniper shot most of his victims near the heart.

Houston McCoy, an Austin police officer, fired two shotgun rounds and killed the twenty-five-year-old. Whitman became a testament to the proverb "He who lives by the sword dies by the sword" when his blood spilled on the observation deck.

The Clock Tower massacre remains a part of America's national consciousness. As an example, "Sniper," Harry Chapin's 1972 song, attempted to create a "psychological profile" of the killer who hated his abusive father.

Dr. M. D. Heatly

Whitman admitted to Dr. M. D. Heatly that he had violent fantasies of killing people from the tower. After a March 1966 consultation, the psychiatrist wrote:

> Although he identifies with his mother in the matter above, his real concern is with himself at the present time. He readily admits having overwhelming periods of hostility with a very minimum of provocation. Repeated inquiries attempting to analyze his exact experiences were

not too successful, with the exception of his vivid reference to "thinking about going up on the tower with a deer rifle and start shooting people."

Heatly determined that Whitman did not present a threat to himself or others, the standard for psychiatric hospitalization. This was several years before the landmark *Tarasoff v. Regents of University of California* case. In 1974 and 1976, the California Supreme Court issued two rulings pertaining to "duty to warn." In *Tarasoff v. Regents of the University of California*, the California Supreme Court ruled that if psychotherapists determine that their patient presents a danger to others, they must warn the intended victim of the threat.

To this day, *Tarasoff* remains ambiguous, with uneven application throughout the fifty states. Still, if it had been enacted, the *Tarasoff* decision might have saved the lives of those University of Texas students. Sadly, all of the warning signs were missed, but doctors discovered a glioblastoma, a highly aggressive brain tumor, when Whitman's body was autopsied. There was added speculation of possible stimulant abuse by the shooter. Found next to the body was a bottle of Dexedrine, an oral form of amphetamine.

Targets

Targets, an obscure film based on Whitman's hate-spawned rampage, represented the confluence of art imitating life. The film was released in 1968, one of

Maxim W. Furek

America's most tumultuous years, when blood flowed from the streets of Saigon to Chicago, a slow trickle, then a grotesque spurting artery. America watched in horror the televised Tet Offensive, the assassinations of Dr. Martin Luther King Jr. and Robert Kennedy, and the Chicago Convention's police brutality.

America was in a state of shock, detailed in newscasts, front-page headlines, and the exploitation film *Targets*. The film was cobbled together by Peter Bogdanovich and Corman. Bogdanovich wrote and directed *Targets* and credited the movie for launching his career. Horror icon Boris Karloff was the film's top-billed star, while omnipresent Corman was the cunning puppet master.

Although based on the Clock Tower shootings, *Targets* had a few other twists. Because Karloff owed Corman two days' work, Corman gave Bogdanovich permission to make any film he wanted, as long as he adhered to three things: (1) feature actor Boris Karloff as the star, (2) keep the film under budget, and (3) incorporate parts of a little-known film, *The Terror*. Produced by Corman, *The Terror*, a 1963 film shot on leftover movie sets, starred Jack Nicholson and the ubiquitous Karloff.

Karloff was one of the greatest masters of horror but was unable to find the dramatic roles he sought during the final days of his career. Some of his last roles included *Bikini Beach* (1964), *Die, Monster, Die!* (1965) with co-star Nick Adams, *The Ghost in the Invisible Bikini* (1966), and *House of Evil* (1968). But *Targets*, featuring Karloff as elderly horror-film star Byron Orlok (named after Max Schreck's vampire Count Orlok in 1922's *Nosferatu*), was viewed as among his finest performances.

In *Targets*, Orlok makes a personal appearance at a San Fernando Valley drive-in and confronts a psychotic Vietnam veteran patterned after Charles Whitman. At the same time, Karloff's *The Terror* plays subtly in the background. In a decisive scene, Karloff warns that the real horror is not the monster on the screen but rather the real-life shooter. Nathan Southern, writing for the All Movie review, agreed with that sad observation that resonates even today:

> For his debut feature, Peter Bogdanovich wrote and directed this shattering, visceral thriller that meditates on the nature of violence in contemporary society, as well as the chasm between real-life horrors and shlocky movie scares that cannot possibly compete with them.

In the book *Roger Corman: How I Made a Hundred Movies in Hollywood and Never Lost a Dime,* director Peter Bogdanovich explained how he made *Targets:*

> My idea was to have Karloff play a retiring horror film actor; the old footage was used as a film-within-a-film he's making at the end of his career. So to contrast the illusion of horror in Karloff's gothic castle with real horror, a deranged Vietnam vet starts sniping at people at a drive-in. This was

a few years after the Texas Tower incident and Charles Whitman.

At the time, Whitman's rampage was the deadliest school shooting in US history. The University of Texas Regents closed the observation deck permanently in 1976. Still, it symbolized lost innocence for the next twenty years, viewed not as a place of academia but as a slaughterhouse.

The tower reopened in 1999 after installing metal detectors and posting security guards on the ground floor and observation deck. Still, some believe Charles Whitman still haunts the site of the massacre. On the fifty-second anniversary of Whitman's slaughter, GhostGhoul, an internet forum, observed:

> Legend has it the tower lights switch on and off at night when the offices are closed, and the tower is vacant. In some cases, the lights turn on and off several times, much to the irritation of onsite security guards. On one occasion, an irritated guard reportedly yelled at Charlie to knock it off, and the lights switched off for good.

Does the ghost of Charles Whitman haunt the Clock Tower? Some say Whitman doesn't just play pranks with the lights, but at times, his image will appear before startled witnesses. In *The Ghosts of Austin,* author Fiona Broome describes Whitman's manifestation as a "fleeting, shadowy form." His spirit may be trapped on the Clock Tower, unable to continue to the next plane.

Ashton Rogers of Fort Worth, Texas, NT Paranormal offered, "We have had some correlation of data suggesting that traumatic events in a location increase the odds that people will have a paranormal experience in the area." Whitman's ghost has not gone away, and some paranormal researchers claim he is responsible for the suicide deaths of nine people who later jumped from the tower's observation deck.

Both Charles Whitman and *Targets* waved a red flag as art imitated life, a reality not lost on horror writer Stephen King. In his interview with Xan Brooks, King observed:

> The world is a scary place, not just America. We're in the spooky house—on the ghost train, if you prefer—for life. The scares come and go, but everyone likes make-believe monsters to stand in for the real ones.

Those make-believe monsters somehow lessened our fears. *Targets* forewarned of a shift from improbable Hollywood monsters to something more sinister. It warned that the beast was not slithering on the movie screen but walking upon our street, shopping in our grocery store, and perching atop a university clock tower. Byron Orlok's warning was clear. *The monster walks among us.*

Chapter 20

Edward J. Conrad:Truth Dispenser

He was more than just an old-school newspaperman working for the Hazleton *Standard-Speaker* and *Shenandoah Herald*. In the tradition of writers like Hunter S. Thompson, Tom Wolfe, and Truman Capote, Ed Conrad was also a gonzo journalist.

Conrad demanded that the Sheppton event be investigated on an academic and scientific level. He singlehandedly brought Sheppton to the attention of prominent scholars and researchers. Because he embedded himself into the story, Conrad provided an invaluable perspective authenticating David Fellin and Henry Throne's story as science rather than science fiction.

Conrad and Fellin became fast friends. He first met Fellin a week before Fellin's eightieth birthday. They met at the wake of a mutual friend. Because of Fellin's age and failing eyesight, Conrad assisted in documenting Fellin's recollections in an array of tape recordings and notarized letters. Fellin signed a particular sworn statement titled "Miraculous Coal-Mine Rescue." The document contained the following text, which supported Fellin's sighting of the Pope during his entombment:

> David Fellin signs an affidavit that Pope John Paul XXIII, who died on June 3, 1963, two months before the cave-in, appeared to him and Hank Throne and remained with them until they were rescued fourteen days after being entombed.

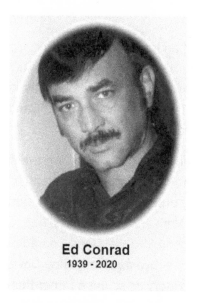

Ed Conrad
1939 - 2020

Gonzo journalist Ed Conrad helped validate the Sheppton mythology on an academic and scientific level. (Mahanoy City Area Historical Society photograph.)

Dr. Elizabeth Kubler-Ross

It was Conrad who drove Dave Fellin to Headwaters, Virginia, in Highland County—"Virginia's Little Switzerland" and the state's least populous territory. Fellin was interviewed by Swiss psychiatrist Dr. Elizabeth Kubler-Ross (1926–2000). Kubler-Ross authored one of the most important psychological studies of the late twentieth century. *On Death and Dying* (1969) explored understanding the five stages of the death process: denial and isolation, anger, bargaining, depression, and acceptance. She gave readers a better understanding of how imminent death affects the patient, doctors and nurses, and the patient's family.

Kubler-Ross remarked on the resilience demonstrated by Fellin and Throne. She called their behavior "a guideline for our miners, soldiers, mountain climbers, and all those at risk to face a similar ordeal one day." Kubler-Ross believed that the miners were truthful about their out-of-body experiences and referred to their resiliency as "a story of faith, courage, and mutual care and respect."

She was convinced that Pope John XXIII had much to do with their survival. "From the moment of the late Pope's appearance until they were moved out of the drillholes, he illuminated their cave with a bluish light radiating from him." Kubler-Ross believed that the miners' miraculous rescue, the appearance of the deceased Pope, and the out-of-body experiences shared by two persons simultaneously were "obviously true." Kubler-Ross concluded that Sheppton represented proof of "life after death," as Pope John XXIII had died before the disaster. Those words were the validation that Fellin and Conrad had sought.

Kubler-Ross gained fame with her studies of people who had been clinically dead, were later revived, and told of having visited a place that was "beautiful beyond description." She described three experiences common to those who had moved to the threshold of death or beyond it—a sense of the soul floating out of the body, feelings of peace and wholeness, and the impression of meeting someone who had previously died.

In 1999, *Time* Magazine named Kubler-Ross one of the "100 Most Important Thinkers" of the past century. On the topic of death, she once said:

> Death is simply a shedding of the physical body, like the butterfly shedding its cocoon. It is a transition to a higher state of consciousness where you continue to perceive, to understand, to laugh, and to be able to grow.

Dr. Bruce Greyson

Dr. Bruce Greyson, a psychiatrist at the University of Connecticut Health Center and editor for the *Journal of Near-Death Studies*, provided additional validation. Greyson, citing the simultaneous paranormal experiences, said: "If they (the miners) can corroborate each other's account, they could provide evidence for the reality of The Other Side beyond anything yet available."

Greyson had become acquainted with the incredible details of the supernatural events only in the last years of Fellin's life, finding them spellbinding, and "intrigued by the simultaneous experiences of Fellin and Throne, who conversed while out of their bodies.

The two miners were interviewed individually, then together by a pair of psychiatrists and a third staff member from the Institute of the University of Pennsylvania in Philadelphia. These intriguing interviews, the subject of an article in the *American Journal of Psychiatry*, offered evidence that both men had been participants in a series of supernatural events, including the appearance of the late pontiff and their collective out-of-body experiences. The miners revealed that their darkened chamber suddenly was illuminated with a bluish light, the deceased pontiff appeared to them, and a large number of humanoids, who were neither miners nor members of the rescue party, could be seen.

Lt. Richard Anderson

Fellin divulged that, shortly after being rescued, he had been interviewed for more than seven hours by the US Navy Survival Team headed by psychiatrist and medical doctor Lt. Richard Anderson. Visiting his hospital room, Anderson told him he was certain his experiences were factual because Throne also had been interviewed for several hours—something Fellin hadn't even been aware of—and their two stories had meshed perfectly. The day after his interview, Fellin recollected:

Dr. Anderson told me our story MUST be true because it would be impossible for two people to concoct a story that would stand up so well during such lengthy interviews.

Pope John XXIII

Conrad called the Pope John XXIII sighting something of "fact" and "definitely not fiction or faith." Says Conrad:

> David Fellin told me perhaps a hundred times that, after Pope John XXIII appeared to both of them at the same time and they briefly discussed his appearance, he never mentioned another word about the Pope to Throne for the duration of their entombment. Fellin explained that since Throne wasn't religious and didn't know the Pope (or that he had died about two months before), he thought it best not to bring more attention to their visitor.

"If Hank knew the 'stranger' was dead, he might've gone berserk," Fellin told me. "If he did, it might've been the death of the both of us. I couldn't have survived without Hank, and likewise, Hank wouldn't have been able to survive without me. We needed each other."

Not another word was made of Pope John XXIII's presence during the remainder of their entombment, even when he was a few short feet away while they were greasing each other before being pulled to the surface."

Fellin and Throne, a devout Roman Catholic and an agnostic, swore they were in the presence of Pope John XXIII. They incontrovertibly believed that the Pope materialized, remained with them for two weeks until their extrication, and saved their lives.

The Other World

Years later, after innumerable privately tape-recorded interviews and public meetings, the miners held to their story of visitations by bizarrely outfitted humanoids and stairwells of white marble.

But what Fellin later confessed to Conrad was the most bizarre in lyric and tone. Fellin spoke of time travel and contact with strange creatures. One of his last testaments would be the most profound. He said that he had clairvoyance and that he knew things and saw things. He confided, "There are more planets with human life in the universe than there are grains of sand on all the beaches of the world."

Conrad wrote "Proof of Life After Death," published in 1990 after Fellin's death. He concluded that the miners shared near-death experiences simultaneously and determined their accounts to be accurate. He decided it was not the result of hallucination, trauma, or a miner's psychosis.

Truth Dispenser

Conrad seemed to enjoy mixing it up with the scientific community. He was much like the brash, opinionated, and confrontational *Amazing Stories'* publisher Ray A. Palmer. A ferocious debater, Conrad was quick to defend his truth and rarely backed down. In 1996 he responded to Chris Brochu from the University of Texas:

> Any scientist in any field—or, for that matter, anyone with an inquiring mind interested in the honest pursuit of scientific truth—is a charlatan if neither is interested or intrigued by what well may be the breakthrough evidence that SEEMS to confirm the possibility of an existence past our physical death.

Conrad held to his belief that Fellin and Throne had witnessed an example of "life after death" and backed up his claim with numerous assertions.

Conrad also shared a strange connection with another Coal Region luminary, Richard Sharpe Shaver—the latter was called an "Outsider Artist," while Conrad labeled himself a "Truth Dispenser." After retirement, Conrad enjoyed climbing Schuylkill County's Bear, Red, and Stone Ridges with "Blue," his husky, looking for fossils while Shaver spent his final years searching for physical evidence of ancient prehistoric races. He claimed to have discovered "rock books" from the ancient Atlanteans.

Both Shaver and Conrad proffered scientifically revolutionary theories. Conrad believed that he had discovered fossils proving that man is older than the scientific community believes. In June 1981, he uncovered an unusual yellow claylike rock with a curved shape resembling the crown of a skull. A local dentist X-rayed a portion of it, convincing Conrad that it was part of a three-hundred-million-year-old petrified skull.

The first primates appeared in the Tertiary Age, about sixty-five million years ago; scientists believe the human species traces its ancestry back about two million years. But Conrad suggested that if his findings are actual hominid bones, they would be about three hundred million years old. Conrad asserted that the petrified bone he discovered was of a primate that preceded man. If proven correct, Conrad's discovery would radically alter Charles Darwin's explanation for the origin of the human species.

Ed Conrad, a Mahanoy City native, was one of the Coal Region's most fascinating characters. He passed away on November 19, 2020, at Shenandoah's Ridgeview Healthcare & Rehabilitation Center. He was eighty-one years old and an important part of the Sheppton Mythology.

Chapter 21

Dr. Frederick L. Santee:
White Witch

Dr. Frederick LaMotte Santee was a genius, acknowledged as "the greatest abstract thinker of the 20th Century." He was a practicing Wiccan and a Christian "white witch." He titled his Faustian book *The Devil's Wager*.

Note: I interviewed Dr. Frederick LaMotte Santee several times during the late 1970s. I used my antique Sony cassette tape recorder and a long list of prepared questions. I was intrigued by Dr. Santee, who at one time was called "the foremost abstract thinker of the 20th Century." Santee's office reeked of medicine and, because of a recent arson at his library, called the Book House, of pungent smoke. Dr. Santee wore his traditional bibbed overalls. He was friendly, gracious, and patient. He spoke with two different voices, one natural, the other articulated through clenched teeth. He said that he appreciated my enthusiasm and curiosity. He presented me with a signed copy of his book *The Devil's Wager*. His inscription read, *Thank you, Max, for a penetrating and successful interview.*

All of the interviews with Dr. Santee included High Priestess Lady Athena, the coven's highest-ranking member. She directed the conversation away from areas she deemed "too sensitive." Still, Santee readily discussed every topic I introduced. I was impressed with his honesty. He demonstrated an impressive body of knowledge and instantaneous recall.

In 1980, I attended his funeral at Wapwallopen's Old River Church. I had a lengthy conversation with David McDowell, Crown Publishing's senior editor. McDowell gave me a personal and intimate insight into his colleague's fascinating literary and academic life. The following is the story of the remarkable child prodigy, doctor, and witch, Dr. Frederick L. Santee.

"A Living Child Prodigy"

The saga of Dr. Frederick L. Santee (1906–1980) is a peek into what paranormal researcher Justin Bamforth has called "high strangeness" and something that defies belief. *Time* magazine named him "a living child prodigy," while a Johns Hopkins University psychological study recognized him as "one of society's genuinely gifted individuals." Santee biographer Blau Stern Schwarz said he "was an amazing man, doctor, scholar, and occultist." Santee was a complex individual—a beautiful mind that discovered truths revealed to only a select few and a hedonist who succumbed to the temptations of the flesh.

He was born September 17, 1906, in Wapwallopen, Pennsylvania, the son of Dr. Charles L. and Verna (Lloyd) Santee. Santee was born in a lineage of four generations of doctors. His grandfather was a Civil War surgeon who helped free runaway slaves. His father was Charles LaMotte Santee, who held MD degrees from Lafayette and Jefferson Colleges.

During his early years, Santee indicated signs of genius. By age three, he could read both English and German. His father would often take him to a local store, sit him on the counter and dazzle the patrons by having the child spell difficult words, such as "Constantinople." He learned Latin from his grandfather's grammar books, and by age eight, he was translating Caesar's *Gallic Wars* from Latin into English and back again to check his grammar.

In his final year, the child prodigy attended Wapwallopen High School and Wilkes-Barre High School. Next, he went to Central High School in Philadelphia for an AB degree (an academic degree conferred by a college upon those who complete the undergraduate curriculum) in Greek. He allegedly had the highest score in the nation.

Interest in the Occult

At fourteen, he was the youngest person to have attended Harvard University, where he graduated magna cum laude. Harvard recognized his first-place ranking for each of his three years.

At age eighteen, he studied at Oxford University, receiving a Bachelor of Arts in 1926 and a Master of Arts in 1928. While at Oxford, Santee met Aleister Crowley (1875–1947), an English occultist, ceremonial magician, and novelist. Crowley was a nineteenth-century religious skeptic and a practitioner of "magick." He called himself *The Beast 666*, and the British popular press labeled him "the wickedest man in the world," denounced for his decadent lifestyle. His most famous saying was, "Do what thou wilt shall be the whole of the law."

Although Crowley may have sparked Santee's interest in the occult, there were others as well. While in England, Santee was introduced to the legendary "white witch" Sybil Leek, who later helped him initiate his Coven of the Catta.

Santee's academic aspirations knew no bounds. After studying at the University of Berlin for one year, he was awarded a Sheldon Fellowship at the American Academy of Rome—where he spent three years reading Latin, Greek, German, and some Sanskrit.

He continued as a classics scholar by utilizing his vast knowledge and critical thinking abilities. He taught at Pennsylvania universities Temple and Lehigh, and Johns Hopkins University Medical School.

He established a medical practice in Baltimore but relocated to Wapwallopen in 1963 after his father's death, taking over his medical practice. He was known as a country doctor who provided free health care to the poor. He was a homeopathic healer who made his medicines and herbal salves and practiced acupuncture when the practice was in its infancy. Some claimed he could diagnose a patient just by being in their presence. He continued to practice medicine until he died in 1980.

Bertrand Russell

Traveling in ever-expanding circles, Santee was introduced to other visionary minds, such as Bertrand Russell, a noted philosopher and mathematician. Russell (1872–1970) was awarded the Order of Merit in 1949 and the Nobel Prize for Literature in 1950. Russell said in a moment of rare tribute, "Santee will be the greatest abstract thinker of the 20th Century." Russell wanted Santee to join his fledgling experimental school at Summerhill. Santee recalled:

I think he overestimated me considerably. He thought that I would be a great asset to that school. He tried to bribe me by trying to teach me all of the mathematics he could remember.

Despite that grand opportunity, Santee turned Russell down, disagreeing with the mathematician's political, social, and educational theories. For example, Russell felt that an individual could be self-motivated in a proper environment. Santee, however, argued that a "proper" environment was nothing without the critical ingredient of discipline. Perhaps a fine point, but one that formed a deep chasm between the symbiosis of two great minds. Of possible significance is that Russell was thirty-four years older than the determined and confident Santee, then around sixteen.

The Coven of the Catta

Nestled in the remote mountain region of northeastern Pennsylvania, Dr. Santee maintained a veil of secrecy between his private life and the curious public. Santee believed in the ancient practice of the Wicca religion, the Craft of the Wise. The country doctor was the high priest and founder of the group, which he named "the Coven of the Catta." He called himself Lord Merlin and was a practicing witch. The doctor's introduction to witchcraft occurred while he was in Europe, according to Santee researcher Blau Stern Schwarz Schlonge:

While at the University of Berlin, he was initiated

into witchcraft at a Coven thirty miles outside Berlin, the coven High Priest being Arnold Reinman. In travels in the Middle East, he met native adepts of the High Art in Egypt, learned from a German adept also in Egypt, and from a Sheik who was High Priest of a "coven" in North Africa.

Santee claimed that (at the time of our interview) there were only about four hundred covens in the United States. The term "witch" comes from the ancient Anglo-Saxon word *wicce*, which translates into "prophet or sorcerer." A gathering of witches constitutes a coven. During the days before the spread of Christianity, common folk passed as doctors, midwives, and healers. All were educated in the healing ways of the craft, learning herbology or homeopathic magic techniques. Among those who have joined Santee's Wapwallopen coven are aviation engineers, homemakers, and ordained ministers; said Santee:

> They participate for varied reasons, but all recognize the craft's positive approach to worldly situations.

"White Witchcraft"

Many still believe that witchcraft is demonic, but Santee emphasized that the Wicca craft is benevolent. His "white witchcraft" is used only for helping and healing. The

Coven of the Catta follows the natural magic of the right-hand path, employing nature's hidden powers.

One such technique is sympathetic magic, performed by making poppet dolls. Here, the patient's hair is affixed to the poppet and anointed in the patient's name. Then needles are pushed into the poppet, hoping to cure the patient's ailments.

Another technique used by the coven is mental magic. Several individuals concentrate on a focal point, attempting to transform their willpower, or combined visualization, onto the person needing healing. The group can only be as strong as its weakest link, so intensive training and discipline are essential for the success of the rites.

Spirits can be conjured up to help in rituals and rites of magic. Friendly spirits are used as "familiars," those go-betweens connecting the witch and the external world. Familiars can be animals or spirits. Sybil Leek used a python as her familiar and also several smaller, more ordinary animals. Santee said:

> No good witch fails to have a familiar. Cats are commonly used, but you can use any animal, even pythons. The animal becomes sensitive to your attitudes, moods, and feelings and reacts to them. And since they have superior sensory powers, in many ways, can warn you of certain dangers or things you might not be aware of.

Lady Phoebe Athena

Researcher Blau Stern Schwarz understood that Edna Jane Kishbaugh Williams urged Santee to initiate the Coven of the Catta in 1956. After meeting Sybil Leek in Europe, he invited her to Covenstead, his Wapwallopen residence. In 1967 they received their charter—named after the cat totem. Santee was initiated as Lord Merlin by Leek, "the World's Most Famous Witch." Leek traced her lineage of witchcraft back to at least 1134. After Britain's Witchcraft Act was repealed in 1951, she began to write about and practice the traditional craft knowledge. In 1969 she published her best-selling autobiography, *Diary of a Witch*. Her citation in *Witch's Almanac* read:

> She often said that she was a Druid, not just a Witch and that Druids were like the priest class while Witches were the working class among Craft practitioners.

Edna was the group's highest-ranking member—High Priestess Lady Phoebe Athena Nimue—employed as the receptionist and secretary of Santee's medical practice. Although she was the highest authority, Lady Athena believed in the democratic process. She often consulted with other witches for input. The Coven of the Catta has thirteen witches, but, if it were to grow larger, it would split into two groups because thirteen is the maximum number allowed.

The Coven of the Catta subscribes to concepts that parallel Christianity's Holy Trinity. They believe in the hierarchy of the Triple Goddess, personified by the Virgin (crescent moon), the Great Mother (full moon), and the Wise Old Woman (waning moon). The importance of the craft's female membership is best explained in terms of the worldly and the spiritual. Wicca practitioners believe that men can best lead women through the world of materialistic values, while women can best lead men through the realms of the spiritual world.

Santee was driven by an insatiable appetite for knowledge. As a regular visitor to New York City, he frequently visited the Magickal Childe bookstore, adding to his expertise of witchcraft. Santee claimed that witchcraft has been around for centuries and was the world's most rapidly spreading religion:

> It increases percentage-wise faster than any others. Almost before any culture, if there was any religion, it was witchcraft. The American Indians, Egyptians, Hindus, and Christians are all founded on the craft which was founded before them.

"Ye shall not suffer a witch to live."

Witchcraft had enemies. Early Christianity set out to vilify, hunt down and kill all witches. Several Bible verses spread that propaganda to a superstitious and ignorant populace. Exodus 22:18 commanded, "Thou shalt not suffer a witch to live," and Leviticus 20:27 provided another horrible rationale. It read, "A man or woman who is a medium or spiritist among you must be put to death. You are to stone them; their blood will be on their own heads."

Witchcraft and folk magic have always been a part of Pennsylvania history, Old World superstitions that followed English and German settlers. In 1684, William Penn presided over the state's only official witch trial, and two hundred years later, accused witch Susan Mummey was shot and killed in her Ringtown Valley home. Residents were convinced that the old woman was a practitioner of a dark art known in Pennsylvania Dutch country as hexerei, the opposite of positive and healing powwowing magic. Mummey's neighbors believed she placed curses on their livestock and themselves. According to "Albert Shinsky and The Witch of Ringtown Valley," an *Unexplained Mysteries* article:

> Mummey was a quarrelsome sort who had feuded with most of her neighbors—something that only exacerbated her sinister occult reputation. She was believed to have turned an "evil eye" on one of her enemies and "hexed" several others. A great sigh of relief went out over Ringwood when it was learned she was dead.

Albert Shinsky, twenty-three, a local Schuylkill County jitney driver, was confident that Mummey had cursed him, later confessing:

> I heard a voice from the sky say, "shoot that woman," and I did. I was hexed. She sent black cats with burning eyes from the skies down at me. Black cats would come into my room and claw at my side. Once, one cat nearly suffocated me with its fur. I had to kill her to break the spell.

Shinsky claimed to have been "prescribed" the "magical bullet" used to kill the elderly Mummey. A local powwow doctor suggested it was the only way to break Mummey's hold over him. But Shinsky was cursed, not by black magic, but by mental illness. Shinsky was diagnosed with dementia praecox, an archaic condition marked by hallucinations and known today as schizophrenia. He was sent to a mental institution, where he later rejected his belief in witches, devil cats, and hexes.

Black Magick

Throughout history, there have been other practitioners of natural magic. The Pennsylvania Dutch folk medicine, known as powwowing, dates back to Europe's Middle Ages. Powwowers were revered for their abilities to heal, lift curses, and find lost objects. The practice rose in the US in the 1700s with the arrival of German-speaking settlers. It used herbs, rituals, and incantations to heal and ward off evil. Powwowing is the positive form of natural magic, while hexerei is the dark form.

Unfortunately, witchcraft's "natural magic" has historically been linked with demonic "black magick." It has given the word "witch" a bad connotation. Demonic magick, called "the left-hand path," uses demon spirits, harmful elements, and devils for evil purposes. Natural magic, "the right-hand path," applies hidden powers in nature. It has been the crux of the benevolent Wicca craft for ages. Santee says his craft is altruistic:

> We're not exactly ascetics, but we do not use the craft for our advantage. The Wicca craft is one of helping people. Wicca believes in a Supreme God, and there's only one God. Wiccans can defend themselves but do not harm others in thought, word, or deed. To do so would make the hardship come back to them tenfold.

Or maybe threefold. New York-based writer and *Allure*'s resident astrologer, Sophie Saint Thomas, says that magick isn't simply good or evil:

> It's a tool. We can all act in ways that are selfish, jealous, and petty from time to time, and, honestly, that's OK. We have good sides that are loving, too. You may have heard of "the rule of threes," or the belief that performing magick with ill intent will come back to you three times, turning the ill intent on you. The neo-pagan religion Wicca holds that "three times what thou givest returns to thee," which can be applied to positive magick as well.

One can immediately perceive similarities between powwowing and Santee's right and left pathways.

Maxim W. Furek

Gretchen Swank, whose great-grandmother was a powwow healer, said:

> The difference between the work of a healer
> (Braucherei) and a witch (Hexerei) in Powwow is
> "intent." A Braucherei becomes a conduit for the
> healing energy of God to do His work while the
> Hexerei works from their own self-interest (ego) to
> benefit themselves or manipulate the situations of
> others for personal gain. A Hexenmeister has a
> firm grasp on the work of a Braucherei, coupled
> with a deeper understanding of the work of a
> Hexerei, which allows the Hexenmeister to
> effectively diagnose, remove, and remedy a Hex.

Just as powwowing uses Christianity at its center, Wicca believes in a Supreme God, and only one God. Although most witches do not accept the existence of the devil, Santee does, but with strong convictions. He said:

> We don't sacrifice animals or humans or do what
> Satanists do. We don't sacrifice virgins. The
> concept of sacrifice is probably present in
> witchcraft, but mainly in the manner of living one's
> life.

Santee was concerned with false narratives promoted by Hollywood, the media, and early Christianity, which became the battle charge for the infamous witch hunters of Salem, Massachusetts, and Pennsylvania. These erroneous portrayals of the craft force covens to maintain

262

a tight veil of secrecy. Without this privacy, attacks would be even more violent than the three fires and burglaries that plagued Santee's property for years.

Deliberate Fires

The first suspected arson case, in 1979, was in Santee's Book House, a cinder-block structure located at 5 River Street in Wapwallopen. The Book House contained possibly one of the finest collections of occult literature in the Northeast and over fifty thousand rare editions of biographies, classic languages, and occultism. Many of these books were either damaged or destroyed in the fire. The second fire, set in his office, completely gutted the lower level of his medical practice. Santee felt it was a deliberate fire set by persons ignorant of the truth and afraid of what they thought Santee represented. But, as Santee related:

> I'm not a person who thinks I have any enemies. I can't find any when I look around, so I have no idea who would do such a thing.

Burglaries too. Thieves took valuable pieces of occult literature dated before 1600. The stolen items included books purchased decades earlier, including *The Golden Bough: A Study in Magic and Religion*, written by the Scottish anthropologist Sir James George Frazer and first published in 1890. Santee estimated the total loss at over five hundred thousand dollars.

Maxim W. Furek

The Devil's Wager

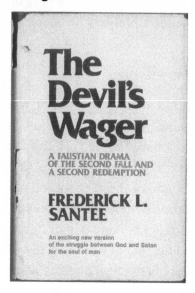

Members of the coven shared their knowledge openly,
opening themselves to criticism from the uninformed.
Santee wrote a newspaper column called "The Country
Doctor," and Lady Athena wrote a column called "The
Witches' Kettle." Santee was also a scholar of the Faust
novels and created his own Faustian story, The *Devil's
Wager,* set in modern times. *The Devil's Wager* deals with
the forces of good and evil, both trying to win possession
of human souls, explained Santee:

> I think my book could not have been published or
> widely read before this new interest in the occult
> or so-called supernatural developed.

One of the most important topics that Santee addressed was the concept of the supernatural. According to Santee, aspects of the supernatural should be viewed as part of the "Laws of Science." Both, he asserts, fall into the natural realm:

> I don't think that our powers, or our studies, are anything more than natural. I think what people call "supernatural" is the same thing that runs through this book as the laws of science. When the connections between the two events cannot be completely discovered and explained, then we call it supernatural, but actually, it's the same thing.

Santee also shed light on topics many have deemed incomprehensible, supernatural themes seemingly outside the realms of science:

> There is only one way of the world. There is no distinction between the occult and the scientific. They are both sciences. In the scientific realm, the connections have all come to life between the cause and the result. In the other case, the supernatural they have not come to life yet, but they're there.

Last Surviving Member

He was an accomplished individual, larger than life and of legendary stature, yet he made his home in the remote village of Wapwallopen, Pennsylvania. Santee employed two nurses and four secretaries, and librarians. The locals believed he was a kind and compassionate doctor, though a bit of an eccentric. He often treated the poor at no charge.

Even after death, Santee's presence is felt. Santee's home was featured on the TV show *The Haunted,* in an episode titled "The Coven of the Catta." In 2005, a man, with his wife and two children, moved into the home built for Santee's nurses. Located directly across the street from Santee's house, the structure was where Coven rituals were performed. On their first night at the house, near Easter, pictures were seen flying off the walls, and shortly after, Easter eggs were flung from the table. One night, while watching TV in bed, the owner witnessed a black form in the shape of a head and shoulders peek in the door at him and then retreat. He heard a voice say, "No. Don't. I'll kill you!" as he brushed his teeth one morning. His children spoke about the man they could see "with the mean eyes."

And according to the Pennsylvania Paranormal Association (PPA), "Reported Activity" at the former Santee Wapwallopen residence included:

> The initial claims ... have reported hearing voices, seeing shadows, and black mass-like figures. Objects moving by themselves have been witnessed. A man has been seen standing at the top of a staircase, looking out a window. Two young children, a boy and a girl, have been seen walking past a doorway. The family dog would

begin to bark aggressively with its hair standing on end for no apparent reason, and a man with mean-looking eyes was reportedly witnessed standing in a hallway.

Santee, the son of the late Dr. Charles L. and Verna Lloyd Santee, was the last surviving member of his immediate family. Santee married Edith Rundle in 1928 and divorced in 1942. They had one child, a daughter, Ruth, born in 1930. He married Betty Addis of Cumberland, Maryland, a poet, who died in 1962. His obituary said:

> Dr. Frederick LaMotte Santee died on April 11, 1980, after a long battle with liver failure. He was seventy-two. His body is buried at the Old River Church, north of Wapwallopen, PA. The Rev. Chelley Laite, the pastor of St. John's United Church of Christ, officiated.

Called "the greatest abstract thinker of the 20th Century," his gravestone cryptically read, "I shall return when Spring's shadow trails."

Chapter 22

Richard Sharpe Shaver

"The truly educated man is that rare individual who can separate reality from illusion."
Author unknown.

Fate brought Raymond Alfred Palmer (1910–1977) and Richard Sharpe Shaver (1907–1975) into each other's lives. This collision of literary minds from a bygone era combined Shaver's pseudoscience with Palmer's entrepreneurial mysticism. Together, they promoted the possibility of alien beings dwelling in subterranean caverns and outer space.

Ray Palmer was only seven years old when a violent accident shattered his spine. His growth was stunted after an unsuccessful operation. He would suffer a lifetime of health-related issues as a deformed hunchback who stood about four feet tall.

(L-R) Richard Sharpe Shaver and RAP
(Ray A. Palmer). During Science Fiction's
Golden Age, the Shaver-Palmer tag team
created "The Shaver Mystery," a national
phenomenon triggering a considerable
cult following and an FBI investigation.
(Photo courtesy of Richard Toronto.)

Although he lived a reclusive, almost paranoid existence,
Palmer found refuge in fantasy. He embraced the world of
1930s science fiction—worlds created not of hard
science and fact but of imagination and possibility.
Palmer inhabited the world of pulp fiction. It was an era
before man walked upon the moon, before thousands of
spy satellites cluttered the skies, and before Kenneth
Arnold saw nine flying discs skipping above Mount
Rainier.

In 1938, Ziff-Davis Publishing acquired *Amazing Stories*
and recruited Palmer to become the editor. Palmer
deserved the job, having already proven his mettle
through *The Comet*, the first science fiction fanzine, and
later *Fantasy Magazine*.

Berwick, Pennsylvania

In 1898 Ziba Rice Shaver married Grace Taylor and found employment at the American Car and Foundry Company in Berwick, Pennsylvania, along the banks of the Susquehanna River. Grace, residing in Shavertown, joined him two years later, and their son, Richard, was born on October 7, 1907. Years later, after teaming with Ray Palmer to form a sci-fi tag team that enthralled the nation and got the attention of the FBI, Shaver would go on to become Berwick's most fantastic personality.

I Remember Lemuria!

Shaver's journey into high strangeness began after he married artist Sophie Gurvich. Her Jewish family did not approve of Richard, and his Protestant family did not approve of Sophie.

Richard found employment at Detroit's Briggs Auto Body Plant, as a welder. Soon, Shaver heard telepathic voices transmitted through his welding gun. He believed the voices were torturing him.

Shaver, an amateur writer, submitted a ten-thousand-word document titled "A Warning to Future Man" to *Amazing Stories*. According to his story, Shaver wrote that, in 1932, while working at the Briggs Auto Plant, he was able to telepathically eavesdrop on "malign entities dwelling in caverns deep within the Earth."

According to messages he inexplicably heard through his welder's gun, a group known as the Elder Race, after fleeing the planet, left behind two groups of offspring—one, the "Teros," a benevolent humanoid group, and the sadistic "Deros," or "detrimental robots."

Shaver learned that the Deros kidnapped and sexually tortured humans and ate the flesh of others. They were especially brutal towards women. Shaver's narrative was strange and rambling. He alleged to have discovered an ancient Proto-World language he called Mantong, the source of all earthly language. Every sound had a hidden meaning, and by applying a formula to any word in any language, one could decode a secret meaning from any word, name, or phrase.

Although Shaver's manuscript was dismissed and thrown into the waste can by an editor, Palmer retrieved it, always looking for the next sensational headline.

Palmer edited and rewrote Shaver's "A Warning to Future Man"—eliminating much of the sadomasochistic content toward women—and retitled the now thirty-one-thousand-word manuscript "I Remember Lemuria!" He published it in the March 1945 issue of *Amazing Stories*.

The issue sold out, and the magazine's circulation increased from about 135,000 to 185,000. Palmer claimed to have received thousands of letters in response from people who alleged to have heard similar voices. "Shaver Mystery Club" societies were created in several cities. The controversy gained some notice in the mainstream press at the time, including a mention in a 1951 issue of *Life* magazine.

Shaver was prolific in his letters to *Amazing Stories,* such as his "Formula from the Underworld," which described the evil Deros as "fearfully anemic jitterbugs, small, with pipestem arms and legs, pot bellies, huge protruding, wide eyes, and idiotically grinning mouths."

Between 1945 and 1948, Palmer published the letters as "The Shaver Mystery." He strongly implied that the stories were authentic accounts of an ancient subterranean civilization. In other words, Palmer implied that Shaver's stories were true. Shaver additionally claimed that the Deros imprisoned and tortured him with their "damnable rays."

For the next few years, much of the content of *Amazing Stories* was related to the Shaver Mystery. Some questioned if Shaver's tale was science fiction or science fact. Shaver always averred that his story was true, although the location of the entrance to this underground world of Titans and Deros was never revealed. Many science fiction fans organized letter-writing campaigns in protest. Palmer printed a number of critical or skeptical letters sent to him and occasionally rebutted or replied to such letters in print. Bruce Lanier Wright notes, "The young Harlan Ellison, later a famously abrasive writer, allegedly badgered [Palmer] into admitting that the Shaver Mystery was a 'publicity grabber.' When the story came out, Palmer angrily responded that this was "hardly the same thing as calling it a hoax."

The Hollow Earth Theory

Richard Sharpe Shaver was not the only one to talk about subterranean civilizations. Throughout recorded history, people have believed in a hollow earth, which has been mentioned in numerous creation myths and in popular literature.

Although accused of perpetuating a classic hoax, it is interesting to trace Shaver's literary inspirations. Shaver's skill resided in the fact that he was a widely read and adept student of pulp fiction and fantasy writers. Other themes by Edgar Rice Burroughs, Jules Verne and H. P. Lovecraft's Cthulhu mythos echo strongly throughout Shaver's stories, including James Churchward's Mu books. Shaver borrowed heavily from H. G. Wells's *Time Machine*—the evil "Dero" hint at H. G. Well's subterranean Morlocks—and often compared them to "the Horla," de Maupassant's invisible tormentor,

He was also familiar with Charles Fort, quoting him frequently, and John Cleves Symmes, recognized as the most famous of the early hollow earth theory advocates. In 1818 Symmes endorsed the idea that the earth was hollow, organizing a private expedition of two sailing vessels, the *Seraph* and the *Annawan*, to embark on a mission to locate the holes leading into this hollow earth. Although newly elected President Andrew Jackson halted the mission, interest in other exploratory ventures remained, and stories of subterranean civilizations persisted.

The hollow earth theory was popular in pre-science times before geologists determined that Earth's core contained a mass of scorching and life-killing magma, rendering the region uninhabitable by any subterranean civilizations.

A 1692 scientific paper by Edmund Halley (of Halley's Comet fame) submitted that Earth consisted of a shell about eight hundred km thick, with two inner concentric shells and an innermost core with the same approximate diameter as the planet Mars. Halley believed that the inner earth could be inhabited. Later, in the seventeenth century, Leonhard Euler proposed that a single-shell hollow earth contained a small sun that provided light and warmth for another inhabited inner-earth civilization.

Others promoted the radical hypothesis. *The Hollow Globe*, published in 1868 by Professor W. F. Lyons, articulated another hollow earth premise. Marshall Gardner's *A Journey to the Earth's Interior* (1913) proposed that an interior sun radiated within the Earth. Gardner even built a working model of his hollow earth and had it patented.

Some of these theories were elaborate hoaxes. Rosicrucian leader Raymond W. Bernard published *The Hollow Earth – the Greatest Geographical Discovery in History Made by Admiral Richard E. Byrd in the Mysterious Land Beyond the Poles – the True Origin of the Flying Saucers* in 1964.

Ypsilanti State Hospital

Palmer and Shaver's relationship intersected between delusion and crass exploitation. To that end, Palmer was more adept at self-promotion than maintaining his friend's confidentiality. Palmer publicly revealed that Shaver was mentally ill. He said that Shaver spent eight years, not in the Cavern World as a prisoner of the Deros but in a mental ward at Michigan's Ypsilanti State Hospital.

The multitalented Shaver is indeed the stuff of legends. However, his greatest accomplishment was advocating against punitive treatment in mental institutions. His Shaver Mystery provided evidence of the cruelty patients endured in the guise of "treatment." Mental institutions have historically used questionable treatment practices, brought to our attention through Hollywood films such as *Bedlam, Girl Interrupted, One Flew Over the Cuckoo's Nest*, and *Shutter Island*. Is it possible that Shaver experienced every bit of that horror at the Ypsilanti State Hospital?

Shaver prolifically wrote about the "damnable rays" that tormented him throughout his life, most likely reflecting the horrors he experienced while hospitalized. Psychiatrists in the 1940s had a primitive understanding of mental illness, commonly using shock and water-based therapies. Effective psychotropic medications had not yet been developed, and severe cases of depression, mania, and schizophrenia were almost untreatable. Physical restraints were standard. According to Encyclopedia.com, for patients suffering from "melancholia" or clinical depression, shock treatment or electroconvulsive therapy (ECT) was generally used:

> The patient would be strapped to a hospital table with electrodes attached to the sides of his or her head. Patients were usually sedated because spasms caused by the shock could injure neck muscles. A current of between seventy and one hundred volts was applied to the head for one-tenth of a second. The shock knocked the patient unconscious but usually revived within a few minutes. This treatment was repeated three times a day for up to eight weeks.

Treatment boiled down to finances. Early shock therapies relied on drugs such as insulin, camphor, or Metrazol. Insulin injections sent patients into a deep coma, while Metrazol caused convulsions and spasms.

ECT, however, was cheaper and more easily controlled than drug therapies. It is still used to treat depression. Although it causes memory loss and confusion and sometimes leaves patients with a sore neck, it is not considered dangerous. Schizophrenic patients like Shaver, however, responded better to the drug treatments, viewing ECT as barbaric and punitive. Concerning Palmer's Ypsilanti State Hospital disclosure, Shaver responded by adhering to his bizarre story about the hollow earth but also addressed the accusations about his mental health:

My problems, I realized, did not stem from cognitive impairment. I wasn't crazy in the traditional sense, even though, at times, I felt like I was being driven mad by the hateful rays that were being beamed at me by the people below. No, I was sane in an insane world.

I have always wondered how many people, who have been institutionalized because they were diagnosed as crazy, were, in fact, victims, such as myself, of the damnable rays. Did they think that they were insane because of the voices they heard in their heads and voluntarily committed themselves? Even today, I wonder if most mental illness forms are not insidious attacks from the world below.

The Shaver Mystery

During Science Fiction's Golden Age, Richard Sharpe Shaver rose to the head of the class as their illustrious sleight-of-hand con artist. Although he provided a meaningful distraction during the war years, Shaver remains unknown to the masses.

The curious tag team of Richard Sharpe Shaver and Raymond Palmer created a cult following that hungered for more. "The Shaver Mystery" became a national phenomenon, providing a positive distraction for a war-weary public and a strange therapy for those who claimed to hear voices.

Shaver's most adept and passionate
researcher, Richard Toronto, is the author
of *War Over Lemuria* (McFarland &
Company, Inc, 2013). For fans of the
hollow earth theory and the Shaver
Mystery, this 256-page document is the
Holy Grail and a must read. Nothing else
compares. Toronto is a former newspaper
reporter with a BA in journalism from
California State University Sacramento.

Critics of the "Shaver Mystery" suspected that its author
suffered from symptoms of paranoid schizophrenia. But
although he heard voices, he was considered somewhat
of a genius. Richard Toronto's book *War Over Lemuria*
listed other literary geniuses, including poet William
Blake, scientist Galileo, and sci-fi writer Philip K. Dick,
who suffered from psychosis.

Nonetheless, Shaver's delusions were implausibly
accepted by many (primarily members of the fanatical
Shaver Mystery Clubs) claiming to have heard the Deros'
voices. Shaver gave birth to the modern-day version of

the hollow earth theory and added to the fabric of Coal Region mythology, thematically linked to the Sheppton mining disaster.

Even stranger was what Palmer and Shaver contributed to the annals of ufology and, because of that, were investigated by the FBI In a 1947 FBI Office memorandum, "Flying discs, Richard Shaver," the FBI concluded that Palmer and Shaver conspired to create the "flying disc hysteria" gripping the nation. They said, "It is possible, therefore, that Palmer and Shaver created the entire flying disc theory."

Outsider Artist

But Shaver had another trick up his sleeve. In the mid-1960s, he moved to Summit, Arkansas, with his wife, Dottie. He spent his final years as an artist. Living in obscurity, he searched for physical evidence of ancient prehistoric races. He claimed to have discovered certain rocks, which he called "rock books"—created by the ancient Atlanteans and embedded with legible pictures and texts.

For years he wrote about the rock books, photographed them, and made paintings of the images. He even organized a mail-order "Rock Book" lending library, mailing slices of polished agate with descriptions of what writings, drawings, and photographs he claimed were archived inside the stone.

About 1,127 miles from his birthplace of Berwick, PA

Shaver died in 1975—his legacy known only to a select few. After his death, he was recognized as an "outsider artist" and a creative talent. A collection of his "Rock Book" artwork and photographs have been exhibited at the California Institute of the Arts, the Santa Monica Museum of Art, the Guggenheim Gallery of Chapman University in Orange County, California, and New York City and San Francisco art galleries. In 2004, a traveling exhibition of "outsider photography" titled *Create and Be Recognized* originated at San Francisco's Yerba Buena Center for the Arts.

He worked as a laborer, a welder, and an artist. Some claimed he was also a genius, pulling off science fiction's biggest con job. Metaphorically, through his Shaver Mystery, he advocated against questionable treatment in mental health institutions, which may have been his most worthy accomplishment and legacy.

Shaver was sixty-eight years old when he died. He is buried in the Layton Cemetery in Yellville, Arkansas, about 1,127 miles from his birthplace of Berwick, Pennsylvania.

Chapter 23
The Philadelphia Experiment

Several books, motion pictures, and documentaries have investigated the USS *Eldridge*, the destroyer believed to have been rendered invisible and teleported to Norfolk, Virginia, during the secret 1943 Philadelphia Experiment. (US Navy archives.)

William L. Moore, Carlos Miguel Allende, and Dr. Morris K. Jessup collectively gave birth to the legend of the Philadelphia Experiment.

Dr. Morris Jessup

Dr. Morris Jessup was an astronomer and paranormal researcher who published four books during the 1950s —*The Case for the UFO* (1955), *The UFO Annual* (1956), *UFOs and the Bible* (1956), and *The Expanding Case for the UFO* (1957). Although he was never awarded a doctorate, many publications called him "Dr. Jessup." Still, his impact on ufology was undeniable, and according to Nick Redfern, *The Case for the UFO* was of special interest:

> His book was a detailed study of theoretical power sources for UFOs: what was it that made them fly? How could they perform incredible aerial feats, such as coming to a complete stop in the skies, hovering at incredible heights? Jessup believed that the vitally important answers lay in the domain of gravity. Or, as he saw it: antigravity.

Jessup's theories took an unexpected turn after one of his readers disclosed information that seemed to validate his nonconventional concepts. It came from ex-merchant mariner Carlos Allende who claimed to have witnessed a strange experiment at the Philadelphia Naval Shipyard sometime around October 28, 1943. At the time he was serving aboard the USS *Furuseth*. According to Allende, the USS *Eldridge*, a destroyer escort, was made invisible and teleported to Norfolk, Virginia, for several minutes and then reappeared in the Philadelphia yard. The ship's crew suffered various side effects, including insanity, intangibility, and being "frozen" in place. Several died in the experiment, according to the story.

Allende, almost single-handedly, was responsible for creating the story. In 1955, he shipped a package marked "Happy Easter" to the US Office of Naval Research. Inside was a copy of Jessup's *The Case for the UFO: Unidentified Flying Saucers,* heavily annotated with handwritten notes written in several shades of blue ink. This package caught the attention of the Navy's "Special Weapons" division, now curious about what Jessup knew about the Philadelphia Experiment.

The plot thickened. Soon after, Allende began sending a series of letters to Jessup, warning him not to investigate the levitation of UFOs. Allende believed that, based on Albert Einstein's unified field theory, Jessup's work was too dangerous. As Jessup himself writes:

> It was written in pencils, ink scribbles, in the middle of a sentence, words could suddenly begin with capital letters, there were a lot of mistakes, punctuation marks were scattered randomly, and some sentences were underlined in different colors. The letter itself had a Pennsylvania stamp.

Despite Allende's childlike sketches and abstract thoughts, Jessup was surprised with the letter's contents, including sections denoting gravitation and propulsion systems. Furthermore, the annotations appeared to detail a debate *among three individuals* discussing Jessup's ideas about flying saucers.

Allende's account of the event has become the stuff of legends. But who was the mysterious Carl Allen or Carlos Miguel Allende? According to William L. Moore's *The Philadelphia Experiment*, Carl Allen was the youngest of three children. He was born to an Irish father and a Gypsy mother, on May 31, 1925, on a farm outside of New Kensington, a small western Pennsylvania town. Allen, who quit school "in his ninth year," was described as moody and a somewhat reckless youngster who "liked to lose himself in books."

Popular Legend

Allende said that countless deaths and horrible mutilations resulted from this experiment, which involved artificially induced electromagnetic force fields and a process known as degaussing. For decades, the US government has denied the Philadelphia Experiment; however, it has been well documented that the Allied powers conducted extensive research with degaussing to evade deadly sea mines in the Atlantic.

Numerous books and motion pictures have been based on this event, while additional researchers and purported witnesses have added to the narrative. Glen Ford, Capt. USNR, movie actor turned producer, released a motion picture about the incident called *The Day Havock Struck*. Others contributing to the account included Charles Berlitz, Dr. Franklin Reno, Dr. Albert Einstein, Riley Crabb, Gray Barker, and Frederick G. Tracy.

Frederick G. Tracy

Frederick G. Tracy, LTCM Ret., served in the United States Navy from 1944 to 1954. Like many sailors serving on the east coast, Tracy heard ominous rumors of the Philadelphia Experiment. These weird stories came from official sources describing a degaussing operation that went haywire, causing widespread destruction

Frederick G. Tracy served aboard the USS *Antietam* (CV-36), an Essex Class aircraft carrier. He was personally involved in a 1945 degaussing operation similar to that of the Philadelphia Experiment—and claimed to have evidence that the secret experiment actually happened. (Maxim W. Furek photograph.)

During World War II, magnetic mines were wreaking havoc on Allied shipping crossing the Atlantic. The degaussing technique, invented in Great Britain, was a secret procedure that neutralized the magnetic field of a ship's hull using electricity generated through massive cables. The method made them less vulnerable to enemy mines and invisible to radar, as it rendered the vessel and its metal parts nonmagnetic.

Tracy recounted that during a degaussing experiment at the Philadelphia Navy Yard, the USS *Eldridge* and its crew were made invisible. After reappearing in Norfolk, Virginia, the ship was teleported back to Philadelphia for a few moments, flicking on and off like an erratic lightbulb.

Serving aboard the USS *Antietam* (CV-36), an Essex Class aircraft carrier, Tracy was personally involved in a 1945 degaussing operation conducted in a top-secret Annapolis, Maryland, installation. The *Antietam* was escorted upriver and secreted alongside a massive power station two hundred and fifty feet wide and five hundred feet long. There, the carrier began to take on shore steam and electricity. Wrapped with three-inch-diameter cables spaced fifteen feet apart, the *Antietam* was bombarded with vast amounts of electricity for three days, time enough to penetrate the eight-inch-thick steel hull.

Unfortunately, the intended degaussing procedure brought about harmful effects. Tracy suffered from bilateral bulla emphysema, a condition requiring him to carry about a supply of liquid oxygen. Tracy was exposed to a dose of intense radiation that rendered his lung capillaries virtually useless. He believed it was connected to the experiments. At sixty years of age, he had shock-white hair and glassy, reddened eyes. Yet he appeared to be years older. The degaussing produced radiation, which excited the basic cell structure, affecting heart rate and respiration. It also caused, according to Tracy, an increase in fungus growth and hair loss. An outbreak of sores among the crew took months to clear up. Tracy remembered that some men resorted to homemade concoctions of raw eggs and Mazola oil as a tonic for their hair and skin dryness.

Tracy claims he experienced the degaussing procedure again while on duty in the Yellow Sea, an exposure equal to two hundred and twenty volts and 6,500 amps of electricity. Over 1,340,000 watts of electricity bombarded Tracy and his mates for three consecutive days. Usually, the force field would begin to break down after thirty days, and then the ship would start up its generators aboard the ship. During the Yellow Sea procedure, however, the generators operated twenty-four hours per day due to the numerous sea mines.

Forrestal's Report

Citing an official document from 1945, Tracy believed he had proof that the Philadelphia Experiment occurred. Due to widespread rumors and low morale, Secretary of the Navy, Admiral Forrestal, issued a directive clarifying the allegations. The crew were sworn to secrecy and repeatedly warned that it would be an act of treason to reveal the directive's contents. This official memo was read to them during the final days of World War II, sometime between May 8, 1945, and May 19, 1945.

Tracy recollected Forrestal's report, acknowledging that the *Eldridge*'s degaussing operation had gone wrong:

Maxim W. Furek

It was then decided to stop the degaussing operation to see what was wrong. The ship could not be seen, although all the electrical cables could still be [seen] in a coil position as if being supported. The boat was not there, nor was any member of its crew present. At the Navy yard, a mist appeared and grew heavy. Finally, the ship reappeared. When the boat was boarded, severe damage was found to the ship and terrible effects on the crew. The names and the logbook were exchanged with that of the USS *Weekiwachee* to prevent the incident from being traced.

Tracy said that in 1949, the Philadelphia incident went before a United States Congress closed session. After hearing all the facts, Congress ordered that all information about the event be buried and the ship destroyed. The vessel was exploded by using a method of controlled C-4 detonation. The remaining pieces were clandestinely buried in the Arizona desert. Years later, writing to Dr. Roger Penrose of the Mathematical Institute of Oxford, England, Tracy stated:

My concern is that of possible adverse detrimental effects of degaussing, which may have put the entire ship's crew in harm's way ... The operation lasted for about three days. The Navy's main concern was the war effort. Unfortunately, the crew didn't count.

Despite eyewitness accounts from Tracy and others, the US Navy maintains that no such experiment was ever conducted, and that the details contradict well-established facts about the USS *Eldridge*. Furthermore, authorities deny that the Philadelphia Experiment ever happened and that the physics the experiment is claimed to be based on is nonexistent.

1988 letter from the National Archives and Records Administration calling the Philadelphia Experiment a practical joke that got out of hand. (Maxim W. Furek collection.)

After contacting the National Archives and Records Administration in Washington, DC, Richard A. von Doenhoff stated to this writer:

> As far as the Department of the Navy can determine, the fictitious story of the destroyer

Maxim W. Furek

(USS *Eldridge*) from the Delaware River off the League Island Navy Yard to Hampton Roads and back in 1943 began as a practical joke among staff members of the Naval Research Laboratory here in Washington. The humorous commentary on a theoretical paper on electromagnetism got out of hand and soon achieved the status of fact and legend.

Something Happened in Philadelphia

In almost every paranormal case, dramatic and erroneous speculation, often rife with extraterrestrial beings and interdimensional travel, thrusts us into the La-La Land of absurdity. Moore's assumptions came closer to science fiction than to scientific methodology, based primarily on correspondence between Allende, the government, and Jessup. And although Moore attracted the mainstream reader, his findings lacked critical peer-reviewed and evidence-based research. According to author Barna William Donovan, the conclusions in Moore's book, *The Philadelphia Experiment: Project Invisibility*:

> ... were dismissed mainly even by the most committed conspiracy and supernatural buffs as nothing more than a shoddy, uncritical repeat of a lingering and completely unsubstantiated urban myth.

Donovan heaped the same criticism on Moore's *The Roswell Incident*, calling it "a collection of wild hearsay," offering second- and thirdhand accounts. Moore's books, although commercially successful, did little to promote the paranormal as a serious scientific topic.

Still, remnants of the truth are out there, waiting to be uncovered. As far as it can be determined, the *Eldridge* was involved in a secret operation using an amplified degaussing technique. The goal was an attempt to confuse the ship's magnetic signature. It was hoped that this degaussing technique would protect the ship from sea mines capable of detecting a ship's magnetic field as it passed near the mine. Contrary to Hollywood movies, most torpedoes didn't hit the sides of boats, they are detonated underneath the vessels with a magnetic trigger that senses the ship's magnetic signature.

While William L. Moore and Charles Berlitz sensationalized the event for commercial gain, Jessup viewed the event through a scientific lens. Jessup believed that the USS *Eldridge* was involved in an experiment producing a time-warp phenomenon, possibly connected to Albert Einstein's unified field theory.

Antigravity

Since Newton published his Theory of Universal Gravitation over four hundred years ago, researchers have desperately attempted to develop an opposing antigravity theory. Antigravity devices represent the Holy Grail promising to break us free from natural laws and transcend the stars and planets.

Newton demonstrated that gravity was a predictable force that acts on all matter in the universe. It is a function of both mass and distance. Each particle of matter attracts every other particle with a force that is directly proportional to the product of their masses and inversely proportional to the square distance between them.

Newton believed that gravity is a force that pulls objects to the ground and keeps the planets in orbit around the sun. Therefore, the farther apart the particles are, the less massive the particles are, and the less the gravitational force. The sun is the most massive body in the solar system, exerting the strongest gravitational pull on the planets. Because Mercury is closest, it experiences the strongest pull. As a result, Mercury is the planet that goes the fastest along its orbit.

Is there a way to counter gravity's influence? The possibility of reducing or canceling gravity's effect is tempting. It is a theme repeated in sundry science-fiction films and the varied incarnations of *Star Trek* and *Star Wars*. An impressive list of individuals have attempted to discover this possible means of propulsion.

Albert Einstein was immersed in his Unified Force Field theory during World War II. This model proposed that the three fundamental universal forces—gravitational, electromagnetic, and nuclear—are all controlled by a single unknown source. Einstein's theory remains controversial and unproven. The US military and the federal government have formally researched antigravity, propellant-less propulsion, and mass-reduction technologies since the 1950s. Their so-called "UFO patents" have involved the American Institute of Physics, NASA, the American Institute of Aeronautics and Astronautics, and the Air Force Research Laboratory. And in 1992, Russian physicist Evgeny Podkletnov, who had claimed to have successfully tested a device that shields an object from gravity, came up empty-handed. There have been others, as well. According to writer Robert Lamb:

> Antigravity technology would revolutionize space exploration and energy production. It would slash the energy demands of travel and transportation. First, however, we'd just have to drastically alter our understanding of physics and figure out how to counter this powerful force.

As such, antigravity technology remains the Holy Grail and a red flag. There's been no shortage of hoaxes, conspiracy theories, and credibility-straining reports regarding its research.

Most scientists believe that because of what we know about physics, aerospace propulsion, and the laws that govern the universe, antigravity isn't possible. Still, there are those who passionately believe the opposite.

Because Jessup was getting closer to the truth, he attracted the government's attention. Jessup was summoned to the Office of Naval Research in 1957 by Captain Sidney Sherby and Commander George W. Hoover. After being presented with the annotated copy of his book, Jessup recognized that the handwriting resembled Allende's.

Dead Men Don't Tell Tales

On April 19, 1959, Jessup contacted his friend, oceanographer Dr. J. Manson Valentine. Claiming to have made a breakthrough regarding the Philadelphia Experiment, Jessup arranged to meet with him the next day. According to Valentine:

> He was convinced that the Navy, in seeking to create a magnetic cloud for camouflage purposes in October 1943, had uncovered a potential that could temporarily, and if strong enough, perhaps permanently, rearrange the molecular structure of people and materials so that they would pass into another dimension with further implications of predictable and as yet uncontrolled teleportation.

Jessup never revealed his breakthrough discovery to the world. His career swirling in controversy, the scientist was found dead the following day. A Florida park attendant discovered the body on April 20, 1959. Jessup's 1958 Chevy Station Wagon was located in Miami's Matheson Hammock Park. The car's engine was still running, and a hosepipe attached to the exhaust had been fed through the driver's side window. All evidence seemed to indicate that Jessup had taken his own life.

What exactly happened during the Philadelphia Experiment? Fred Tracy, Dr. Morris Jessup, and others believe there was a horrible accident that has never been fully revealed. What we are left with is a widespread disinformation campaign and unproven speculation. Researcher William L. Moore, co-author of *The Philadelphia Experiment,* contended that the Navy successfully rendered the USS *Eldridge* invisible and then teleported the vessel over two hundred miles—killing two men in the process.

But Moore's conclusion leaves much to be desired. After over seventy-five years, the Philadelphia Experiment remains one of the most obscure wartime mysteries and an anomaly that simply refuses to go away. And although Jessup's death was considered an apparent suicide, some believed he had been murdered for what he knew about UFOs, antigravity propulsion, and the Philadelphia Experiment.

Chapter 24
Strange Highways

"Strange Highways" is the end of the journey. This final chapter is an attempt to tie together any loose ends and provide some last-minute additional information. It will also serve as a sort of regional index. The following paranormal areas, receiving the most coverage in this text, are as follows: Philadelphia Zone I, the Coal Region, Zone II, the Chestnut Ridge Zone III, and Lancaster Zone IV.

ZONE I: Bill Baldini, *The Blob,* Gary Heidnik, the Pennhurst Asylum, the Philadelphia Experiment, Fred Tracy, UFOs.

In 1959, when the first episode of *The Twilight Zone* aired, "two out of three Americans listed the possibility of nuclear war as the nation's most urgent problem." There was widespread fear of nuclear conflict between the United States and the Soviet Union and of radioactive fallout. This fear manifested itself in popular culture in mutant monster movies like *Them!* (1954) and *Godzilla* (1956).

The Blob (1958) was another radiation-spawned-monster movie churned out for the insatiable teenage market. Paramount Pictures distributed it as a double feature with *I Married a Monster from Outer Space*.

In Steve McQueen's film debut, a meteorite's alien lifeform crashes to earth. Growing as large as a house, the organism consumes everything in its path in the small communities of Phoenixville and Downingtown, Pennsylvania. The monstrosity appears at the Colonial Theater ("Healthfully Air Conditioned"), oozing into the auditorium during a midnight screening of *Daughter of Horror*.

The Blob, like *The Philadelphia Experiment*, had some factual basis. According to *Mental Floss*'s Jake Rossen, police officers Joe Keenan and John Collins claimed to have seen something falling from the Philadelphia skies on September 26, 1950:

> Searching the area, they found a curious ooze dangling from a telephone pole that seemed to move. When Collins reached out to touch it— apparently, he was not well-versed in the rules of horror movies—it left behind a sticky residue and then simply evaporated.

Ester Inglis-Arkell wrote that various accounts give it different gelatinous qualities:

It seemed to be about six feet in diameter, purple, filled with strange crystals and giving off a mist. Naturally, one of the police officers put his hand right in it. It left a "odorless sticky residue" on his hand, but fortunately didn't eat him and his fellow officers, giving the terrified populace no choice but to freeze it and fly it to the arctic. Instead, it seemed to sense that it wasn't wanted and sadly dissolved into nothing, supposedly leaving the grass underneath it unbent.

Although no explanation was ever presented as to the substance's origin, two more police officers and the FBI were called to help deal with the mystery. Eight years later, local filmmakers Jack Harris and Irvine H. Millgate created *The Blob*. Though not explicitly based on the 1950 incident, their proximity to it meant they would have been aware of it. Irvin Yeaworth directed the cult film remade in 1988 with Kevin Dillon.

The Pennhurst Asylum

Along with Gettysburg, the Pennhurst State School and Hospital has the reputation of being the Commonwealth's most haunted place. Pennhurst was originally known as the Eastern Pennsylvania State Institution for the Feeble-Minded and Epileptic. The hospital admitted its first patient in 1908 during a time when treatment was more akin to torture—a similar ordeal experienced by artist Richard Sharp Shaver, as noted in chapter 22. The Pennhurst State School and Hospital was intended to be an asylum for the mentally and physically handicapped but lapsed into one of the most torturous places in America. For decades, the hospital, located in Spring City, operated under abysmal conditions. Here, criminals, orphans, and even immigrants were housed, deemed "unfit for citizenship." There was no curative treatment. Typically, the patients were locked away until they died.

Twenty-six-year-old Bill Baldini was a local WCAU Channel 10 reporter who got a tip on the abuse at Pennhurst. In a five-part television series, Baldini helped break the news of the Pennhurst nightmare. One doctor admitted asking about which injection could cause his patients the most pain without permanent injury.

He revealed that he had a hard time even keeping his video crew working, as they were so repulsed and sickened by what they saw that nobody wanted to return.

Baldini's shocking television disgusted his viewers. His exposé described wards of young children in metal cages, lying, for days, in their own waste. In another harsh exposé, Philadelphia writer Kim Magaraci described the squalor:

> The series aired in Philadelphia in 1968. Naked, starving residents, children tied to beds, and doctors admitting horrible acts shocked the public, who had long ignored the isolated asylum. Though it was clear that Pennhurst needed to be shut down, it took nearly twenty years for the asylum to finally be shut down. In those twenty years, abuse

remained rampant, children and adults were treated horribly, and Pennhurst became known as "The Shame of Pennsylvania."

Pennhurst Asylum stayed open until 1987. It was reopened to the public as a haunted house attraction, convincing patrons that the abandoned building is haunted by the spirits of former patients.

Now, with visions of a financial windfall, Pennhurst has evolved into a successful commercial venture. The company's website reads:

> Pennhurst, the legendary haunted hospital complex, has opened its doors after being abandoned for 25 years! Pennhurst haunted asylum is Pennsylvania's Scariest destination haunted house! The fear is real at Pennhurst!

ZONE II: Nick Adams, the Bagunk, Centralia, Ed Conrad, the Haunted Hinsdale House, Pope John XXIII, Father Daniel Ignatius McDermott, Dr. Frederick LaMotte Santee, Richard Sharpe Shaver, Sheppton, *Silent Hill*, the Smurl haunting, Rev. Alphonsus Trabold, Ed and Lorraine Warren.

It is possible that Carlos M. Allende and Richard Sharpe Shaver were among Pennsylvania's foremost hoaxers— con artists who worked the rich loam of science fiction and the paranormal. Both gentlemen operated during the unsettling days of the 1940s, as the world came together with modern-day swords and spears, intent on destroying each other.

While Shaver was reciting his tale of being abducted by subterranean ghoulies, Allende told of a US Navy experiment that rendered a destroyer invisible. Both had us believing the impossible. In an era before computers and instantaneous communications, they bridged the gap between pseudoscience and scientific fact, taking their audience on a trip that has never been replicated.

While Allende remains an obscure footnote, Shaver influenced writers, including Harlan Ellison and Phillip K. Dick. UFO researcher Timothy Green Beckley said that Shaver predicted the advent of flying saucers before Kenneth Arnold's 1947 sighting. Additionally, according to Beckley, Shaver described ancient astronauts visiting the Earth, claiming that man's "Gods" were travelers from outer space—decades before Erich von Daniken achieved worldwide fame with *Chariots of the Gods*.

The Berwick guy pulled it off with his sleight-of-hand, rabbit-in-the-hat trick.

Dr. Frederick LaMotte Santee

In "A Biography of Dr. Frederick LaMotte Santee," Blau Stern Schwarz transformed the fascinating story of Santee into unsubstantiated mythology. According to Schwarz, Santee was employed as Adolf Hitler's homeopathic doctor.

But Schwarz, who claims to have researched Santee extensively, is incorrect. At that time, Santee was not a practicing medical doctor but a student of classical languages. Santee was about twenty-one years old (from 1926 to 1927) when he studied in Germany. He did not begin his pre-medical program at Vanderbilt University until 1934, receiving his MD from Johns Hopkins University in 1938.

Hitler would have been thirty-eight years old in 1927, six years from his rise to power. Hitler was chancellor of Germany from 1933 to 1945.

The truth is that Theodor Gilbert Morell (1886–1948) was heavily into homeopathic medicine. Morell was Hitler's physician and was recognized for his unconventional treatments. For example, Morell regularly injected Hitler with a solution that he called "Vitamultin," which contained methamphetamine.

Daughter Tao

Schwarz also writes that Santee adopted Tao, the daughter of Hitler and an Englishwoman who escaped Germany before World War II. But again, there is no record of this child, but according to extensive documentation, Hitler did father a child.

A Frenchwoman, Charlotte Lobjoie, claimed her son, Jean-Marie Loret, was the child of Adolf Hitler. Lobjoie admitted that she and the Fuhrer had an affair when she was only sixteen years old, and he was still just a twenty-eight-year-old German soldier. In 1916, Hitler, a German army corporal, broke from fighting the French in the Picardy region. Jean-Marie Loret was born not long after the affair began in March 1918. His father, Adolf Hitler, had already crossed the border back to Germany. Lobjoie put her son up for adoption in the 1930s, and Jean-Marie Lobjoie became Jean-Marie Loret.

Further documentation was provided in the online reference *Hitler's Children*:

> According to military documents, cash deliveries were made to Lobjoie when Germany occupied France. They also found paintings with Hitler's signature in her attic, and there was a painting Hitler had done that looks just like the woman claiming to have his son.

Loret wrote a memoir in 1981 called *Your Father's Name was Hitler*. However, no official record of this relationship has been made, and Germany's official document still states that Hitler had no children. Loret died in 1985 before DNA testing was an option.

Schwarz did correctly document at least one of Santee's traits. The doctor's well-known obsession with the female leg was witnessed by countless patients who visited his Wapwallopen office. As documented by Schwarz, "He required his nurses and librarians to wear skirts, nylons, and high heels." Sexual proclivities aside, other unproved stories circulated that the Soviet Union hunted Santee because of special knowledge they believed he had obtained about military secrets.

Ed Conrad

Ed Conrad devoted his final days verifying aspects of the Sheppton mythology. By interviewing Dave Fellin, he introduced themes breathing the ether of time travel and ancient aliens.

Fellin had the amazing gift of total recall. Before his death, he left a plethora of notarized letters and taped interviews detailing paranormal experiences. They included his familiar themes of out-of-body experiences and life after death. But there were additional stories, equally bizarre. Fellin testified that he had experienced time travel, witnessing monumental historical events as they actually occurred, and watched the construction of the Egyptian pyramids:

> It was nowhere near the gargantuan task as is generally theorized. It did not require thousands of men working for hundreds of years because not a single multi-ton rock had to be hauled to the site from a great distance. Several blocks were being built at the same time. Each block had twenty to twenty-five Egyptian-looking men carrying pails of what looked like water and what looked like sand, and they were pouring the contents into a wooden form—as concrete is poured today.

Fellin said he traveled with Christopher Columbus as he sailed to America. Columbus was Tyrolean, not Italian, and had yellow hair and a red beard. The secret of his navigational success was simply because he had mastered the use of the compass.

Time travel, flight of the soul, and life after death are the uncanny legacy of Shenandoah's "Truth Dispenser," Ed Conrad, and Sheppton's Dave Fellin.

ZONE III: Carlos M. Allende, Eric Altman, Bigfoot, Chestnut Ridge, Stan Gordon, Gary Heidnik, Kecksburg, Pennsylvania Bigfoot Association, *Silence of the Lambs*, UFOs.

According to Eric Altman, president of the Pennsylvania Bigfoot Association, Pennsylvania ranks #three regarding the prevalence of Bigfoot sightings. Most have been sighted in western Pennsylvania, an area known for the bizarre. Chestnut Ridge, the creepy mountain region south of Pittsburgh, has been the epicenter of UFOs, Bigfoot, and sightings of other anomalies. Portions of Thomas Harris's 1991 psychological horror classic *The Silence of the Lambs* were filmed near Connellsville, in Fayette County. The three-story Victorian house was the fictitious home of serial killer Buffalo Bill, a character based on Gary Heidnik, the real-life Philadelphia serial killer. Heidnik starved and tortured women in an underground pit, a virtual house of horrors.

The 1965 Kecksburg UFO flap wallowed in the same morass of redacted information, government disinformation, and cover-up as did Roswell.

But on a saner note, Kecksburg did not embrace the hysteria that consumed the nation on October 30, 1938, when *The War of the Worlds* was broadcast on Halloween Eve. Orson Welles's *Mercury Theatre on the Air*'s radio program mixed fiction with supposed factual reports of an alien invasion. It is rumored to have caused mass panic and alleged suicides.

ZONE IV: Albatwitches, Bigfoot, hexes, Dean Koontz, Pennsylvania Dutch, powwowing, Tim Renner, Trotterheads, UFOs.

The Commonwealth is noted for an abundance of cryptids, including dogman, the Waterford Sheepman, and the Haycock Mountain mutant albinos, sighted by numerous individuals but never proven to exist. Other anomalies include thunderbirds, mountain lions, and giant snakes. Hayley Williams states:

> Contrary to popular belief, cryptids don't have to be supernatural, mythical or even all that strange— though many popular creatures acquire these characteristics as their legends grow.

In his article, "Top Ten Cryptids Still Roaming Around Pennsylvania," Ricky Rodson asserts:

> Because of the large cities in Pennsylvania, a lot of people question whether or not any of the Cryptids could actually survive in the state. But the truth is that Pennsylvania is the perfect location for cryptids to live. With its dense woodlands, high

mountains, and freshwater streams, the state offers the creatures plenty of places to high [*sic*] and an ample amount of animal life to feed on. And while Pennsylvania may have a large population, most of the people tend to remain in the urban areas far removed from the prowling grounds of these mysterious animals.

These legends are plentiful, beginning with Native Americans and continued by paranormal-loving European immigrants. According to Luzerne County folklore (northwest of Lancaster), the red-eyed Bagunk is a nocturnal creature that has been sighted at St. Michael's and St. Andrew's Cemetery in Glenn Lyon and the old Newport Center Cemetery near Sheatown. Origins vary. One legend states that in the 1970s, a teenager was crushed to death while stripping parts from an abandoned car. The resulting sound of the car jack landing on his chest sounded like BAGUNK! Another possible origin is an unsolved coal miner's murder near Glen Lyon.

In Lancaster County, many residents believe in hexerei, or "witchcraft." The region has long been the hotbed of Pennsylvania Dutch folklore, including rites of powwowing and hexes, themes straddling superstition and commercialism. Colorful hex signs are commonly seen on the sides of barns and houses. Hex signs have many meanings. A cross painted on the handlebar of a door latch is believed to prevent the devil from entering. The signs are understood to cleanse evil and promote good health, fertility, and happiness. Some think they will start or stop the rain.

Strange creatures have been seen in this area as well. Called the "Little Bigfoot," the Albatwitch is a possible verbal corruption of "apple snitcher." According to Amish legend, the shiny and diminutive creature is often described as standing five feet tall. It is said to roam the region near the mysterious Chickies Rock Park area near Columbia, Pennsylvania, and parts of Eastern Pennsylvania along the Susquehanna River. Traditional stories tell that the Albatwitch sits in trees and snacks on apples stolen from unsuspecting people, throwing the digested apple cores at the same people.

The Dutch weren't the only ones to have spotted the creature. The Susquehannock Native Americans tribe depicted the apelike creature on their battle shields.

Eric Altman of the Pennsylvania Bigfoot Association notes, "The Susquehannock Indians of the Lancaster County area shared legends of a small hair-covered man-like creature that inhabited the woods along the Susquehanna River. They called it the Albatwitch or Apple Snatcher."

Albatwitches announce their presence by making a sound like a cracking whip but can also communicate over long distances by smacking flat rocks together. Unfortunately, these "Little Bigfoot" creatures may not still exist. Legend says they were driven to near extinction in the later 1900s.

Trotterhead is another regional cryptid. Because of the monster's ability to run through property and dark trees, the verb "trot" has become incorporated into its name. Also, because it can ruin people's dreamscapes, giving them nightmares, the cryptid has been referred to as a "sleep demon." An excellent description can be found in Patrick J. Donmoyer's book *Powwowing in Pennsylvania: Braucherei and the Ritual of Everyday Life*:

> One of the most celebrated of all written blessings used to protect the house and home from the influence of ... an entity known as the *Trotterkopf*— a name that is not easily translated into English but has been sometimes called "Trotterhead." Among the Pennsylvania Dutch, it was perceived that the Trotterkopf may represent the spiritual form of a witch.

The Hex Book of the Pennsylvania Dutch, The Long Lost Friend, offered a comprehensive protection prayer to keep the Trotterhead from doing harm:

> Trotter head, I forbid thee my house and premises; I forbid thee my horse and cow stable; I forbid thee my bedstead, that thou mayst not breathe upon me; breathe into some other house, until thou hast ascended every hill until thou has counted every fencepost, and until thou hast crossed every water. And thus dear day my come again into my house, in the name of God, the Father, the son, and the Holy Ghost. Amen.

Destined to Remain Unknown

Some things are destined to remain unknown. Seekers of the truth continue to scrutinize anomalies that fall beyond the grasp of science and the failure of words.

Our journey commenced with the *Night of the Living Dead,* a real-life metaphor far removed from the stench and horror of the undead and having nothing to do with zombies. It ended with the Philadelphia Experiment, criticized as an inane science fiction hoax. Nevertheless, some believe something happened during this secret 1943 experiment, still hidden beneath denial and official cover-ups. Researcher William Moore wrote that, in 1951, the Navy, in a review of its wartime experiments, "Discovered that twenty-one of the forty participants had died of fatal heart attacks. These were men in their late 20s and early 30s." Moore said that, despite the government's concealment, the experiment had two significant results:

> The first was mind control, inducing confusion in the enemy. The second was the secret stealth technology that we've since developed to disguise airplanes against radar. The experiment was the grandfather of our whole range of electronic countermeasures.

As a fitting conclusion, many thanks to Pennsylvania-born horror master Dean Koontz for taking a side trip into a Centralia-like ghost town and suggesting our title.

Strange Highways is his 1995 book aptly described as "a journey into subterranean depths where the darkness of the human soul breeds in every conceivable form."

Nothing stays the same, even the tenets of science change, as wind currents shift, icebergs melt, and planets rotate slightly away from their regular spin, being pulled closer to the sun. Science helps us understand the natural realm, but science has limitations. It cannot explain the world of the supernatural and things that go bump in the night. These aspects of weirdness slot conveniently into a category that defies explanation and are themes touched upon in *Coal Region Hoodoo*.

On a personal note, the Men in Black have suggested that I post the following message:

> Whether you loved or hated *Coal Region Hoodoo*, please post something on Amazon and Goodreads. They can be an author's best friend— and we need all the help we can get. Thank you for reading my book. I hope that at least some of it it met with your approval.

Peace,

Maxim W. Furek

Bibliography

1.Night of the Living Dead

"30 Essential Zombie Movies." Rotten Tomatoes (2018). Retrieved from https://editorial.rottentomatoes.com/guide/essential-zombie-movies/

Axelrod, J. "Living Dead Museum Rising Again at Monroeville Mall." *USNews* (February 20, 2021).Retrieved from https://www.usnews.com/news/best-states/pennsylvania/articles/2021-02-20/living-dead-museum-rising-again-at-monroeville-mall

Beldin, F. "She-Devils on Wheels (1968)." AllMovie (January 29, 2022). Retrieved from https://www.allmovie.com/movie/she-devils-on-wheels-v44236/review

Brunson, M. "View From the Couch: *The Silence of the Lambs*, *Wonder*, etc." Film Frenzy (September 1, 2021). Retrieved from https://thefilmfrenzy.com/2018/02/14/the-bird-with-the-crystal-plumage-the-silence-of-the-lambs-wonder-among-new-home-entertainment-titles/

Burkholder, L. "Jan. 22 marks dark anniversary of Budd Dwyer's public suicide." WGAL TV (January 22, 2022). Retrieved from https://www.wgal.com/article/budd-dwyer-public-suicide-pennsylvania-state-treasurer-1642785747/38845511

Ebert, R. "The Night of the Living Dead." Rogerebert.com (January 5, 1969). Retrieved from https://www.rogerebert.com/reviews/the-night-of-the-living-dead-1968

Furek, M. W. *Somebody Else's Dream: Dakota, the Buoys, & "Timothy."* Mechanicsburg, PA: Sunbury Press, 2021.

George A. Romero Foundation. (January26, 2022). Retrieved from https://georgearomerofoundation.org/biography

Kain, E. "'The Walking Dead' Creator Reveals The Origin Of The Zombie Apocalypse." *Forbes* (January 24, 2020). Retrieved from https://www.forbes.com/sites/erikkain/2020/01/24/the-walking-dead-creator-reveals-the-origin-of-the-zombie-apocalypse/?sh=68fb39e055d1

Bibliography

Paquet, C. "Examining the socio-political influences behind Night of the Living Dead." *The Concordian* (October 29, 2019). Retrieved from https://theconcordian.com/2019/10/influence-behind-night-of-the-living-dead/

Zinkhann, Dean Mayor of Evans City, PA. Personal phone conversation. (February 1, 2022).

2. The Howard Beale Effect

Horvat, J. "What is the Cause of Our Angry politics?" Intellectual Takeout (June 22, 2016).Retrieved from http://www.intellextualtakeout.org

Jacob, R. I. "Where is Bernard Goetz Now?" The Cinamaholic (May 9, 2020). Retrieved from https://thecinemaholic.com/where-is-bernhard-goetz-now/

3. Ripperology

Brooks, X. Stephen King: 'I have outlived most of my critics. It gives me great pleasure.' *The Guardian*. (September 7, 2019). Retrieved from https://www.theguardian.com/books/2019/sep/07/stephen-king-interview-the-institute

Burton, N. "Jung: The Man and His Symbols." *Psychology Today* (April 8, 2012). Retrieved from https://www.psychologytoday.com/us/blog/hide-and-seek/201204/jung-the-man-and-his-symbols

"Carl Jung and the Shadow: A Guide to the Dark Side of the Mind." Arts of Thought (November 17, 2020). Retrieved from https://artsofthought.com/2020/11/17/carl-jung-and-the-shadow-a-guide-to-the-dark-side-of-the-mind/

Cherry, K. "What Are the Jungian Archetypes?" Very Well Mind (May 2, 2022). Retrieved from https://www.verywellmind.com/what-are-jungs-4-major-archetypes-2795439

Coolidge, F. L. "Why We Enjoy Horror Films." *Psychology Today* (October 23, 2021). Retrieved from https://www.psychologytoday.com/us/blog/how-think-neandertal/202110/why-we-enjoy-horror-films

Cornwell, P. *Portrait of a Killer, Jack the Ripper: Case Solved*. New York: G. P. Putnam's Sons, 2002.

Faurholt, G. "Self as Other. The Doppelganger." Aarhus University (Summer 2009). Retrieved from https://www.doubledialogues.com/article/self-as-other-the-doppelganger/

"Gary Heidnik: Case Study." ReadBakery.com. Retrieved from https://www.readbakery.com/various/infciq-twin-sisters/?utm_campaign=54hrixw9&utm_medium=cpc&utm_source=google&utm_term=forensicreader.com&gclid=EAIaIQobChMI-dDekZ7I-wIVHhmzAB3_9Ql7EAEYASAAEgLg3fD_BwE

Hall, C. S. *A Primer of Freudian Psychology*. New York: The World Publishing Company, 1954.

"Healing Heart and Mind." *Daily Reflections* (May 1, 2022): 130.

Hedegaard, E. "Manson today: The final confessions of America's most notorious psychopath." *Rolling Stone*, S1197 (December 5, 2013): 72–96

Janos, A. "Gary Heidnik's Unspeakable Crimes: An Interview With the Serial Killer's Attorney." A&E True Crime (January 14, 2021). Retrieved from https://www.aetv.com/real-crime/gary-heidnik

Lebeau, V. "The Strange Case of Dr. Jekyll and Mr. Hyde." Britannica (May 14, 2020). Retrieved from https://www.britannica.com/topic/The-Strange-Case-of-Dr-Jekyll-and-Mr-Hyde

Murphy, J. "Gary Heidnik's execution in 1999 stands as the last time a death sentence was carried out in PA." Pennlive.com (January 7, 2015). Retrieved from https://www.pennlive.com/midstate/2015/01/gary_heidniks_execution_in_199.html

Oliver, M. "Serial Killer Gary Heidnik: The Real-Life Buffalo Bill Who Fed One of His Victims To His Prisoner." AllThatsInteresting.com (November 4, 2022). Retrieved from https://allthatsinteresting.com/gary-heidnikhttps://

Petherick, W., and G. Sinnamon. *The Psychology of Criminal and Antisocial Behavior*. Cambridge, MA: Academic Press, 2017.

Poe, E. A. "William Wilson." In *Selected Tales*. New York: Penguin Popular Classics, 1994.

Stevenson, R. L. *The Strange Case of Dr. Jekyll and Mr. Hyde*. London: Palazzo Editions, 2020.

"Walter Sikert. (British, 1860–1942)." Artnet (July 23, 2022). Retrieved from http://www.artnet.com/artists/walter-richard-sickert/

"Was Renowned English Painter Walter Sickert Actually Jack the Ripper?" All That's Interesting (April 8, 2022). Retrieved from https://allthatsinteresting.com/walter-sickert

Wulff, T. J. "Recover Yourself: A Different Perspective on Addiction and

Recovery." *Counselor: The Magazine for Addiction and Behavioral Health Professionals*, 20 (3) (June 2019): 33–37.

4. Sheppton

"Final Report of Collapse of Slope Pillar Accident and Rescue of Two of the Three Entombed Men. Oneida No. 2 Slope. Fellin Mining Company. Oneida, Schuylkill County, Pennsylvania. (August 13, 1963)." United States Department of the Interior Bureau of Mines. District A.

Furek, M. W. *Sheppton: The Myth, Miracle & Music*. Charleston, SC: CreateSpace, 2015.

Furek, M. W. "The Strange and Paranormal Events of Sheppton." *Fate,* 733 (December 2018): 34–38.

Gilger, M., Jr. "Author's book revisits Sheppton mine disaster." Pottsville *Republican Herald* (March 6, 2016): A3, A5.

Goodman, J. A. *Two Weeks Under: The Sheppton Mine Disaster/Miracle*. Bloomsburg, PA: Coal Hole Productions, 2003.

Henritzy, H. M. "Eternally Grateful Dave Fellin has Mission." Hazleton *Standard-Speaker* (September 5, 1963): 6.

Jackson, K. "Sheppton mine story is retold Down Under." *Standard Speaker* (June 29, 2019).

Monitz, K. "Marked Forever." Hazleton *Standard-Speaker* (August 23, 2015): A1, A8.

Newton, M. *Strange Pennsylvania Monsters*. Atglen, PA: Schiffer Publishing Ltd., 2012.

Nickell, J. "The Trapped Miner's Holy Visions: Investigating The Sheppton 'Miracle.'" *The Skeptical Inquirer* Vol. 43, No. 3 (May/June 2019).

Robinson, H. "Quecreek mine disaster survivors reunite 20 years after 'miracle' rescue." *New York Post* (July 30, 2022). Retrieved from https://nypost.com/2022/07/30/quecreek-miners-reunite-20-years-after-miracle-rescue/

Sando, R. *The Famous Sheppton Mine Rescue. The Untold Story: The Blood and Sweat of the Rescue Team*. Baltimore: Publish America, 2006.

Schmeer, B. "The entombed miners' staircase to heaven." *Fate* (March 1965): 23–37.

Shector, A. *Centralia PA: Devils Fire*. Berwick, PA: Shector Enterprises Inc., 2016.

"Sheppton PA was the site of an historic mine disaster in August 1963." CoalSpeaker (August 22, 2020). Retrieved from https://coalspeaker.com/2020/08/22/sheppton-pa-was-the-site-of-an-historic-mine-disaster-in-august-1963/

Smiles, J. "Trapped in a Mine." *Citizen's Voice* (January 31, 2016): C1, C8.

Terwilliger, V. "Author digs into myths, mysteries of mine disaster." Pottsville *Republican Herald* (January 10, 2016): C1.

Terwilliger, V. A new perspective. "Author's latest release focuses on Sheppton mine disaster." Pottsville *Republican Herald* (January 3, 2016): C1, C4.

"The Famous Sheppton Mine Rescue. Fellin Mining Company. Oneida No. 2 Slope Cave-in." United States Mine Rescue Association (April 10. 2022). Retrieved from https://usminedisasters.miningquiz.com/saxsewell/sheppton.htm

5. Alferd Packer's Flesh Eaters

Vidar. "Alferd Packer: The Man Who Consumed Five Democrats." History of Yesterday (April 29, 2021). Retrieved from https://historyofyesterday.com/alferd-packer-the-man-who-consumed-five-democrats-6b1dd80edbd2

Furek, M. W. "Cannibalism's Unspeakable Reality." *Fate* 734 (January 2019): 34–39.

Kristof, N. D. "The Grotesque Vocabulary in Congo." *New York Times* (2010). Retrieved from http://www.nytimes.com/2010/02/11/opinion/11kristof.html?scp=1&sq=grotesque%20vocabulary%20in%20congo&st=cse

"Pennsylvania: Start of a Legend?" *Time* (1963). Retrieved from http://www.time.com/time/magazine/article/0,9171,870450,00.html

Sando, J. R. *The Famous Sheppton Mine Rescue: The Untold Story: The Blood and Sweat of the Rescue Team*. Frederick, MD: PublishAmerica, 2006.

"Sheppton Mine Disaster and Rescue." HMdb.org (November 8, 2019). Retrieved from https://www.hmdb.org/m.asp?m=87542

Throne, H. "Throne's Account: Throne Tells How He and Fellin Survived Entombment." Pottsville *Republican* (1963). Retrieved from http://

www.eastuniontownship.com/index.php?option=com_content&view=article&id=84&Itemid=95

Trembath, B. K. "Alferd Packer: The Truth is Out There (or Right Here)." History.DenverLibrary.org (October 21, 2015). Retrieved from https://history.denverlibrary.org/news/alferd-packer-truth-out-there

Wallace, P. A. W. "Indians in Pennsylvania." Pennsylvania Historical and Museum Commission (1970).

Mazzula, F. M. *Al Packer, A Colorado Cannibal.*

6. The Third Man Factor

Adams, C. J. *Coal Country Ghosts. Legends and Lore.* Reading, PA: Exeter House Books, 2004.

Andrews, E. "10 Fascinating Facts About Charles Lindbergh." History.com (September 1, 2018). Retrieved from https://www.history.com/news/10-fascinating-facts-about-charles-lindbergh

Bucher, M. "What Does the Bible Say about Guardian Angels?" I Believe (February 26, 2021). Retrieved from https://www.ibelieve.com/faith/what-does-the-bible-say-about-guardian-angels.html

Eliot, T. S. *The Waste Land.* New York: Boni & Liveright, 1922.

"Flying With Angels: The Curious Story of Charles Lindbergh." Anomalien.com (December 12, 2020). Retrieved from https://anomalien.com/charles-lindbergh-angels/

Furek, M. W. "Davey Fellin and the Third Man Factor." Normal Paranormal (April 2021).

Gaines, J. "Shackleton's Third Man." (July 29, 2012). Retrieved from https://theglyptodon.wordpress.com/2012/07/29/shackletons-third-man/

Geiger, J. *The Third Man Factor: Surviving the Impossible.* New York: Weinstein Books, 2009.

MacDonald, H. *When Angels Appear.* New York: Harper, 1982.

Mayer, S. "The Ultimate Guide to Marian Apparitions." Ascension Press (May 30, 2020). Retrieved from https://media.ascensionpress.com/2020/05/30/the-ultimate-guide-to-marian-apparitions/#what-is-it

Shackleton, E. *South: The ENDURANCE Expedition.* London: William Heinemann, 1919.

"What Does the Bible Say About Guardian Angels?" 21st Century Catholics (October 26, 2021). Retrieved from https://

21stcenturycatholicevangelization.org/catholicism-101/what-does-the-bible-say-about-guardian-angels/

7. Roman Catholic Mysticism

"A miracle has been attributed to John XXIII but not for his canonization." LaStampa (April 24, 2014). Retrieved from https://www.lastampa.it/vatican-insider/en/2014/04/24/news/a-miracle-has-been-attributed-to-john-xxiii-but-not-for-his-canonization-1.35769929

Allegri, R. "An uncontested miracle." Messenger of Saint Anthony (March 4, 2003). Retrieved from https://www.messengersaintanthony.com/content/uncontested-miracle

Clemente-Arnaldo, N. V. "Pope John XXIII: The Good Pope." Totus Tuus, Maria (2009). Retrieved from http://www.all-about-the-virgin-mary.com/pope-john-xxiii.html

Conrad, E. "The Second Greatest Story Ever Told." (1990). Retrieved from http://www.edconrad.org/lifeafterdeath/page2_files/body.html

Furek, M. W. Sheppton: The Myth, Miracle, & Music. North Charleston, SC: CreateSpace, 2015.

Goodman, J. A. Two Weeks Under: The Sheppton Mine Disaster/Miracle. Bloomsburg, PA: Coal Hole Productions, 2003.

Monitz, K. "Locals recall Sheppton's story." Standard-Speaker (August 15, 2013).

Nadeau, B. L. "Popes, Saints, Miracles, Weird Relics and Odd Omens Converge on Rome." The Daily Beast (April 26, 2014). Retrieved from http://www.thedailybeast.com/articles/2014/04/26/popes-saints-miracles-weird-relics-and-odd-omens-converge-on-rome.html

Ney, F. "Sheppton Mine Disaster: 40 Years Later." News Item (2003).

Nickell, J. "The Trapped Miners' Holy Visions: Investigating The Sheppton 'Miracle.'" Skeptical Inquirer, 43 (3) (May/June 2019).

O'Grady, D. "Almost A Saint: Pope John XXIII." St. Anthony Messenger (November 1996). Retrieved from http://www.americancatholic.org/Messenger/Nov1996/feature1.asp

Petroff, D., and N. Windfield. "Vatican sees historic day of 4 popes." Associated Press (April 28, 2014).

Piechota, M. "Religion and Ufology." IRAAP Messenger (2005).

Ragan, T. "Authors recount famous two weeks." *Standard-Speaker* (August 15, 2013).

Reed, J. "Great Gift of New Saints Reminds Us of Our Call to Holiness, Bishop Says as Diocese Celebrates Canonizations." *Catholic Witness* (May 9, 2014).

Rocca, F. X. "Pope Francis, with Retired Pope Benedict. Canonizes Sts. John XXIII and John Paul II." *Catholic Witness*, 10 (May 9, 2014).

Rychlak, R. J. "A War Prevented: Pope John XXIII and the Cuban Missile Crisis." *Crisis Magazine* (November 11, 2011). Retrieved from https://www.crisismagazine.com/2011/preventing-war-pope-john-xxiii-and-the-cuban-missile-crisis

Sando, J. R. *The Famous Sheppton Mine Rescue: The Untold Story: The Blood and Sweat of the Rescue Team.* Frederick, MD: PublishAmerica, 2006.

Schmeer, B. "The Entombed Miners' Staircase to Heaven." In *The World's Strangest Stories*. Clark Publishing, 1983.

"Standards for sainthood: what defines a 'miracle'?" The Conversation (May 1, 2014). Retrieved from https://theconversation.com/standards-for-sainthood-what-defines-a-miracle-26160

Throne, H. "Throne's Account: Throne Tells How He and Fellin Survived Entombment." Pottsville *Republican* (1963). Retrieved from http://www.eastuniontownship.com/index.php?option=com_content&view=article&id=84&Itemid=95

Waller, M. "Sheppton Folks Recall Mine Disaster: Throne's death finds Sheppton folks recall mine disaster vividly. Rescue put patch in international spotlight." Pottsville *Evening Herald* (1998).

"Vatican II." Vatican.com (May 22, 2018). Retrieved from https://vatican.com/Vatican-II/

8. St. Teresa of Avila

"Amazing Levitating Saints." CaringCatholicConvert (February 7, 2022). Retrieved from http://www.caringcatholicconvert.com/_sites/wordpress/articles/saints/amazing-levitating-saints/

Blai, A. "The Saints Who Levitated: Extraordinary and Concrete Miracles." Catholic Exchange (May 24, 2021). Retrieved from https://catholicexchange.com/the-saints-who-levitated-extraordinary-and-concrete-miracles/

"Four stages of Mystical Prayer in Teresa of Avila." Explore the Faith

(October 16, 2016). Retrieved from https://explorethefaith.com/
four-stages-of-mystical-prayer-in-teresa-of-avila/

McColman, C. "Teresa of Avila: A Passionate Mystic of The Love of
God." AnamChara (September 24, 2019). Retrieved from https://
anamchara.com/teresa-of-avila-a-passionate-mystic-of-the-love-
of-god/

"Mystical state. Trance." Britannica.com. Retrieved from https://www.
britannica.com/topic/mysticism/Mystical-states.

Rudy, L. J. "Ancient and Modern Mysticism and Mystics." Learn
Religions (September 26, 2019).

"St. Teresa of Avila." Catholic Miracles (October 4, 2022). Retrieved
from http://catholicmiracles.org/saint-miracles/st-teresa-of-avila/

"St. Teresa of Avila." EWTN (October 4, 2022). Retrieved from https://
www.ewtn.com/catholicism/saints/teresa-of-avila-780

"Saint Teresa Of Avila And Her Life Of Mysticism And Reform." The
Historian's Hut (August 24, 2017). Retrieved from https://
thehistorianshut.com/2017/08/24/saint-teresa-of-avila-and-her-
life-of-mysticism-and-reform/?fbclid=IwAR1m7SqoErsbqjjfu0qYj
Qeuu5j71CILzsDdnUc2b9zg2EHKL-qdTIaumgE

"St. Teresa of Avila. Spanish mystic." Britannica.com (October 4,
2022). Retrieved from https://www.britannica.com/biography/Saint-
Teresa-of-Avila

"The Protestant Reformation." *National Geographic* (October 5, 2022).
Retrieved from https://education.nationalgeographic.org/resource/
protestant-reformation

"What was the Spanish inquisition?" World Atlas (October 5, 2022).
Retrieved from https://www.worldatlas.com/articles/what-was-the-
spanish-inquisition.html

9. Ed & Lorraine Warren: Demonologists

Alu, M. E. "Valley's own horror tale wafts into bookstores." *Times
Leader* (March 6, 1988): 3A.

Corbett, S. "The Smurls. They're back." *Times Leader* (May 5,
1991): 3A.

Curran, R. "Penning Book Tedious Task." *Sunday Independent* (April
14, 1991): 1.

Curran, R., Ed and Lorraine Warren, and Jack and Janet Smurl. *The
Haunted: One Family's Nightmare.* New York: St. Martin's Press,

1988.

Flannery, J. X. "Smurls Got help From Diocese." Scranton *Times-Tribune* (May 18, 1991): 3.

Furek, M. W. "Ed and Lorraine Warren & The Smurl Haunting." Normal Paranormal (August 2020).

Furek, M. W. "The Warrens & the Smurl Haunting." *Fate* (February 28, 2022).

Janes, D. A. "Nightmare on Chase Street: The Smurl Family Haunting." The Lineup (May 25, 2016). Retrieved from https://the-line-up.com/smurl-family-haunting

Marusak, J. "It 'stinks,' concludes reviewer." *Times Leader* (March 6, 1988): 3A.

Marusak, J. "'Haunted' faulted as 'sad' saga." *Times Leader* (January 1, 1989): 1G.

Merrow, M. "Couple Buys Rhode Island home that inspired horror film 'The Conjuring.'" *Boston Globe* (July 8, 2019). Retrieved from https://www.bostonglobe.com/lifestyle/names/2019/07/08/couple-buys-rhode-island-home-that-inspired-horror-film-the-conjuring/6QtYFSELZO0pWmlKXJlB6I/story.html

Merryweather, C. "10 Most Haunting Cases Investigated by Ed And Lorraine Warren." ListVerse (April 25, 2019). Retrieved from https://listverse.com/2019/04/25/10-most-haunting-cases-investigated-by-ed-and-lorraine-warren/

"Paranormal investigator who probed Smurl house dies at 92." Citizens Voice (April 19, 2019).

Ravenhurst, Barrett, owner, the Victorian Palace Theatre, Jim Thorpe, PA. Personal correspondence (October 12, 2019).

"Reviewers Accord High Marks to Bob Curran's 'The Haunted.'" *Sunday Independent* (May 5, 1991).

Smiles, J. "The Conjuring: Tale of demon-filled home draws media, curious to West Pittston." *Citizens' Voice* (August 14, 2016): C1–C6.

Stockton, C. "Ed and Lorraine Warren Movies: Films Inspired by the Paranormal Investigators." Creepy Catalog (September 6, 2022). Retrieved from https://creepycatalog.com/ed-and-lorraine-warren-movies/

Sullivan, G., and H. Aronson. *High Hopes: The Amityville Murders*. New York: Coward, McCann & Geoghegan, 1981.

"'The Haunted' to Star Sally Kirkland." *Sunday Independent* (April 14, 1991): 1.

The Haunted. Made-for-TV movie starring Sally Kirkland and Jeffrey DeMunn. Director Robert Mandel. (May 6, 1991).

Warren, Ed and Lorraine. Personal communications circa 1988 to 1990.

Warren, Ed and Lorraine. Personal interview and photo shoot. The Victorian Palace Theatre, Jim Thorpe, PA. (July 19, 1988).

White, A. "6 Paranormal Cases Investigated by Ed and Lorraine Warren That We Can't Stop Talking About." The Lineup (November 10, 2017). Retrieved from https://the-line-up.com/ed-and-lorraine-warren-paranormal-cases

Wolkomir, J., and R. Wolkomir. "Ghost Busters." *McCall's* (July 1989): 104, 106, 109.

10. Fr. Alphonsus Trabold

"Father Gabriele Amorth." Occult World (September 10, 2021). Retrieved from https://occult-world.com/father-gabriele-amorth/

Davey, G. C. L. "'Spirit Possession' and Mental Health." *Psychology Today* (December 31, 2014). Retrieved from https://www.psychologytoday.com/us/blog/why-we-worry/201412/spirit-possession-and-mental-health

Davies, L. "Popes John Paul II and John XXIII declared saints in double canonization." *The Guardian* (April 27, 2014). Retrieved from https://www.theguardian.com/world/2014/apr/27/popes-john-paul-ii-and-john-xxiii-saints-canonisation

"Fr. Alphonsus' 'Spooks' Class." St. Bonaventure University: A Haunted History (August 28, 2021). Retrieved from https://hauntedhistorysbu.weebly.com/spooks-class.html

Furek, M. W. "'Spooks' Trabold: Exorcist in Academia." *Paranormal Underground* 15 (1) *(January 2022):* 22–24.

Klass, D, T. Joyce, and E. R. Vernor. Hinsdale House: an American Haunting. Fort Wayne, Indiana: Dark Moon Press, 2016.

Miller, J. "Fr. Alphonsus A. Trabold, OFM." (August 19, 1925–April 5, 2005). The BonaVenture (April 8, 2005). Retrieved from http://archives.sbu.edu/Biographies/Trabold/index.html

Nicholas, C. "Hinsdale Haunting, Western New York's Greatest Historical Folly." ObscureCaseBook (2017). Retrieved from https://

www.obscurecasebook.com/single-post/2014/05/01/FROZEN-RIVER

Pelton, R. W. *In My Name shall they cast out devils.* New Haven, CT: A. S. Barnes, 1976.

Ramos Diaz, A. W. "How John Paul II infuriates the devil." Aleteia (October 30, 2016). Retrieved from https://aleteia.org/2016/10/30/how-john-paul-ii-infuriates-the-devil/

"Rite of Exorcism." Catholic Doors (September 10, 2021). Retrieved from https://www.catholicdoors.com/prayers/english/p01975b.htm

"*Rituale Romanum.*" (September 10, 2021). Retrieved from http://www.liturgica.net/rituale/inside.html

Wilde, V. "Famous Catholic Exorcist (Loosely) Weaves a Dangerous Tale in New Book." Friendly Atheist (April 4, 2020). Retrieved from https://friendlyatheist.patheos.com/2020/04/04/famous-catholic-exorcist-loosely-weaves-a-dangerous-tale-in-new-book/

Winfield, M. "Elegy for an Exorcist—In Memoriam: Father Alphonsus Trabold (1925–2005)." Buffalo Rising. (April 26, 2015). Retrieved from https://www.buffalorising.com/2015/04/elegy-for-an-exorcist-in-memoriam-father-alphonsus-trabold-1925-2005/

11. Centralia: Gateway to Hell

Centralia, PA. "Spooky Centralia Pennsylvania: Ghosts and Silent Hill." (October 31, 2014). Retrieved from https://www.centraliapa.org/spooky-centralia-pennsylvania-ghosts-silent-hill/

Clawser, B. "Of the Season: 5 Fascinating Ghost Towns." *Susquehanna Life* (August 31, 2021). Retrieved from https://www.susquehannalife.com/2021/08/31/366960/of-the-season-5-fascinating-ghost-towns

Forsyth, B. "The 'Silent Hill' church – Last church standing in Centralia." Canadian Military History (September 2019). Retrieved from https://militarybruce.com/the-silent-hill-church-last-church-standing-in-centralia/

Furek, M. W. "Centralia: Gateway to Hell." Normal Paranormal (June 2020).

Furek, M. W. *Sheppton: The Myth, Miracle & Music.* Charleston, SC: CreateSpace, 2015.

Hangley, B. "The Church that Wouldn't Burn." *Readers Digest* (December 18/January 19).

"Is Centralia Haunted?" OffRoaders.com (May 12, 2021). Retrieved from http://www.offroaders.com/album/centralia/haunted.htm

Ivory, K. *Pennsylvania Disasters*. Guilford, CT: Morris Book Publishing, Inc., 2007.

Knutson, J. "The End of Centralia's Abandoned, Colorful, Anarchic 'Graffiti Highway.'" Atlas Obscura (September 14, 2020). Retrieved from https://www.atlasobscura.com/articles/centralia-graffiti-highway-buried

Koontz, D. *Strange Highways*. New York: Brandon Tartikoff Books, 1995.

Machado, K. "Is Centralia's Fire Still Burning? This Is What Happened to The Pennsylvania Ghost Town." The Travel (October 11, 2020). Retrieved from https://www.thetravel.com/is-the-centralia-fire-still-burning/

Mocarsky, S. "Real or not, Molly Maguires left an impression." *Times Leader* (March 11, 2012): 7A.

Swartz, S. "New Graffiti Highway pitched." *Press Enterprise* Vol 120, (120) (June 28, 2021): 1.

Symon, E. V. "I Live in Centralia, PA: It's America's Creepiest Ghost Town." Cracked Newsletter (October 23, 2017). Retrieved from https://www.cracked.com/personal-experiences-2537-i-live-in-centralia-pa-its-americas-creepiest-ghost-town.html

"History." The Old Jail Museum (2019). Retrieved from http://www.theoldjailmuseum.com/history.html

Williams, D. "Pennsylvania's colorful 'Graffiti Highway' is being shut down for good." CNN (April 8, 2020). Retrieved from https://www.cnn.com/travel/article/graffiti-highway-closing-trnd/index.html

12. TWA Flight 800

Butler, C., and M. Caldwell. "Montoursville Remembers Lives Lost in Flight 800 Crash." PA HomePage (July 17, 2016). Retrieved from https://www.pahomepage.com/news/montoursville-remembers-lives-lost-in-flight-800-crash/

Cashill, J. *TWA 800: The Crash, the Cover-Up, and the Conspiracy*. Washington, DC: Regnery History, 2016.

Chung, J. "TWA Flight 800 Was Totally Shot Down, Says Veteran Airline Pilot." Gothamist (April 16, 2015). Retrieved from https://

gothamist.com/news/twa-flight-800-was-totally-shot-down-says-veteran-airline-pilot

Colbert, C. "Wreckage from TWA Flight 800 to be destroyed years after explosion." CNN (February 27, 2021). Retrieved from https://www.cnn.com/2021/02/27/us/twa-flight-800-wreckage-destroyed-trnd/index.html

Danziger, A. (April 15, 2015). Former Obama pilot: TWA Flight 800 was not blown up by a faulty fuel tank; it was shot down. I'll always believe that, and here's why. New York *Daily News*. Retrieved from https://www.nydailynews.com/new-york/obama-pilot-twa-flight-800-shot-article-1.2186329

"Flight 800." TWA Museum (June 11, 2021). Retrieved from http://www.twamuseum.com/flight-800/

Furek, M. W. "The Internet Age's First Conspiracy." Normal Paranormal (September 2021).

Goglia, J. "NTSB Denies TWA 800 Conspiracy Theory Petition." *Forbes* (July 2, 2014). Retrieved from https://www.forbes.com/sites/johngoglia/2014/07/02/ntsb-denies-twa-800-conspiracy-theory-petition/?sh=7d1ca6be5b78

Hadad, C. "5 things you didn't know about the crash of TWA Flight 800." CNN (July 15, 2014). Retrieved from https://www.cnn.com/2014/07/14/us/twa-flight-800-five-things/index.html

Madsen, W. "Former Navy official: Missile from USS Seawolf submarine shot down TWA flight 800." SOTT (July 28, 2014). Retrieved from https://www.sott.net/article/286528-Former-Navy-official-Missile-from-USS-Seawolf-submarine-shot-down-TWA-Flight-800

Purdy, M. "Flight 800 Theories Come Out of the Woodwork." *New York Times* (April 13, 1997). Retrieved from https://www.nytimes.com/1997/04/13/weekinreview/flight-800-theories-come-out-of-the-woodwork.html

Smallwood, D. "Make No Mistake About It – TWA Flight 800 Was Shot Down by the United States Navy." Military Corruption.com (July 12, 2018). Retrieved from https://militarycorruption.com/flight-800/

"TWA Flight 800 Conspiracy Theories: The Dubious Explosion of Flight 800." Conspiracies.net (April 11, 2017). Retrieved from https://www.conspiracies.net/dubious-explosion-flight-800/

Zimmer, D. "'First conspiracy of the internet age': How the TWA Flight 800 explosion sparked online rumors for years." *USA Today* (July 15, 2021). Retrieved from https://www.yahoo.com/news/first-conspiracy-internet-age-twa-090216342.html

13. Unidentified Aerial Phenomena

Andrew, S. "The US Navy just confirmed these UFO videos are the real deal." CNN (September 18, 2018). Retrieved from https://www.cnn.com/2019/09/18/politics/navy-confirms-ufo-videos-trnd/index.html

Bender, B. "Republican lawmaker presses Navy on UFO sightings." *Politico* (July 30, 2019). Retrieved from https://www.politico.com/story/2019/07/30/navy-mark-walker-ufo-1441105

Bowman, V. "Aliens exist but we may simply not see them, says first British astronaut into space." *The Telegraph* (January 6, 2020). Retrieved from https://www.yahoo.com/news/aliens-exist-living-among-us-173131625.html

Gorman, S. "NASA's UFO panel convenes to study unclassified sightings." Reuters (October 24, 2022). Retrieved from https://frontier.yahoo.com/news/nasas-ufo-panel-convenes-study-003226536.html

"Government report has no answers about UFOs." Associated Press *Press-Enterprise* (June 26, 2021): 4.

Kay, S. "How Takoma Gave the World the Flying Saucer." *Grit City Magazine* (October 2019). Retrieved from https://gritcitymag.com/2019/10/how-tacoma-gave-the-world-the-flying-saucer/

"Kenneth Arnold Sighting." UFO Databank. Retrieved from http://www.ufodatabank.com/arnold.htm

Lacitis, E. "An Eastern WA man records 180,000 UFO sightings, even if others debunk them." *Seattle Times* (October 14, 2022). Retrieved from https://www.seattletimes.com/pacific-nw-magazine/as-one-eastern-wa-man-records-ufo-sightings-others-debunk-them/

"Luis Elizondo reveals that our military has experienced alien abductions and implants." *The Gate to Strange Phenomena* vol 38 (1) (July 2022): 1–2.

Mead, M. "UFO: Visitors from Outer Space?" *Redbook* (September 1974): 57.

Bibliography

MacIsaac, T. "4 Pilots Who Say They've Seen UFOs." *Epoch Times* (November 18, 2013). Retrieved from https://www.ufocasebook.com/2013/4-pilots-see-ufos.html

Merlan, A. "Americans Now Correctly Believe UFOs Could Be Alien Craft." Vice News (August 20, 2021). Retrieved from https://www.vice.com/en/article/bvzbw3/more-americans-now-correctly-believe-ufos-could-be-alien-craft-from-outer-space

Shannon, J. "'We can't ignore this': UFO sightings spark concern from more than just conspiracy theorists." *USA Today* (June 1, 2021). Retrieved from https://www.yahoo.com/news/t-ignore-ufo-sightings-spark-100116674.html

Swiatek, Susan, MUFON, Virginia State director. Personal correspondence (April 2020).

The UFO Phenomenon. Alexandria, VA: Time-Life Books, 1987.

"To the Stars Academy of Arts and Science Acknowledges the Pentagon's Official Release of UAP Video Footage." TTSA (September 1, 2022). Retrieved from https://tothestars.media/blogs/press-and-news/to-the-stars-academy-of-arts-science-acknowledges-the-pentagons-official-release-of-uap-video-footage

14. Kecksburg

Booth, B. J. "The Kecksburg UFO Crash." UFO Evidence.org (2011). Retrieved from http://ufoevidence.org/documents/doc1294.htm

Dickinson, D. "Spot failed Soviet Venus probe Kosmos 482 in Earth orbit." *Universe Today* (March 20, 2019). Retrieved from https://phys.org/news/2019-03-soviet-venus-probe-kosmos-earth.html

Dinkel, M. "Acorn from Space: The Kecksburg Incident." Pennsylvania Center for the Book (2010). Retrieved from https://pabook.libraries.psu.edu/literary-cultural-heritage-map-pa/feature-articles/acorn-space-kecksburg-incident

Dudding, G. *The Kecksburg UFO Incident*. Spencer, WV: GSD Publications, 2013.

Furek, M. W. "Revisiting the Kecksburg UFO Incident." *Paranormal Underground* (May 2022): 38–40.

Gordon, S. "Kecksburg, PA UFO Incident: Some Interesting Details 56 Years Later." Phantoms and Monsters (December 10, 2021). Retrieved from https://www.phantomsandmonsters.com/2021/12/kecksburg-pa-ufo-incident-some.html

"Kecksburg Crash UFO: Undoubted Federal Object." The Quester Files (September 24, 2021). Retrieved from http://www.thequesterfiles.com/html/kecksburg_crash_ufo--_undoubte.html

Shelton, J. "The Kecksburg Incident: Mysterious UFO Crash of The '60s." Groovy History.com (December 10, 2020). Retrieved from https://groovyhistory.com/kecksburg-incident-ufo-crash

Snow, K. "Kecksburg Crash 1965." The National Paranormal Society (2016). Retrieved from http://national-paranormal-society.org/kecksburg-crash-1965/

15. Bigfoot

Beckley, T. G. "America's Abominable Swampman." *Saga* vol 49, No 6. (March 1975): 36–74.

Belinski, M. "Not Real: Sasquatch Watch." *The Morning Call* (October 17, 2022): 1.

Bemis, R. "Reports of Bigfoot's death may be exaggerated." *Eureka Times Herald* (September 27, 2022). Retrieved from http://www.bigfootencounters.com/articles/times_standard.htm

Bernard, L. "Bigfoot sightings in the Pennsylvania wilds." Pennsylvania Wilds (May 24, 2019). Retrieved from https://pawilds.com/bigfoot-sightings-pennsylvania-wilds/

Coleman, L. "Ray Wallace's Bigfoot Fakery: Cautionary Tale's 10th Anniversary." Cryptozoonews (December 5, 2012.) Retrieved from http://www.cryptozoonews.com/wallace-10/

Cronin, E. W., Jr. "On the Trail of the Abominable Snowman." *The Atlantic Monthly* (March 1976): 149–156.

Cutchin, J., and T. Renner. *Where the Footprints End: High Strangeness and the Bigfoot Phenomenon. Volume II: Evidence.* Red Lion, Pennsylvania: Dark Holler Arts, 2020.

Emerson, T., and M. Litvin. "The Hunt for 'Wildman.'" *Newsweek* 730 (November 26, 1990).

"Forensic Expert Says Bigfoot Is Real." *National Geographic* (October 23, 2003). Retrieved from https://www.nationalgeographic.com/culture/article/forensic-expert-says-bigfoot-is-real

Gordon, S. *Silent Invasion. The Pennsylvania UFO-Bigfoot Casebook.* www.stangordon.com, 2010.

Guiley, R. E. "The Bigfoot Alien Connection." Interview (January 27, 2019).

Bibliography

Irwin, W. "Why I Believe in Bigfoot." *Psychology Today* (May 15, 2015). Retrieved from https://www.psychologytoday.com/us/blog/plato-pop/201505/why-i-believe-in-bigfoot

Jackson, K. "Tabloids crown Bigfoot with 'respectability.'" *Dallas Morning News* (March 9, 1992): 3B.

Kane, M. "Is Bigfoot an extraterrestrial visitor? Some researchers think so". Masslive (October 19, 2015). Retrieved from https://www.masslive.com/news/worcester/2015/10/is_bigfoot_an_extraterrestrial.html

Keel, J. *The Mothman Prophecies*. New York: Tom Doherty Associates, 1991.

Little, B. "Bigfoot was Investigated by the FBI. Here's What They Found." History.com (January 22, 2020). Retrieved from https://www.history.com/news/bigfoot-fbi-file-investigation-discovery

Margaritoff, M. "Astounding Bigfoot Facts That Delve Into The Legend Of The Notorious Ape-Man." AllThatsInteresting (April 27, 2021). Retrieved from https://allthatsinteresting.com/bigfoot-facts

Monsters: Myth or Fact? NBC Smithsonian Special narrated by Rod Serling (January 20, 1977).

Morello, C. "Unbelievable: Strange sights are common along Chestnut Ridge." *Philadelphia Inquirer* (February 12, 1989): B1, 7B.

Newton, M. *Strange Pennsylvania Monsters*. Atglen, PA: Schiffer Publishing Ltd., 2012.

"Pacific Northwest's Bigfoot is still a mystery after 160 years." Berwick *Press Enterprise* (January 23, 1974).

"Patterson-Gimlin Film – Hoax Allegations – Ray Wallace." Primidi.com. Retrieved from https://www.primidi.com/patterson-gimlin_film/hoax_allegations/ray_wallace

Pennsylvania Bigfoot Society. PBS (September 1, 2022). Retrieved from https://www.pabigfoot.com

Redfern, N. "More on the Mysterious Bigfoot: The UFO Connection." Mysterious Universe (September 17, 2020). Retrieved from https://mysteriousuniverse.org/2020/09/more-on-the-mysterious-bigfoot-the-ufo-connection/

Renner, T. *Apparitions: Illustrations of The Other*. Red Lion, Pennsylvania: Strange Familiars/Dark Holler Arts, LLC, 2020.

Renner, T. *Bigfoot in Pennsylvania*. Red Lion, Pennsylvania: Dark Holler

Arts, 2017.

Robertson, R. "Bigfoot." *Campus Life* (March 1977): 61–63.

Ruehl, F. "Is Bigfoot Possibly an Alien Entity?" *HuffPost* (August 7, 2012). Retrieved from https://www.huffpost.com/entry/is-bigfoot-possibly-an-alien_b_1578844

The Bigfoot Alien Connection Revealed. Centre Communications, Inc., 2020.

"The Ray Wallace-Rant Mullins Mess." *Vancouver Sun* (December 7, 2002). Retrieved from http://www.bigfootencounters.com/articles/wallace.htm

Schneck, M. "Is Bigfoot in Pennsylvania? Parts of the state have several reported Sasquatch sightings." *PatriotNews* (June 18, 2019). Retrieved from https://www.pennlive.com/life/2019/06/where-are-pennsylvanias-bigfoot-hotspots.html

Scott, J. "Tracking Bigfoot." *Argosy* (April 1975): 16–30.

Speigel, L. "Bigfoot Hunter Rick Dyer Confesses Again To Duping The Public." *HuffPost* (December 6, 2017). Retrieved from https://www.huffpost.com/entry/bigfoot-hoax-rick-dyer-confesses_n_5079861

Susman, R. L. "*Oreopithecus bambolii*: an unlikely case of hominid-like grip capability in a Miocene ape." National Library of Medicine (October 10, 2003). Retrieved from https://pubmed.ncbi.nlm.nih.gov/14698686/

Stump, A. "The Man Who Tracks 'Bigfoot.'" *True* (May 1975): 28–77.

"UFOs and Bigfoot; Evidence of an Inter-Dimensional Connection." *Gaia* (March 27, 2020). Retrieved from https://www.gaia.com/article/ufos-bigfoot-evidence-interdimensional-connection

White, E. "Who Are the Nephilim? The Mysterious Beings of Genesis 6." Bible History Daily (August 18, 2022). Retrieved from https://www.biblicalarchaeology.org/daily/biblical-topics/hebrew-bible/who-are-the-nephilim/

17. Nick Adams

Adams, A. Daughter of Nick Adams. Personal correspondence (December 30, 2016).

Adams, N. "I Was Wild and Weak." *Modern Screen* 51 (5) (May 1957).

Adams, N. *The Rebel & the King: Expanded Edition. More Elvis*. Columbia, SC: Water Dancer Press, 2012.

"All About Hollywood." TV Film Stars (February 1956).

"American Stars in Japanese Films: Nick Adams in *Godzilla Vs. Monster Zero*." Brian Camp's Film and Anime Blog (September 6, 2018). Retrieved from https://briandanacamp.wordpress.com/2015/09/06/american-stars-in-japanese-films-nick-adams-in-godzilla-vs-monster-zero/

Austin, J. *Hollywood's Unsolved Mysteries*. New York: Wings Books, 1991.

Beath, W. N. *The Death of James Dean*. New York City: Grove Press, 1986.

"Catherine Adamshock, Mom to TV's Nick Adams, the Rebel." Kearny Works, Kearnygram (April 1960).

Day, C. "James Dean: Forever young, forever cool." The Orlando Sentinel (September 19, 2000): 51.

DeBlasio, I. "Laurel Canyon—The Dark Side: The 'Rebel Without a Cause' Curse." Patch.com (December 11, 2011). Retrieved from https://patch.com/california/studiocity/bp--laurel-canyonthe-dark-side-the-rebel-without-a-cause-curse

"Dennis Hopper: Easy Rider." The Criterion Collection (February 25, 2022). Retrieved from https://www.criterion.com/films/27528-easy-rider

Dickinson, K. Founder, Pennsylvania Nurses Assistance Program (PNAP). Personal communications (May 17, 2017).

"Everyone Loves Nick." *Hollywood Stars* (February 1956).

Furek, M. W. "Adams rests in Berwick cemetery." *Sunday Independent* (June 11, 1989).

Furek, M. W. "Author chronicles Adams-Dean friendship." *Sunday Independent* (October 7, 1990).

Furek, M. W. "The Final Days of The Rebel." *Counselor, The Magazine for Addiction & Behavioral Health Professionals* 18 (5) (October 2017): 10–11.

Harris, W. G. *Natalie & R.J. Hollywood's Star-Crossed Lovers*. New York City: Doubleday, 1988.

Jacob, R. M. "What Happened Between Natalie Wood and Christopher Walken?" The Cinemaholic (May 5, 2020). Retrieved from https://thecinemaholic.com/natalie-wood-christopher-walken/

Johnson, L. "The Murder of Actor Sal Mineo: From '50s heartthrob to a homicide victim." Medium (March 5, 2021). Retrieved from https://

loriajohnston.medium.com/the-murder-of-actor-sal-mineo-cd2605349f4e

Kern, B. "My friend, Nick Adams." Berwick *Enterprise* (April 22, 1968).

Martinetti, R. *The James Dean Story*. New York City: Pinnacle Books, Inc., 1975.

Meares, H. "What Really Happened to 1960s Starlet Jenny Maxwell?" *Los Angeles Magazine* (April 2, 2021). Retrieved from https://www.lamag.com/culturefiles/jenny-maxwell-murder/

Mission Mars. IMDb (February 21, 2022). Retrieved from https://www.imdb.com/title/tt0063311/

Mosby's Marauders. TheDisneyWiki (February 21, 2022). Retrieved from https://disney.fandom.com/wiki/Mosby%27s_Marauders

"Nick Adams Funeral Rites in Berwick." Hazleton *Standard-Speaker* (February 10, 1968).

"Nick Adams: Obituary." *Variety* (February 14, 1968).

"Promazine (Sparine) Data Sheet." PsyWeb.com (December 2, 2015). Retrieved from http://www.psyweb.com/drughtm/jsp/sparine.jsp

Raup, J. "Watch: Robert Altman's Documentary Exploring the Life and Career of James Dean." The Film Stage (February 8, 2014). Retrieved from https://thefilmstage.com/watch-three-documentaries-explore-the-life-and-career-of-james-dean/

"'Rebel' Actor Nick Adams Found Dead in Coldwater Canyon Home 1968." RIP Los Angles (February 7, 2011). Retrieved from http://rip-losangles.blogspot.com/2011/02/actor-nick-adams-found-dead-in.html

Roberto, J. R. "Kaiju Conversations: An Interview with Henry G. Saperstein." *G-Fan* (Fall 1995).

Shelton, J. "Rebel Without A Cause: Curse, Trivia, And More." History Daily (February 26, 2022). Retrieved from https://historydaily.org/rebel-without-a-cause-curse-trivia

Schow, D. J. "The Outer Limits: And now a word from our censor. The Twilight Zone." [PN2] (August 1984).

Schow, D. J., and J. Frentzen. "The Outer Limits: Part Four. The Twilight Zone." [PN3] (August 1984).

"The Killing Bottle." Letterboxd (February 20, 2022). Retrieved from https://letterboxd.com/film/the-killing-bottle/

Winkler, P. "Nick Adams: His Hollywood Life and Death." Crime

Magazine.com (October 30, 2009). Retrieved from http://www.crimemagazine.com/nick-adams-his-hollywood-life-and-death

Yapp, N. "*Die, Monster, Die!* (1965)." Classic-Horror.com (January 29, 2008). Retrieved from https://classic-horror.com/reviews/die_monster_die_1965.html

19. Roger Corman and the Texas Clock Tower

Brooks, X. "Stephen King: 'I have outlived most of my critics. It gives me great pleasure.'" *The Guardian* (September 7, 2019). Retrieved from https://www.theguardian.com/books/2019/sep/07/stephen-king-interview-the-institute

Bullock, P. "Tales of Terror: Roger Corman's Poe Cycle." *Starburst Magazine* (September 14, 2011). Retrieved from https://www.starburstmagazine.com/features/tales-of-terror-roger-cormans-poe-cycle

"Charles Whitman University of Texas Tower Shooting." My Crime Library (November 22, 2019). Retrieved from https://mycrimelibrary.com/charles-whitman-university-of-texas-tower-shooting/

Corman, R., and J. Jerome. *Roger Corman: How I Made a Hundred Movies in Hollywood and Never Lost a Dime*. New York: Random House, 1990.

Erickson, E. "*Targets*." Rotten Tomatoes (August 19, 2020). Retrieved from https://www.rottentomatoes.com/m/targets

Furek, M. W. "America's First Mass Murderer." *Counselor, The Magazine for Addiction & Behavioral Health Professionals* 17 (3) (June 2016): 14–17.

Furek, M. W. "Roger Corman and the Ghost of Charles Whitman." *Paranormal Underground* (July 2021).

Furek, M. W. "The Deadly Legacy of The Texas Clock Tower Massacre." *Counselor, The Magazine for Addiction Professionals* 14 (4) (August 2013): 34–39.

Heatly, M. D. "Text of Psychiatrist's Notes on Sniper." *New York Times* (August 3, 1966). Retrieved from http://partners.nytimes.com/library/national/080366tx-shoot.html

Hlavaty, C. "47 years later, Whitman's tower shooting still a haunting memory for Texans." Chron (August 1, 2013). Retrieved from https://blog.chron.com/thetexican/2013/08/47-years-later-whitmans-tower-shooting-still-a-haunting-memory-for-texans/

Macleod, M. "Charles Whitman: The Texas Bell Tower Sniper." Crime Library (2013). Retrieved from http://www.trutv.com/library/crime/notorious_murders/mass/whitman/preparations_4.html

Moraes, F. "The Roger Corman Poe Cycle." Psychotronic Review (June 6, 2017). Retrieved from https://psychotronicreview.com/films/roger-corman-poe/

Nevin, D. "The Eagle Scout Who Grew Up with a Tortured Mind." *Life* 28D (August 12, 1966).

"Officer who stopped 1966 UT clock tower sniper rampage dies." Associated Press (December 27, 2012). Retrieved from http://abclocal.go.com/ktrk/story?section=news/state&id=8933697

Palladini, M. *Drugs of abuse: From doctors to dealers, users and healers.* Beaver, PA: Three Sons Publishing, 2011.

Popovits, R. M. "HHS 'duty to warn' letter highlights conflicting privacy laws." Behavioral Healthcare (March 14, 2013). Retrieved from http://www.behavioral.net/article/hhs-duty-warn-letter-highlights-conflicting-privacy-laws?WA_MAILINGLEVEL_CODE=&spMailingID=41162324&spUserID=NzYwMTY5ODMxS0&spJobID=181133978&spReportId=MTgxMTMzOTc4S0#node-20692

Ashton Rogers. NT Paranormal. Personal correspondence (June 3, 2021).

Small, L. B. "Psychotherapists duty to warn: Ten years After Tarasoff." *Golden Gate University Law Review* Volume 15, Issue #2 (September 7, 2010). Retrieved from http://digitalcommons.law.ggu.edu/cgi/viewcontent.cgi?article=1367&context=ggulrev

Southern, N. "Boris Karloff in *Targets*." All Movie (August 19, 2020). Retrieved from https://www.allmovie.com/movie/targets-v48670/review

"The Texas Tower Sniper Ghost." GhostGhoul (August 1, 2018). Retrieved from https://ghostsnghouls.com/texas-tower-sniper-ghost/

20. Ed Conrad: Truth Dispenser

Conrad, E. "Cave-in survivors saw deceased pope." Hazleton *Standard-Speaker* (May 30, 1990): 16, 18.

Conrad, E. "Proof of Life After Death." (February 9, 2015). Retrieved from http://www.edconrad.org/lifeafterdeath/index_files/body.html

Conrad, E. "The Famous Sheppton Mine Disaster." Hazleton *Standard-Speaker* (August 16, 2007).

Conrad, E. "The Second Greatest Story Ever Told." (1990). Retrieved from http://www.edconrad.org/lifeafterdeath/page2_files/body.html

Conrad, E. "Trapped miner recalls miracles of Sheppton rescue." Hazleton *Standard Speaker* (August 13, 1988): 5.

Devlin, R. "Collector: Find Changes Evolution Scientists: 'Skull Fossil' is Quartz." *The Morning Call* (September 28, 1986). Retrieved from https://www.mcall.com/news/mc-xpm-1986-09-28-2532363-story.html

Edward J. Conrad Obituary (1939–2020). Retrieved from https://www.legacy.com/us/obituaries/schuylkill/name/edward-conrad-obituary?id=7827453

Furek, M. W. *Sheppton: The Myth, Miracle, and Music.* Charleston, SC: CreateSpace, 2015.

Hart, J. "Beyond the Grave." Shenandoah *Evening Herald* (July 2, 1976): 4.

Plagenz, G. "Heaven, Hell are debated." *York Dispatch* (February 20, 1988): 8.

Shorey, A. "Psychiatrist, author who theorized five stages of grief dies at 78." *Standard-Speaker* (August 26, 2004): 2.

Whalen, J. "Retired Standard-Speaker reporter Ed Conrad remembered." Hazleton *Standard-Speaker* (November 22, 2020).

21. Dr. Santee: White Witch

"A Biography of Dr. Frederick LaMotte Santee." Deadline Paranormal (June 11, 2021). Retrieved from https://hatchet5855.wixsite.com/deadline-paranormal/blank-c7cq

"Albert Shinsky and the Witch of Ringtown Valley." Unexplained Mysteries (November 22, 2016). Retrieved from https://coolinterestingstuff.com/the-witch-of-ringtown-valley-and-albert-shinsky

"Albert Shinsky: The Murderer of the Witch of Ringtown Valley." Anomalien.com (March 25, 2021). Retrieved from https://anomalien.com/albert-shinsky-the-murderer-of-the-witch-of-ringtown-valley/

"Aleister Crowley: British occultist." *Encyclopaedia Britannica* (October

8, 2022).Retrieved from https://www.britannica.com/biography/
Aleister-Crowley

Russell, Bertrand. Stanford Encyclopedia of Philosophy. (May 27,
2020). Retrieved from https://plato.stanford.edu/entries/russell/

Bovsun, M. "'Witch' murdered in Pennsylvania Dutch country—killer
thought she'd cursed him." New York *Daily News* (December 10,
2016). Retrieved from https://www.nydailynews.com/news/crime/
witch-murdered-pennsylvania-dutch-country-hex-article-1.2906278

"Dr. Charles Santee, 88, Dies at His Home in Wapwallopen." Hazleton
Standard-Speaker (April 17, 1963): 20.

Fenstermacher, T. "Frederick Santee was both unusual and gifted."
Press Enterprise (April 9, 1990).

Fenstermacher, T. "Witch in Wapwallopen." *Times-Tribune* (October
29, 1967): 12.

Santee, Frederick L. "Wapwallopen Doctor Dies." *Standard-Speaker*
(April 15, 1980).

Santee, Frederick L. Personal interviews (1976, 1977, 1979).

"Hitler's Children." (April 23, 2022.) Retrieved from http://www.
hitlerschildren.com/article/591-did-hitler-have-children

Hoke, G. L. *A History of Dr. Frederick LaMotte Santee and the Coven
of the Catta*. Morrisville, North Carolina: Lulu, 2010.

"File No: 09-03-014." Investigation of former Santee residence,
Wapwallopen, PA. Pennsylvania Paranormal Association (February
14, 2009).

Saint Thomas, S. "We Asked Real Modern Witches To Debunk Magick's
Biggest Misconceptions." *Allure* (December 17, 2021). Retrieved
from https://www.allure.com/contributor/sophie-saint-thomas

Santee, F. L. *The Devil's Wager*. Hicksville, New York: Exposition Press,
1979.

Schwarz, B. S. "A Biography of Dr. Frederick LaMotte Santee." (2012).

Smith, C. "Did Hitler Have a Secret Son? Evidence Supports Alleged
Son's Claims." ABC News. (February 21, 2012). Retrieved from
https://abcnews.go.com/blogs/headlines/2012/02/did-hitler-have-
a-secret-son-evidence-supports-alleged-sons-claims

Swank, G. "The Art of My Ancestors- Becoming a Pennsylvania Dutch
Powwow." Suurata Reiki (February 18, 2021). Retrieved from https://

www.suuratareiki.org/post/the-art-of-my-ancestors-becoming-a-pennsylvania-dutch-powwow

Leek, Sybil. The Witches Almanac (2021). Retrieved from https://thewitchesalmanac.com/pages/sybil-leek/

22. Richard Sharpe Shaver

Brown, S. L. "Newly opened files at Public Record Office Victoria reveal life in 1940s mental hospitals." ABC RN (December 31, 2018). Retrieved from https://www.abc.net.au/news/2019-01-01/newly-opened-files-reveal-life-in-1940s-mental-hospitals/10671498

Budd, D. "Trapped Miners Meet the Paranormal." BellaOnline: The Voice of Women (2013). Retrieved from http://www.bellaonline.com/ArticlesP/art55544.asp

"Caverns, Dungeons and Labyrinths." The Watcher Files (May 5, 2014). Retrieved from http://www.thewatcherfiles.com/cosmicconflict/caverns.htm

Furek, M. W. Sheppton: The Myth, Miracle & Music. Charleston, SC: CreateSpace, 2015.

Furek, M. W. "The Hollow Earth Theory & The Shaver Mysteries." Paranormal Underground (August 2022): 12–14.

Holzer, H. Ghosts: True Encounters with the World Beyond. New York: Black Dog & Leventhal Publishers, Inc., 1997.

"John Cleves Symmes, Hollow Earth Theory, and Edmond Halley." American History (June 29, 2017). Retrieved from https://worldhistory.us/american-history/john-cleves-symmes-hollow-earth-theory-and-edmond-halley.php

Norman, E. The Under-People. New York: Award Books, 1969.

Piechota, M. "Religion and Ufology." IRAAP Messenger (2005).

"Richard Sharpe Shaver (1907–1975)." Encyclopedia of Arkansas (June 6, 2022). Retrieved from https://encyclopediaofarkansas.net/entries/richard-sharpe-shaver-4462/

"Richard Sharpe Shaver, UFO Hoaxter." Howstuffworks (June 6, 2022). Retrieved from https://science.howstuffworks.com/space/aliens-ufos/maury-island-incident.htm

"The 1940s Medicine and Health: Topics in the News." Encyclopedia.com (2019). Retrieved from https://www.encyclopedia.com/social-sciences/culture-magazines/1940s-medicine-and-health-topics-news

Toronto, R. *The War Over Lemuria*. Jefferson, North Carolina: McFarland, 2013.

23. The Philadelphia Experiment

Berlitz, C., and J. M. Valentine. *Without A Trace*. Garden City, NY: Doubleday, 1977.

Donovan, B. W. *Conspiracy Films: A Tour of Dark Places in the American Conscious*. Jefferson, North Carolina: McFarland, 2011.

East, M. "The Truth About: The Philadelphia Experiment." The Mystery Box (November 3, 2020). Retrieved from https://medium.com/the-mystery-box/the-truth-about-the-philadelphia-experiment-c768993610c0

Gordon, B. "Degaussing: The demagnetization of ships." *Electronics and Power* (June 1984).

"History of USS *Eldridge* (DE 173)." Ships Section, Office of Public Information, Navy Department (Received 1988).

"Is there any truth in the 'Philadelphia Experiment'?" Worldopo (April 20, 2020). Retrieved from https://medium.com/@worldopo.io/is-there-any-truth-in-the-philadelphia-experiment-a1ce6e5800e1

Lamb, R. "What is antigravity?" HowStuffWorks. Retrieved from https://science.howstuffworks.com/innovation/science-questions/antigravity.htm

Lambert, A. "Fantastic story of Dr. Morris K. Jessup, professor, astrophysicist, and the real invisible Man." *Bluebook* (date unknown).

Moore, W. L. *The Philadelphia Experiment: An Update.* (Revised Edition). Burbank, CA: William L. Moore Publications & Research, 1987.

Moore, W. L, and C. Berlitz. *The Philadelphia Experiment*. New York: Fawcett Crest, 1979.

Redfern, N. "UFO researcher Morris Jessup: Murdered For What He Knew." Mysterious Universe (January 13, 2021). Retrieved from https://mysteriousuniverse.org/2021/01/ufo-researcher-morris-jessup-murdered-for-what-he-knew/

Serena, K. "How The Philadelphia Experiment Became Famous Despite Never Happening." ATI (July 22, 2021). Retrieved from https://allthatsinteresting.com/philadelphia-experiment

Tingley, B., and T. Rogoway. "Scientist Behind the Navy's 'UFO Patents' Has Now Filed One For A Compact Fusion Reactor." The War Zone

(December 1, 2019). Retrieved from https://www.thedrive.com/the-war-zone/30256/scientist-behind-the-navys-ufo-patents-has-now-filed-one-for-a-compact-fusion-reactor

Tracey, F. Personal correspondence and physical meeting (January 8, 1989).

von Doenhoff, R. A. National Archives, Military Reference Branch. Personal correspondence (December 13, 1988).

Weeks, J. "When the supernatural touches reality." *Houston Post* (August 5, 1984): 14F.

24. Strange Highways

Conrad, E. "How the Pyramids were REALLY Built (and How Columbus Discovered America)." Narkive (November 25, 2022). Retrieved from https://alt.fan.ed-conrad.narkive.com/v8RErrwY/how-the-pyramids-were-really-built-and-how-columbus-discovered-america

Donmoyer, P. J. *Powwowing in Pennsylvania: Braucherei and the Ritual of Everyday Life*. Kutztown University: Masthof Press & Pennsylvania German Cultural Heritage Center, 2018.

Dragonstar, The Long-Lost Friend, T. R. Swartz, and King Zaltron. *Gypsy Witch Book Of Old Pennsylvania Dutch Pow-Wows And Hexes*. New Brunswick, NJ: Global Communications, 2012.

Inglis-Arkell, E. "The Blob Was Based on a True Story." Gizmodo (August 18, 2014). Retrieved from https://gizmodo.com/the-true-story-behind-the-blob-1623120977

Keel, J. *The Mothman Prophecies*. New York: Tom Doherty Associates, LLC, 1991.

Koontz, D. *Strange Highways*. New York: Warner Books, Inc., 1995.

The Long-Lost Friend. *The Hex Book of the Pennsylvania Dutch*. (Date unknown.)

Magaraci, K. "This Asylum Near Philadelphia Has A Dark And Evil History That Will Never Be Forgotten." Philadelphia (September 15, 2017). Retrieved from https://www.onlyinyourstate.com/states/pennsylvania/philadelphia/

Nocek, B. "Out of the mists of night in Newport Township slithers the red-eyed creature known as ... The Bagunk stories of origin vary, but the tale has long endured." *Times Leader* (October 31, 1997): 1A.

Pinela, R. "Is Pennhurst Asylum Actually haunted?" Distractify

(October 31, 2019). Retrieved from https://www.distractify.com/p/is-pennhurst-asylum-haunted

Rodson, R. "Top 10 Cryptids Still Roaming Around Pennsylvania." HubPages (October 30, 2020). Retrieved from https://discover.hubpages.com/education/Top-10-Cryptids-Still-Roaming-Around-Pennsylvania

Rossen, J. "The Real-Life Creepy Blob That Inspired The Blob." Mental Floss (May 5, 2021). Retrieved from https://www.mentalfloss.com/article/639625/the-blob-horror-movie-true-story

Swancer, B. "Some Very Weird mystery Monsters from Pennsylvania." Mysterious Universe (July 4, 2018). Retrieved from https://mysteriousuniverse.org/2018/07/some-very-weird-mystery-monsters-from-pennsylvania/

"The legend of the Bagunk." Deadline Paranormal (2011). Retrieved from https://hatchet5855.wixsite.com/deadline-paranormal/blank-cxr2

About the Author

Photo of Evans City Mayor Dean Zinkhann and author Maxim W. Furek. Evans City, located north of Pittsburgh, was the location for Night of the Living Dead. *(Photograph by Patricia A. Furek.)*

An avid student of the paranormal, Maxim W. Furek's eclectic background includes aspects of psychology, addictions, and rock journalism. He has a master's degree in Communications from Bloomsburg University and a bachelor's degree in Psychology from Aquinas College.

The author has been interviewed on *Exploring the Bizarre* with the legendary Timothy Green Beckley (Mr. UFO) and Tim R. Swartz (Commander X), and on Dave Schrader's *Paranormal 60*. In addition, he is a contributor to *Fate*

Magazine, Normal Paranormal, and *Paranormal Underground.*

www.maximfurek.com

 facebook.com/maxim.furek
instagram.com/maximwfurek

Printed in the USA
CPSIA information can be obtained
at www.ICGtesting.com
LVHW090333250324
775412LV00002B/238